CW00803029

The Jeffers(

The Life and Morals of
Jesus of Nazareth
by Thomas Jefferson

The Complete Sayings of
Jesus Christ
by Arthur Hinds

The Jefferson Bible:
The Life and Morals of
Jesus of Nazareth

The Complete Sayings of
Jesus Christ

©2008 Wilder Publications
This book is a product of its time and does not reflect the same values as it would if it were written today. Parents might wish to discuss with their children how views on race, gender, sexuality, ethnicity, and interpersonal relations have changed since this book was written before allowing them to read this classic work.

All rights reserved. Printed in the United States of America. No part of this book may be used or reproduced in any manner without written permission except for brief quotations for review purposes only.

A & D Publishing
PO Box 3005
Radford VA 24143-3005
www.wilderpublications.com

ISBN 10: 1-60459-433-0
ISBN 13: 978-1-60459-433-1

First Edition

Table of Contents

PREFACE.

In 1803, while "overwhelmed with other business," Mr. Jefferson cut from the evangelists such passages as he believed would best present the ethical teaching of Jesus, and "arranged them, on the pages of a blank book, in a certain order of time or subject." He called it "The Philosophy of Jesus of Nazareth, extracted from the account of his life and doctrines, as given by Matthew, Mark, Luke and John; being an abridgment of the New Testament for the use of the Indians, unembarrassed with matters of fact or faith beyond the level of their comprehension." In a letter to his friend, Mr. Charles Thompson, after describing this work, he said: "If I had time I would add to my little book the Greek, Latin and French texts in columns, side by side." Some time afterwards he carried out the design thus expressed, giving the texts in the four languages, "in a handsome morocco-bound volume, labeled on the back 'Morals of Jesus.'" This is the volume called "The Jefferson Bible," which is now owned by the Government, and the publication of which has been recently ordered by Congress. While this volume was still in the possession of Mr. Jefferson's oldest grandson, Colonel Thomas Jefferson Randolph, an accurate copy of its table of contents was made, and from that copy the English text is reproduced in the following pages. As a fit introduction to it, a letter to Dr. Benjamin Rush, and a comparison of the doctrines of Jesus with those of others, are published, giving, perhaps, the fullest expression of his religious views ever made by Mr. Jefferson himself. Say nothing of my religion. It is known to my God and myself alone. Its evidence before the world is to be sought in my life; if that has been honest and dutiful to society, the religion which has regulated it cannot be a bad one.
—Thomas Jefferson.

RELIGIOUS VIEWS OF THOMAS JEFFERSON.

In a letter to his daughter, written in 1803, Mr. Jefferson said: "A promise made to a friend some years ago, but executed only lately, has placed my religious creed on paper. I have thought it just that my family, by possessing this, should be enabled to estimate the libels published against me on this, as on every other possible subject." The "religious creed" to which he referred was a comparison of the doctrines of Jesus with those of others, prepared in fulfillment of a promise made to Dr. Benjamin Rush. This paper, with the letter to Dr. Rush which accompanied it is a fit introduction to the "Jefferson Bible."

Washington, April 21, 1803.

Dear Sir: In some of the delightful conversations with you, in the evenings of 1798-99, and which served as an anodyne to the afflictions of the crisis through which our country was then laboring, the Christian religion was sometimes our topic; and I then promised you that one day or other, I would give you my views of it. They are the result of a life of inquiry and reflection, and very different from that Anti-Christian system imputed to me by those who know nothing of my opinions. To the corruptions of christianity I am indeed opposed; but not to the genuine precepts of Jesus himself. I am a Christian in the only sense in which he wished any one to be; sincerely attached to his doctrines, in preference to all others; ascribing to himself every human excellence, and believing he never claimed any other.

At the short intervals since these conversations, when I could justifiably abstract my mind from public affairs, this subject has been under my contemplation; but the more I considered it, the more it expanded beyond the measure of either my time or Information. In the moment of my late departure from Monticello, I received from Dr. Priestly his little treatise of "Socrates and Jesus Compared." This being a section of the general view I had taken of the field, it became a subject of reflection while on the road, and unoccupied otherwise. The result was to arrange in my mind a syllabus, or outline, of such an estimate of the comparative merits of Christianity, as I wished to see executed by some one of more leisure and information for the task than myself. This I now send you, as the only discharge of my promise I can probably ever execute. And in confiding it to you, I know it will not be exposed to the malignant perversions of those who make every word from me a text for new misrepresentations and calumnies.

I am moreover averse to the communication of my religious tenets to the public; because it would countenance the presumption of those who have endeavored to draw them before that tribunal, and to seduce public opinion to erect itself into that inquisition over the rights of conscience which the laws have so justly proscribed. It behooves every man who values liberty of conscience for himself to resist invasions of it in the case of others, or their case may, by change of circumstances, become his own. It behooves him, too, in his own case, to give no example of concession, betraying the right of independent opinion by answering questions of faith, which the laws have left between God and himself.

Accept my affectionate salutations.

SYLLABUS OF AN ESTIMATE OF THE DOCTRINES OF JESUS, COMPARED WITH THOSE OF OTHERS.

In a comparative view of the ethics of the enlightened nations of antiquity, of the Jews, and of Jesus, no notice should be taken of the corruptions of reason among the ancients, to wit, the idolatry and superstition of the vulgar, nor of the corruptions of Christianity by the learned among its professors. Let a just view be taken of the moral principles inculcated by the most esteemed of the sects of ancient philosophy, or of their individuals; particularly Pythagoras, Socrates, Epicurus, Cicero, Epictetus, Seneca, Antoninus.

I. PHILOSOPHERS.

1. Their precepts related chiefly to ourselves, and the government of those passions which, unrestrained, would disturb our tranquility of mind. In this branch of philosophy they were really great.

2. In developing our duties to others, they were short and defective. They embraced indeed the circles of kindred and friends, and inculcated patriotism, or the love of country in the aggregate, as a primary obligation: towards our neighbors and countrymen they taught justice, but scarcely viewed them as within the circle of benevolence. Still less have they inculcated peace, charity, and love to our fellow-men, or embraced with benevolence the whole family of mankind.

II. JEWS.

1. Their system was Deism, that is, the belief in one only God; but their ideas of him and of his attributes were degrading and injurious.

2. Their ethics were not only imperfect, but often irreconcilable with the sound dictates of reason and morality, as they respect intercourse with those around us; and repulsive and anti-social as respecting other nations. They needed reformation, therefore, in an eminent degree.

III. JESUS.

In this state of things among the Jews, Jesus appeared. His parentage was obscure; his condition poor; his education null; his natural endowments great; his life correct and innocent. He was meek, benevolent, patient, firm, disinterested, and of the sublimest eloquence. The disadvantages under which his doctrines appear are remarkable.

1. Like Socrates and Epictetus, he wrote nothing himself.

2. But he had not, like them, a Xenophon or an Arrian to write for him. I name not Plato, who only used the name of Socrates to cover the whimsies of his own brain.

On the contrary, all the learned of his country, entrenched in its power and riches, were opposed to him, lest his labors should undermine their advantages; and the committing to writing of his life and doctrines fell on unlettered and ignorant men; who wrote, too, from memory, and not till long after the transactions had passed.

3. According to the ordinary fate of those who attempt to enlighten and reform mankind, he fell an early victim to the jealousy and combination of the altar and the throne, at about 33 years of age, his reason having not yet attained the maximum of its energy, nor the course of his preaching, which was but of three years at most, presented occasions for developing a complete system of morals.

4. Hence the doctrines which he really delivered were defective, as a whole, and fragments only of what he did deliver

have come to us mutilated, misstated, and often unintelligible.

5. They have been still more disfigured by the corruptions of schismatizing followers, who have found an interest in sophisticating and perverting the simple doctrines he taught, by engrafting on them the mysticisms of a Grecian Sophist (Plato), frittering them into subtilties and obscuring them with jargon, until they have caused good men to reject the whole in disgust, and to view Jesus himself as an impostor. Notwithstanding these disadvantages, a system of morals is presented to us which, if filled up in the true style and spirit of the rich fragments he left us, would be the most perfect and sublime that has ever been taught by man. The question of his being a member of the Godhead, or in direct communication with it, claimed for him by some of his followers, and denied by others, is foreign to the present view, which is merely an estimate of the intrinsic merits of his doctrines.

1. He corrected the Deism of the Jews, confirming them in their belief of one only god, and giving them juster notions of his attributes and government.

2. His moral doctrines, relating to kindred and friends, were more pure and perfect than those of the most correct of the philosophers, and greatly more so than those of the Jews; and they went far beyond both in inculcating universal philanthrophy, not only to kindred and friends, to neighbors and countrymen, but to all mankind, gathering all into one family, under the bonds of love, charity, peace, common wants and common aids. A development of this head will evince the peculiar superiority of the system of Jesus over all others.

3. The precepts of philosophy and of the Hebrew code laid hold of action only. He pushed his scrutinies into the heart of man; erected his tribunal in the region of his thought, and purified the waters at the fountain head.

4. He taught emphatically the doctrine of a future state, which was either doubted or disbelieved by the Jews; and wielded it with efficacy as an important incentive, supplementary to the other motives to moral conduct.

I, too, have made a wee-little book from the same materials (The Gospels) which I call the Philosophy of Jesus. It is a paradigma of his doctrines, made by cutting the texts out of the book and arranging them on the pages of a blank book, in a certain order of time or subject. A more beautiful or precious morsel of ethics I have never seen. It is a document in proof that I am a REAL CHRISTIAN, that is to say, a disciple of the doctrines of Jesus, very different from the Platonists, who call ME infidel and THEMSELVES Christians and preachers of the Gospel, while they draw all their characteristic dogmas from what its author never said nor saw. They have compounded from the heathen mysteries a system beyond the comprehension of man, of which the great reformer of the vicious ethics and deism of the Jews, were he to return on earth, would not recognize one feature.—Jefferson to Mr. Charles Thompson.

I. Joseph and Mary go to Bethlehem, Where Jesus is Born.

AND it came to pass in those days, that there went out a decree from Caesar Augustus, that all the world should be taxed.

2 (And this taxing ways first made when Cyrenius was governor of Syria.)

3 And all went to be taxed, every one into his own city.

4 And Joseph also went up from Galilee, out of the city of Nazareth, into Judaea, unto the city of

David, which is called Bethlehem, (because he was of the house and lineage of David,)

5 To be taxed with Mary his espoused wife, being great with child.

6 And so it was, that, while they were there, the days were accomplished that she should be delivered.

7 And she brought forth her firstborn son, and wrapped him in swaddling clothes, and laid him in a manger; because there was no room for them in the inn.

II. He is Circumcised and Named and They Return to Nazareth.

AND when eight days were accomplished for the circumcising of the child, his name was called JESUS.

2 And when they had performed all things according to the law of the Lord, they returned into Galilee, to their own city Nazareth.

III. At Twelve Years of Age He Accompanies His Parents to Jerusalem and Returns.

AND the child grew, and waxed strong in spirit, filled with wisdom: and the grace of God was upon him.

2 And when he was twelve years old, they went up to Jerusalem after the custom of the feast.

3 And when they had fulfilled the days, as they returned, the child Jesus tarried behind in Jerusalem; and Joseph and his mother knew not of it.

4 But they, supposing him to have been in the company, went a day's journey; and they sought him among their kinsfolk and acquaintance.

5 And when they found him not, they turned back again to Jerusalem, seeking him.

6 And it came to pass, that after three days they found him in the temple, sitting in the midst of the doctors, both hearing them, and asking them questions.

7 And all that heard him were astonished at his understanding and answers.

8 And when they saw him, they were amazed: and his mother said unto him, Son, why hast thou thus dealt with us? behold, thy father and I have sought thee sorrowing.

9 And he went down with them, and came to Nazareth, and was subject unto them: but his mother kept all these sayings in her heart.

10 And Jesus increased in wisdom and stature, and in favour with God and man.

IV. John Baptizes in Jordan.

NOW in the fifteenth year of the reign of Tiberius Caesar, Pontius Pilate being governor of Judaea, and Herod being tetrarch of Galilee, and his brother Philip tetrarch of Ituraea and of the region of Trachonitis, and Lysanias the tetrarch of Abilene,

2 Annas and Caiaphas being the high priests, the word of God came unto John the son of Zacharias in the wilderness.

3 John did baptize in the wilderness, and preach the baptism of repentance for the remission of sins.

4 And the same John had his raiment of camel's hair, and a leathern girdle about his loins; and his meat was locusts and wild honey.

5 ¶ Then went out to him Jerusalem, and all Judaea, and all the region round about Jordan;

6 And were baptized of him in Jordan, confessing their sins.

V. Jesus is Baptized at 30 Years of Age.

THEN cometh Jesus from Galilee to Jordan unto John, to be baptized of him.

2 And Jesus himself began to be about thirty years of age, being (as was supposed) the son of Joseph, which was the son of Heli.

VI. Drives the Traders Out of the Temple.

AFTER this he went down to Capernaum, he, and his mother, and his brethren, and his disciples: and they continued there not many days.

2 ¶ And the Jews' passover was at hand, and Jesus went up to Jerusalem;

3 And found in the temple those hat sold oxen and sheep and doves, and the changers of money sitting:

4 And when he had made a scourge of small cords, he drove them all out of the temple, and the sheep, and the oxen; and poured out the changers' money, and overthrew the tables;

5 And said unto them that sold doves, Take these things hence; make not my Father's house an house of merchandise.

VII. He Baptizes, but Retires into Galilee on the Death of John.

AFTER these things came Jesus and his disciples into the land of Judaea; and there he tarried with them, and baptized.

2 ¶ Now when Jesus had heard that John was cast into prison, he departed into Galilee;

3 For Herod himself had sent forth and laid hold upon John, and bound him in prison for Herodias' sake, his brother Philip's wife: for he had married her.

4 For John had said unto Herod, It is not lawful for thee to have thy brother's wife.

5 Therefore Herodias 'had a quarrel against him, and would have killed him; but she could not:

6 For Herod feared John, knowing that he was a just man and an holy, and observed him; and when he heard him, he did many things, and heard him gladly.

7 And when a convenient day was come, that Herod on his birthday made a supper to his lords, high captains, and chief estates of Galilee;

8 And when the daughter of the said Herodias came in, and danced, and pleased Herod and them that sat with him, the king said unto the damsel, Ask of me whatsoever thou wilt, and I will give it thee.

9 And he sware unto her, Whatsoever thou shalt ask of me, I will give it thee, unto the half of my kingdom.

10 And she went forth, and said unto her mother, What shall I ask? And she said, The head of John the Baptist.

11 And she came in straightway with haste unto the king, and asked, saying, I will that thou give me by and by in a charger the head of John the Baptist.

12 And the king was exceeding sorry; yet for his oath's sake, and for their sakes which sat with him, he would not reject her.

13 And immediately the king sent an executioner, and commanded his head to be brought: and he went and beheaded him in the prison,

14 And brought his head in a charger, and gave it to the damsel: and the damsel gave it to her mother.

VIII. He Teaches in the Synagogue.

AND they went into Capernaum; and straightway on the sabbath day he entered into the synagogue, and taught.

2 And they were astonished at his doctrine: for he taught them as one that had authority, and not as the scribes.

IX. Explains the Sabbath.

AT that time Jesus went on the sabbath day through the corn; and his disciples were an hungred, and began to pluck the ears of corn, and to eat.

2 But when the Pharisees saw it, they said unto him, Behold, thy disciples do that which is not lawful to do upon the sabbath day.

3 But he said unto them, Have ye not read what David did, when he was an hungred, and they that were with him;

4 How he entered into the house of God, and did eat the shew-bread, which was not lawful for him to eat, neither for them which were with him, but only for the priests?

5 Or have ye not read in the law, how that on the sabbath days the priests in the temple profane the sabbath, and are blameless?

6 ¶ And when he was departed thence, he went into their synagogue:

7 And, behold, there was a man which had his hand withered. And they asked him, saying, Is it lawful to heal on the sabbath days? that they might accuse him.

8 And he said unto them, What man shall there be among you, that shall have one sheep, and if it fall into a pit on the sabbath day, will he not lay hold on it, and lift it out?

9 How much then is a man better than a sheep? Wherefore it is lawful to do well on the sabbath days.

10 And he said unto them, The sabbath was made for man, and not man for the Sabbath.

11 ¶ Then the Pharisees went out, and held a council against him, how they might destroy him.

12 But when Jesus knew it, he withdrew himself from thence: and great multitudes followed him, and he healed them all.

X. Call of His Disciples.

AND it came to pass in those days, that he went out into a mountain to pray, and continued all night in prayer to God.

2 And when it was day, he called unto him his disciples: and of them he chose twelve, whom also he named apostles;

3 Simon, (whom he also named Peter,) and Andrew his brother, James and John, Philip and Bartholomew,

4 Matthew and Thomas, James the son of Alphaeus, and Simon called Zelotes,

5 And Judas the brother of James, and Judas Iscariot, which also was the traitor.

6 And he came down with them, and stood in the plain, and the company of his disciples, and a great multitude of people out of all Judaea and Jerusalem, and from the sea coast of Tyre and Sidon, which came to hear him, and to be healed of their diseases.

XI. The Sermon on the Mount.

AND seeing the multitudes, he went up into a mountain: and when he was set, his disciples came unto him:

2 And he opened his mouth, and taught them, saying,

3 Blessed are the poor in spirit: for theirs is the kingdom of heaven.

4 Blessed are they that mourn: for they shall be comforted.

5 Blessed are the meek: for they shall inherit the earth.

6 Blessed are they which do hunger and thirst after righteousness: for they shall be filled.

7 Blessed are the merciful: for they shall obtain mercy.

8 Blessed are the pure in heart: for they shall see God.

9 Blessed are the peacemakers; for they shall be called the children of God.

10 Blessed are they which are persecuted for righteousness' sake: for theirs is the kingdom of heaven.

11 Blessed are ye, when men shall revile you, and persecute you, and shall say all manner of evil against you falsely, for my sake.

12 Rejoice, and be exceeding glad: for great is your reward in heaven: for so persecuted they the prophets which were before you.

13 But woe unto you that are rich! for ye have received your consolation.

14 Woe unto you that are full! for ye shall hunger. Woe unto you that laugh now! for ye shall mourn and weep.

15 Woe unto you, when all men shall speak well of you! for so did their fathers to the false prophets.

16 ¶ Ye are the salt of the earth: but if the salt have lost his savour, wherewith shall it be salted? it is thenceforth good for nothing, but to be cast out, and to be trodden under foot of men.

17 Ye are the light of the world. A city that is set on an hill cannot be hid.

18 Neither do men light a candle, and put it under a bushel, but on a candlestick; and it giveth light unto all that are in the house.

19 Let your light so shine before men, that they may see your good works, and glorify your Father which is in heaven.

20 ¶ Think not that I am come to destroy the law, or the prophets: I am not come to destroy, but to fulfil.

21 For verily I say unto you, Till heaven and earth pass, one jot or one tittle shall in no wise pass from the law, till all be fulfilled.

22 Whosoever therefore shall break one of these least commandments, and shall teach men so, he shall be called the least in the kingdom of heaven: but whosoever shall do and teach them, the same shall be called great in the kingdom of heaven.

23 For I say unto you, That except your righteousness shall exceed the righteousness of the scribes and Pharisees, ye shall in no case enter into the kingdom of heaven.

24 ¶ Ye have heard that it was said by them of old time, Thou shalt not kill; and whosoever shall kill shall be in danger of the judgment:

25 But I say unto you, That whosoever is angry with his brother without a cause shall be in danger of the judgment: and whosoever shall say to his brother, Raca, shall be in danger of the council; but whosoever shall say, Thou fool, shall be in danger of hell fire.

26 Therefore if thou bring thy gift to the altar, and there rememberest that thy brother hath ought against thee;

27 Leave there thy gift before the altar, and go thy way; first be reconciled to thy brother, and then come and offer thy gift.

28 Agree with thine adversary quickly, whiles thou art in the way with him; lest at any time the adversary deliver thee to the judge, and the judge deliver thee to the officer, and thou be cast into prison.

29 Verily I say unto thee, Thou shalt by no means come out thence, till thou hast paid the uttermost farthing.

30 ¶ Ye have heard that it was said by them of old time, Thou shalt not commit adultery:

31 But I say unto you, That whosoever looketh on a woman to lust after her hath committed adultery with her already in his heart.

32 And if thy right eye offend thee, pluck it out, and cast it from thee: for it is profitable for thee that one of thy members should perish, and not that thy whole body should be cast into hell.

33 And if thy right hand offend thee, cut it off, and cast it from thee: for it is profitable for thee that one of thy members should perish, and not that thy whole body should be cast into hell.

34 ¶ It hath been said, Whosoever shall put away his wife, let him give her a writing of divorcement:

35 But I say unto you, That whosoever shall put away his wife, saving for the cause of fornication, causeth her to commit adultery: and whosoever shall marry her that is divorced committeth adultery.

36 ¶ Again, ye have heard that it hath been said by them of old time, Thou shalt not forswear thyself, but shalt perform unto the Lord thine oaths:

37 But I say unto you, Swear not at all; neither by heaven; for it is God's throne:

38 Nor by the earth; for it is his footstool: neither by Jerusalem; for it is the city of the great King.

39 Neither shalt thou swear by thy head, because thou canst not make one hair white or black.

40 But let your communication be, Yea, yea; Nay, nay: for whatsoever is more than these cometh of evil.

41 ¶ Ye have heard that it hath been said, An Oil eye for an eye, and a tooth for a tooth:

42 But I say unto you, That ye resist not evil: but whosoever shall smite thee on thy right cheek, I. turn to him the other also.

43 And if any man will sue thee at the law, and take away thy coat, let him have thy cloak also.

44 And whosoever shall compel thee to go a mile, go with him twain.

45 Give to him that asketh thee, and from him that would borrow of thee

turn not thou away.

46 ¶ Ye have heard that it hath been said, Thou shalt love thy neighbour, and hate thine enemy.

47 But I say unto you, Love your enemies, bless them that curse you, do good to them that hate you, and pray for them which despitefully use you, and persecute you;

48 That ye may be the children of your Father which is in heaven: for he maketh his sun to rise on the evil and on the good, and sendeth rain on the just and on the unjust.

49 For if ye love them which love you, what reward have ye? do not even the publicans the same?

50 And if ye salute your brethren only, what do ye more than others? do not even the publicans so?

51 And if ye lend to them of whom ye hope to receive, what thank have ye? for sinners also lend to sinners, to receive as much again.

52 But love ye your enemies, and do good, and lend, hoping for nothing again; and your reward shall be great, and ye shall be the children of the Highest: for he is kind unto the unthankful and to the evil.

53 Be ye therefore merciful, as your Father also is merciful.

54 Take heed that ye do not your alms before men, to be seen of them: otherwise ye have no reward of your Father which is in heaven.

55 Therefore when thou doest thine alms, do not sound a trumpet before thee, as the hypocrites do in the synagogues and in the streets, that they may have glory of men. Verily I say unto you, They have their reward.

56 But when thou doest alms, let not thy left hand know what thy right band doeth:

57 That thine alms may be in secret: and thy Father which seeth in secret himself shall reward thee openly.

58 ¶ And when thou prayest, thou shalt not be as the hypocrites are: for they love to pray standing in the synagogues and in the corners of the streets, that they may be seen of men. Verily I say unto you, They have their reward.

59 But thou, when thou prayest, enter into thy closet, and when thou hast shut thy door, pray to thy Father which is in secret; and thy Father which seeth in secret shall reward thee openly.

60 But when ye pray, use not vain repetitions, as the heathen do: for they think that they shall be heard for their much speaking.

61 Be not ye therefore like unto them: for your Father knoweth what things ye have need of, before ye ask him.

62 After this manner therefore pray ye: Our Father which art in heaven, Hallowed be thy name.

63 Thy kingdom come. Thy will be done in earth, as it is in heaven.

64 Give us this day our daily bread.

65 And forgive us our debts, as we forgive our debtors.

66 And lead us not into temptation, but deliver us from evil: For thine is the kingdom, and the power, and the glory, for ever. Amen.

67 For if ye forgive men their trespasses, your heavenly Father will also forgive you:

68 But if ye forgive not men their trespasses, neither will your Father

forgive your trespasses.

69 ¶ Moreover when ye fast, be not, as the hypocrites, of a sad countenance: for they disfigure their faces, that they may appear unto men to fast. Verily I say unto you, They have their reward.

70 But thou, when thou fastest, anoint thine head, and wash thy face;

71 That thou appear not unto men to fast, but unto thy Father which is in secret: and thy Father, which seeth in secret, shall reward thee openly.

72 ¶ Lay not up for yourselves treasures upon earth, where moth and rust doth corrupt, and where thieves break through and steal:

73 But lay up for yourselves treasures in heaven, where neither moth nor rust doth corrupt, and where thieves do not break through nor steal.

74 For where your treasure is, there will your heart be also.

75 The light of the body is the eye: if therefore thine eye be single, thy whole body shall be full of light.

76 But if thine eye be evil, thy whole body shall be full of darkness. If therefore the light that is in thee be darkness, how great is that darkness!

77 No man can serve two masters: for either he will hate the one, and love the other; or else he will hold to the one, and despise the other. Ye cannot serve God and mammon,

78 Therefore I say unto you, Take no thought for your life, what ye shall eat, or what ye shall drink; nor yet for your body, what ye shall put on. Is not the life more than meat, and the body than raiment?

79 Behold the fowls of the air: for they sow not, neither do they reap, nor gather into barns; yet your heavenly Father feedeth them. Are ye not much better than they?

80 Which of you by taking thought can add one cubit unto his stature?

81 And why take ye thought for raiment? Consider the lilies of the field, how they grow; they toil not, neither do they spin:

82 And yet I say unto you, That even Solomon in all his glory was not arrayed like one of these.

83 Wherefore, if God so clothe the grass of the field, which today is, and tomorrow is cast into the oven, shall he not much more clothe you, O ye of little faith?

84 Therefore take no thought, saying, What shall we eat? or, What shall we drink? or, Wherewithal shall we be clothed?

85 (For after all these things do the Gentiles seek:) for your heavenly Father knoweth that ye have need of all these things.

86 But seek ye first the kingdom of God, and his righteousness; and all these things shall be added unto you.

87 Take therefore no thought for the morrow: for the morrow shall take thought for the things of itself. Sufficient unto the day is the evil thereof.

88 Judge not, that ye be not judged.

89 For with what judgment ye judge, ye shall be judged: and with what measure ye mete, it shall be measured to you again.

90 Give, and it shall be given unto you; good measure, pressed down, and shaken together, and running over, shall men give into your bosom. For with the same measure that ye mete withal it shall be measured to you again.

91 And why beholdest thou the mote that is in thy brother's eye, but

considerest not the beam that is in thine own eye?

92 Or how wilt thou say to thy brother, Let me pull out the mote out of thine eye; and, behold, a beam is in thine own eye?

93 Thou hypocrite, first cast out the beam out of thine own eye; and then shalt thou see clearly to cast out the mote out of thy brother's eye.

94 ¶ Give not that which is holy unto the dogs, neither cast ye your pearls before swine, lest they trample them under their feet, and turn again and rend you.

95 ¶ Ask, and it shall be given you; seek, and ye shall find; knock, and it shall be opened unto you:

96 For every one that asketh receiveth; and he that seeketh findeth; and to him that knocketh it shall be opened.

97 Or what man is there of you, whom if his son ask bread, will he give him a stone?

98 Or if he ask a fish, will he give him a serpent?

99 If ye then, being evil, know how to give good gifts unto your children, how much more shall your Father which is in heaven give good things to them that ask him?

100 Therefore all things whatsoever ye would that men should do to you, do ye even so to them: for this is the law and the prophets,

101 ¶ Enter ye in at the strait gate; for wide is the gate, and broad is the way, that leadeth to destruction, and many there be which go in thereat:

102 Because strait is the gate, and narrow is the way, which leadeth unto life, and few there be that find it.

103 ¶ Beware of false prophets, which come to you in sheep's clothing, but inwardly they are ravening wolves.

104 Ye shall know them by their fruits. Do men gather grapes of thorns, or figs of thistles?

105 Even so every good tree bringeth forth good fruit; but a corrupt tree bringeth forth evil fruit.

106 A good tree cannot bring forth evil fruit, neither can a corrupt tree bring forth good fruit.

107 Every tree that bringeth not forth good fruit is hewn down, and cast into the fire.

108 Wherefore by their fruits ye shall know them.

109 A good man out of the good treasure of the heart bringeth forth good things: and an evil man out of the evil treasure bringeth forth evil things.

110 But I say unto you, That every idle word that men shall speak, they shall give account thereof in the day of judgment.

111 For by thy words thou shalt be justified, and by thy words thou shalt be condemned.

112 ¶ Therefore whosoever heareth these sayings of mine, and doeth them, I will liken him unto a wise man, which built his house upon a rock:

113 And the rain descended, and the floods came, and the winds blew, and beat upon that house; and it fell not: for it was founded upon a rock.

114 And every one that heareth these sayings of mine, and doeth them not, shall be likened unto a foolish man, which built his house upon the sand:

115 And the rain descended, and the floods came, and the winds blew and

beat upon that house; and it fell: and great was the fall of it.

116 ¶ And it came to pass, when Jesus had ended these sayings, the people were astonished at his doctrine:

117 For he taught them as one having authority, and not as the scribes.

XII. Exhorts.

WHEN he was come down from the mountain, great multitudes followed him.

2 And he marvelled because of their unbelief. And he went round about the villages, teaching.

3 ¶ Come unto me, all ye that labour and are heavy laden, and I will give you rest.

4 Take my yoke upon you, and learn of me; for I am meek and lowly in heart: and ye shall find rest unto your souls.

5 For my yoke is easy, and my burden is light.

XIII. A Woman Annointeth Him.

AND one of the Pharisees desired him that he would eat with him. And he went into the Pharisee's house, and sat down to meat.

2 And, behold, a woman in the city, which was a sinner, when she knew that Jesus sat at meat in

the Pharisee's house, brought an alabaster box of ointment,

3 And stood at his feet behind him weeping, and began to wash his feet with tears, and did wipe them with the hairs of her head, and kissed his feet, and anointed them with the ointment.

4 Now when the Pharisee which had bidden him saw it, he spake within himself, saying, This man, if he were a prophet, would have known who and what manner of woman this is that toucheth him: for she is a sinner.

5 And Jesus answering said unto him, Simon, I have somewhat to say unto thee. And he saith, Master, say on.

6 There was a. certain creditor which had two debtors: the one owed five hundred pence, and the other fifty.

7 And when they had nothing to pay, he frankly forgave them both. Tell me therefore, which of them will love him most?

8 Simon answered and said, I suppose that he to whom he forgave most. And he said unto him, Thou hast rightly judged.

9 And he turned to the woman, and said unto Simon, Seest thou this woman? I entered into thine house, thou gavest me no water for my feet: but she hath washed my feet with tears, and wiped them with the hairs of her head.

10 Thou gavest me no kiss: but this woman since the time I came in hath not ceased to kiss my feet.

11 My head with oil thou didst not anoint: but this woman hath anointed my feet with ointment.

12 Wherefore I say unto thee, Her sins, which are many, are forgiven; for she loved much: but to whom little is forgiven, the same loveth little.

13 And he said unto her, Thy sins are forgiven.

14 And they that sat at meat with him began to say within themselves, Who is this that forgiveth sins also?

15 And he said to the woman, Thy faith hath saved thee; go in peace.

XIV. Precepts.

THERE came then his brethren and his mother, and, standing without, sent unto him, calling him.

2 And the multitude sat about him, and they said unto him, Behold, thy mother and thy brethren without seek for thee.

3 And he answered them, saying, Who is my mother, or my brethren?

4 And he looked round about on them which sat about him, and said, Behold my mother and my brethren!

5 For whosoever shall do the will of God, the same is my brother, and my sister, and mother.

6 In the mean time, when there were gathered together an innumerable multitude of people, insomuch that they trode one upon another, he began to say unto his disciples first of all, Beware ye of the leaven of the Pharisees, which is hypocrisy.

7 For there is nothing covered, that shall not be revealed; neither hid, that shall not be known.

8 Therefore whatsoever ye have spoken in darkness shall be heard in the light; and that which ye have spoken in the ear in closets shall be proclaimed upon the housetops.

9 And I say unto you my friends, Be not afraid of them that kill the body, and after that have no more that they can do.

10 But I will forewarn you whom ye shall fear: Fear him, which after he hath killed hath power to cast into hell; yea, I say unto you, Fear him.

11 Are not five sparrows sold for two farthings, and not one of them is forgotten before God?

12 But even the very hairs of your head are all numbered. Fear not therefore; ye are of more Ë value than many sparrows.

13 ¶ And one of the company said unto him, Master, speak to my brother, that he divide the inheritance with me.

14 And he said unto him, Man, who made me a judge or a divider over you?

15 And he said unto them, Take heed, and beware of covetousness: for a man's life consisteth not in the abundance of the things which he possesseth.

XV. Parable of the Rich Man.

AND he spake a parable unto them, saying, The ground of a certain rich man brought forth plentifully:

2 And he thought within himself, saying, What shall I do, because I have no room where to bestow my fruits?

3 And he said, This will I do: I will pull down my barns, and build greater; and there will I bestow all my fruits and my goods.

4 And I will say to my soul, Soul, thou hast much goods laid up for many years; take thine ease, eat, drink, and be merry.

5 But God said unto him, Thou fool, this night thy soul shall be required of thee: then whose shall those things be, which thou hast provided?

6 So is he that layeth up treasure for himself, and is not rich toward God.

XVI. Precepts.

AND he said unto his disciples, Therefore I say unto you, Take no thought for your life, what ye shall eat; neither for the body, what ye shall put on.

2 The life is more than meat, and the body is more than raiment.

3 Consider the ravens: for they neither sow nor reap; which neither have storehouse nor barn; and God feedeth them: how much more are ye better than the fowls?

4 And which of you with taking thought can add to his stature one cubit?

5 If ye then be not able to do that thing which is least, why take ye thought for the rest?

6 Consider the lilies how they grow; they toil not, they spin not; and yet I say unto you, that Solomon in all his glory was not arrayed like one of these.

7 If then God so clothe the grass, which is today in the field, and tomorrow is cast into the oven; how much more will he clothe you, O ye of little faith?

8 And seek not ye what ye shall eat, or what ye shall drink, neither be ye of doubtful mind.

9 For all these things do the nations of the world seek after: and your Father knoweth that ye have need of these things.

10 But rather seek ye the kingdom of God; and all these things shall be added unto you.

11 Fear not, little flock; for it is your Father's good pleasure to give you the kingdom.

12 Sell that ye have, and give alms; provide yourselves bags which wax not old, a treasure in the heavens that faileth not, where no thief approacheth, neither moth corrupteth.

13 For where your treasure is, there will your heart be also.

14 Let your loins be girded about, and your lights burning;

15 And ye yourselves like unto men that wait for their lord, when he will return from the wedding; that when he cometh and knocketh, they may open unto him immediately.

16 Blessed are those servants, whom the lord when he cometh shall find watching; verily I say unto you, that he shall gird himself, and make them to sit down to meat, and will come forth and serve them.

17 And if he shall come in the second watch, or come in the third watch, and find them so, blessed are those servants.

18 And this know, that if the goodman of the house had known what hour the thief would come, he would have watched, and not have suffered his house to be broken through.

19 Be ye therefore ready also: for the Son of man cometh at an hour when ye think not.

20 ¶ Then Peter said unto him, Lord, speakest thou this parable unto us, or even to all?

21 And the Lord said, Who then is that faithful and wise steward, whom his lord shall make ruler over his household, to give them their portion of meat in due season?

22 Blessed is that servant, whom his lord when he cometh shall find so doing.

23 Of a truth, I say unto you, that he will make him ruler over all that he hath.

24 But and if that servant say in his heart, My lord delayeth his coming; and shall begin to beat the menservants and maidens, and to eat and drink, and to be drunken;

25 The lord of that servant will come in a day when he looketh not for him, and at an hour when he is not aware, and will cut him in sunder, and will appoint him his portion with the unbelievers.

26 And that servant, which knew his lord's will, and prepared not himself, neither did according to his will, shall be beaten with many stripes.

27 But he that knew not, and did commit things worthy of stripes, shall be beaten with few stripes. For unto whomsoever much is given, of him shall be much required: and to whom men have committed much, of him they will ask the more.

28 ¶ And he said also to the people, When ye see a cloud rise out of the west, straightway ye say, There cometh a shower; and so it is.

29 And when ye see the south wind blow, ye say, There will be heat; and it cometh to pass.

30 Ye hypocrites, ye can discern the face of the sky and of the earth; but how is it that ye do not discern this time?

31 Yea, and why even of yourselves judge ye not what is right?

32 ¶ When thou goest with thine adversary to the magistrate, as thou art in the way, give diligence that thou mayest be delivered from him; lest he hale thee to the judge, and the judge deliver thee to the officer, and the officer cast thee into prison.

33 I tell thee, thou shalt not depart thence, till thou hast paid the very last mite.

34 There were present at that season some that told him of the Galileans, whose blood Pilate had mingled with their sacrifices.

35 And Jesus answering said unto them, Suppose ye that these Galileans were sinners above all the Galileans, because they suffered such things?

36 I tell you, Nay: but, except ye repent, ye shall all likewise perish.

37 Or those eighteen, upon whom the tower in Siloam fell, and slew them, think ye that they were sinners above all men that dwelt in Jerusalem?

38 I tell you, Nay: but, except ye repent, ye shall all likewise perish.

XVII. Parable of the Fig Tree.

HE spake also this parable; A certain man had a fig tree planted in his vineyard; and he came and sought fruit thereon, and found none.

2 Then said he unto the dresser of his vineyard, Behold, these three years I come seeking fruit on this fig tree, and find none: cut it down; why cumbereth it the ground?

3 And he answering said unto him, Lord, let it alone this year also, till I shall dig about it, and dung it:

4 And if it bear fruit, well: and if not, then after that thou shalt cut it down.

XVIII. Precepts.

AND as he spake a certain Pharisee besought him to dine with him: and he went in, and sat down to meat.

2 And when the Pharisee saw it, he marvelled that he had not first washed before dinner.

3 And the Lord said unto him, Now do ye Pharisees make clean the outside of the cup and the platter; but your inward part is full of ravening and wickedness.

4 Ye fools, did not he that made that which is without make that which is within also?

5 But rather give alms of such things as ye have; and, behold, all things are clean unto you.

6 But woe unto you, Pharisees! for ye tithe mint and rue and all manner of herbs, and pass over judgment and the love of God: these ought ye to have done, and not to leave the other undone.

7 Woe unto you, Pharisees! for ye love the uppermost seats in the synagogues, and greetings in the markets.

8 Woe unto you, scribes and Pharisees, hypocrites! for ye are as graves which appear not, and the men that walk over them are not aware of them.

9 Then answered one of the lawyers, and said unto him, Master, thus saying thou reproachest us also.

10 And he said, Woe unto you also, ye lawyers! for ye lade men with burdens grievous to be borne, and ye yourselves touch not the burdens with one of your fingers.

11 Woe unto you, lawyers! for ye have taken away the key of knowledge: ye entered not in yourselves, and them that were entering in ye hindered.

12 And as he said these things unto them, the scribes and the Pharisees began to urge him vehemently, and to provoke him to speak of many things:

13 Laying wait for him, and seeking to catch something out of his mouth, that they might accuse him.

XIX. Parable of the Sower.

THE same day went Jesus out of the house, and sat by the sea side.

2 And great multitudes were gathered together unto him, so that he went into a ship, and sat; and the whole multitude stood on the shore.

3 And he spoke many things unto them in parables, saying, Behold, a sower went forth to sow;

4 And when he sowed, some seeds fell by the way side, and the fowls came and devoured them up:

5 Some fell upon stony places, where they had not much earth: and forthwith they sprung up, because they had no deepness of earth:

6 And when the sun was up, they were scorched; and because they had no root, they withered away.

7 And some fell among thorns; and the thorns sprung up, and choked them:

8 But other fell into good ground, and brought forth fruit, some an hundredfold, some sixtyfold, some thirtyfold.

9 Who hath ears to hear, let him hear.

10 ¶ And when he was alone, they that were about him with the twelve asked of him the parable.

11 ¶ Hear ye therefore the parable of the sower.

12 When any one heareth the word of the kingdom, and understandeth it not, then cometh the wicked one, and catcheth away that which was sown in his heart. This is he which received seed by the way side.

13 But he that received the seed into stony places, the same is he that heareth the word, and anon with joy receiveth it;

14 Yet hath he not root in himself, but dureth for a while; for when tribulation or persecution ariseth because of the word, by and by he is offended.

15 He also that received seed among the thorns is he that heareth the word; and the care of this world, and the deceitfulness of riches choke the word, and he becometh unfruitful.

16 But he that received seed into the good ground is he that heareth the word, and understandeth it; which also beareth fruit, and bringeth forth, some an hundredfold, some sixty, some thirty.

XX. Precepts.

AND he said unto them, Is a candle brought to be put under a bushel, or under a bed? and not to be set on a candlestick?

1 For there is nothing hid, which shall not be manifested; neither was any thing kept secret, but that it should come abroad.

2 If any man have ears to hear, let him hear.

XXI. Parable of the Tares.

ANOTHER parable put he forth unto them, saying, The kingdom of heaven is likened unto a man which sowed good seed in his field.

2 But while men slept, his enemy came and sowed tares among the wheat, and went his way.

3 But when the blade was sprung up, and brought forth fruit, then appeared the tares also.

4 So the servants of the householder came and said unto him, Sir, didst not thou sow good seed in thy field? from whence then hath it tares?

5 He said unto them, An enemy hath done this. The servants said unto him, Wilt thou then that we go and gather them up?

6 But he said, Nay; lest while ye gather up the tares, ye root up also the wheat with them.

7 Let both grow together until the harvest: and in the time of harvest I will say to the reapers, Gather ye together first the tares, and bind them in bundles to burn them: but gather the wheat into my barn.

8 if Then Jesus sent the multitude away, and went into the house: and his disciples came unto him, saying, Declare unto us the parable of the tares of the field.

9 He answered and said unto them, He that soweth the good seed is the Son of man;

10 The field is the world; the good seed are the children of the kingdom; but the tares are the children of the wicked one;

11 The enemy that sowed them is the devil; the harvest is the end of the world; and the reapers are the angels.

12 As therefore the tares are gathered and burned in the fire; so shall it be in the end of this world.

13 The Son of man shall send forth his angels, and they shall gather out of his kingdom all things that offend, and them which do iniquity.

14 And shall cast them into a furnace of fire: there shall be wailing and gnashing of teeth.

15 Then shall the righteous shine forth as the sun in the kingdom of their Father. Who hath ears to hear, let him hear.

16 ¶ Again, the kingdom of heaven is like unto treasure hid in a field; the which when a man hath found, he hideth, and for joy thereof goeth and selleth all that he hath, and buyeth that field.

17 ¶ Again, the kingdom of heaven is like unto a merchant man, seeking goodly pearls:

18 Who, when he had found one pearl of great price, went and sold all that he had, and bought it,

19 ¶ Again, the kingdom of heaven is like unto a net, that was cast into the sea, and gathered of every kind:

20 Which, when it was full, they drew to shore, and sat down, and gathered the good into vessels, but cast the bad away.

21 So shall it be at the end of the world: the angels shall come forth, and sever the wicked from among the just,

22 And shall cast them into the furnace of fire: there shall be wailing and gnashing of teeth.

23 Jesus saith unto them, Have ye understood all these things? They say unto him, Yea, Lord.

24 Then said he unto them, Therefore every scribe which is instructed unto the kingdom of heaven is like unto a man that is an householder, which bringeth forth out of his treasure things new and old.

XXII. Precepts.

AND he said, So is the kingdom of God, as if a man should cast seed into the ground;

2 And should sleep, and rise night and day, and the seed should spring and grow up, he knoweth not how.

3 For the earth bringeth forth fruit of herself; first the blade, then the ear, after that the full corn in the ear.

4 But when the fruit is brought forth, immediately he putteth in the sickle, because the harvest is come.

5 ¶ And he said, Whereunto shall we liken the kingdom of God? or with what comparison shall we compare it?

6 It is like a grain of mustard seed, which, when it is sown in the earth, is less than all the seeds that be in the earth:

7 But when it is sown, it groweth up, and becometh greater than all herbs, and shooteth out great branches; so that the fowls of the air may lodge under the shadow of it.

8 And with many such parables spake he the word unto them, as they were able to hear it.

9 But without a parable spake he not unto them; and when they were alone, he expounded all things to his disciples.

10 ¶ And it came to pass, that, as they went in the way, a certain man said unto him, Lord, I will follow thee whithersoever thou goest.

11 And Jesus said unto him, Foxes have holes, and birds of the air have nests; but the Son of man hath not where to lay his head.

12 And he said unto another, Follow me. But he said, Lord, suffer me first to go and bury my father.

13 Jesus said unto him, Let the dead bury their dead: but go thou and preach the kingdom of God.

14 And another also said, Lord, I will follow thee; but let me first go bid them farewell, which are at home at my house.

15 And Jesus said unto him, No man, having put his hand to the plough and looking back, is fit for the kingdom of God.

16 ¶ And after these things he went forth, and saw a publican named Levi, sitting at the receipt of custom: and he said unto him, Follow me.

17 And he left all, rose up, and followed him.

18 And Levi made him a great feast in his own house; and it came to pass, that, as Jesus sat at meat in his house, many publicans and sinners sat also together with Jesus and his disciples: for there were many, and they followed him.

19 And when the scribes and Pharisees saw him eat with publicans and sinners, they said unto his disciples, How is it that he eateth and drinketh with publicans and sinners?

20 When Jesus heard it, he saith unto them, They that are whole have no need of the physician, but they that are sick: I came not to call the righteous, but sinners to repentance.

XXIII. Parable of New Wine in Old Bottles.

AND he spake also a parable unto them; No man putteth a piece of a new garment upon an old; if otherwise, then both the new maketh a rent, and the piece that was taken out of the new agreeth not with the old.

2 And no man putteth new wine into old bottles; else the new wine will burst the bottles, and be spilled and the bottles shall perish.

3 But new wine must be put into new bottles; and both are preserved.

4 No man also having drunk old wine straightway desireth new: for he saith, The old is better.

XXIV. A Prophet Hath no Honor in his Own Country.

AND it came to pass, that when Jesus had finished these parables, he departed thence.

2 And when he was come into his own country, he taught them in their synagogue, insomuch that they were astonished and said, Whence hath this man this wisdom, and these mighty works?

3 Is not this the carpenter's son? is not his mother called Mary? and his brethren James, and Joses, and Simon, and Judas?

4 And his sisters, are they not all with us? Whence then hath this man all these things?

5. And they were offended in him. But Jesus said unto them, A prophet is not without honour, save in his own country, and in his own house.

XXV. Mission Instructions, Return of Apostles.

BUT when he saw the multitudes, he was moved with compassion on them, because they fainted and were scattered abroad, as sheep having no shepherd.

2 ¶ And he called unto him the twelve, and began to send them forth by two and two; and gave them power over unclean spirits;

3 These twelve Jesus sent forth, and commanded them, saying, Go not into the way of the Gentiles, and into any city of the Samaritans enter ye not:

4 But go rather to the lost sheep of the house of Israel.

5 Provide neither gold, nor silver, nor brass in your purses,

6 Nor scrip for your journey, neither two coats, neither shoes, nor yet staves: for the workman is worthy of his meat.

7 And into whatsoever city or town ye shall enter, enquire who in it is worthy; and there abide till ye go thence.

8 And when you come into an house, salute it.

9 And if the house be worthy, let your peace come upon it: but if it be not worthy, let your peace return to you.

10 And whosoever shall not receive you, nor hear your words, when ye depart out of that house or city, shake off the dust of your feet.

11 Verily I say unto you, It shall be more tolerable for the land of Sodom and Gomorrah in the day of judgment, than for that city.

12 ¶ Behold, I send you forth as sheep in the midst of wolves: be ye therefore wise as serpents, and harmless as doves.

13 But beware of men: for they will deliver you up to the councils, and they will scourge you in their synagogues;

14 And ye shall be brought before governors and kings for my sake, for a testimony against them and the Gentiles.

15 But when they persecute you in this city, flee ye into another: for verily I say unto you, Ye shall not have gone over the cities of Israel, till the Son of man be come.

16 Fear them not therefore: for there is nothing covered, that shall not be revealed; and hid, that shall not be known.

17 What I tell you in darkness, that speak ye in light: and what ye hear in the ear, that preach ye upon the housetops.

18 And fear not them which kill the body, but are not able to kill the soul: but rather fear him which is able to destroy both soul and body in hell.

19 Are not two sparrows sold for a farthing? and one of them shall not fall on the ground without your Father.

20 But the very hairs of your head are all numbered.

21 Fear ye not therefore, ye are of more value than many sparrows.

22 And they went out, and preached that men should repent.

23 ¶ And the apostles gathered themselves together unto Jesus, and told him all things, both what they had done, and what they had taught.

XXVI. Precepts.

AFTER these things Jesus walked in Galilee: for he would not walk in Jewry, because the Jews sought to kill him.

2 Then came together unto him the Pharisees, and certain of the scribes, which came from Jerusalem.

3 And when they saw some of his disciples eat bread with defiled, that is to say, with unwashen, hands, they found fault.

4 For the Pharisees, and all the Jews, except they wash their hands oft, eat not, holding the tradition of the elders.

5 And when they come from the market, except they wash, they eat not. And many other things
there be, which they have received to hold, as the washing of cups and pots, brazen vessels, and of tables.

6 Then the Pharisees and scribes asked him, Why walk not thy disciples according to the tradition of the elders, but eat bread with unwashen hands?

7 ¶ And when he had called all the people unto him, he said unto them, Hearken unto me every one of you, and understand:

8 There is nothing from without a man, that entering into him can defile him: but the things which come out of him, those are they that defile the man.

9 If any man have ears to hear let him hear.

10 And when he was entered into the house from the people, his disciples asked him concerning the parable.

11 And he saith unto them, Are ye so without understanding also? Do ye not perceive, that whatsoever thing from without entereth into the man, it cannot defile him;

12 Because it entereth not into his heart, but into the belly, and goeth out into the draught, purging all meats?

13 And he said, That which cometh out of the man, that defileth the man.

14 For from within, out of the heart of men, proceed evil thoughts, adulteries, fornications, murders,

15 Thefts, covetousness, wickedness, deceit, lasciviousness, an evil eye, blasphemy, pride, foolishness:

10 All these evil things come from within, and defile the man.

17 ¶ And from thence he arose, and went into the borders of Tyre and Sidon, and entered into an house, and would have no man know it: but he could not be hid.

18 At the same time came the disciples unto Jesus, saying, Who is the greatest in the kingdom of heaven?

19 And Jesus called a little child unto him, and set him in the midst of them,

20 And said, Verily I say unto you, Except ye be converted, and become as little children, ye shall not enter into the kingdom of heaven.

21 Whosoever therefore shall humble himself as this little child, the same

is greatest in the kingdom of heaven.

22 ¶ Woe unto the. world because of offences! for it must needs be that offences come; but woe to that man by whom the offence cometh!

23 Wherefore if thy hand or thy foot offend thee, cut them off, and cast them from thee: it is better for thee to enter into life halt or maimed, rather than having two hands or two feet to be cast into everlasting fire.

24 And if thine eye offend thee, pluck it out, and cast it from thee: it is better for thee to enter into life with one eye, rather than having two eyes to be cast into hell fire.

25 How think ye? if a man have an hundred sheep, and one of them be gone astray, Both he not leave the ninety and nine, and goeth into the mountains, and seeketh that which is gone astray?

26 And if so be that he find it, verily I say unto you, he rejoiceth more of that sheep, than of the ninety and nine which went not astray.

27 Even so it is not the will of your Father which is in heaven, that one of these little ones should perish.

28 Moreover if thy brother shall trespass against thee, go and tell him his fault between thee and him alone: if he shall hear thee, thou hast gained thy brother.

29 But if he will not hear thee, then take with thee one or two more, that in the mouth of two or three witnesses every word may be established.

30 And if he shall neglect to hear them, tell it unto the church: but if he neglect to hear the church, let him be unto thee as an heathen man and a publican.

31 ¶ Then came Peter to him, and said, Lord, how oft shall my brother sin against me, and I forgive him? till seven times?

32 Jesus saith unto him, I say not unto thee, Until seven times: but, Until seventy times seven.

XXVII. Parable of the Wicked Servant.

THEREFORE is the kingdom of heaven likened unto a certain king, which would take ac count of his servants.

2 And when he had begun to reckon, one was brought unto him, which owed him ten thousand talents.

3 But forasmuch as he had not to pay, his lord commanded him to be sold, and his wife, and children, and all that he had, and payment to be made.

4 The servant therefore fell down, and worshipped him, saying, Lord, have patience with me, and I will pay thee all.

5 Then the lord of that servant was moved with compassion, and loosed him, and forgave him the debt.

6 But the same servant went out, and found one of his fellow-servants, which owed him an hundred pence: and he laid hands on him, and took him by the throat, saying, Pay me that thou owest.

7 And his fellow-servant fell down at his feet, and besought him, saying, Have patience with me, and I will pay thee all.

8 And he would not: but went and cast him into prison, till he should pay the debt.

9 So when his fellow-servants saw what was done, they were very sorry, and came and told unto their lord all that was done.

10 Then his lord, after that he had called him, said unto him, O thou wicked servant, I forgave thee all that debt, because thou desiredst me;

11 Shouldest not thou also have had compassion on thy fellow-servant, even as I had pity on thee?

12 And his lord was wroth, and delivered him to the tormentors, till he should pay all that was due unto him.

13 So likewise shall my heavenly Father do also unto you, if ye from your hearts forgive not every one his brother their trespasses.

XXVIII. Mission of the Seventy.

AFTER these things the Lord appointed other seventy also, and sent them two and two before his face into every city and place, whither he himself would come.

2 Therefore said he unto them, The harvest truly is great, but the labourers are few: pray ye therefore the Lord of the harvest, that he would send forth labourers into his harvest.

3 Go your ways: behold, I send you forth as lambs among wolves.

4 Carry neither purse, nor scrip, nor shoes: and salute no man by the way.

5 And into whatsoever house ye enter, first say, Peace be to this house.

6 And if the son of peace be there, your peace shall rest upon it: if not, it shall turn to you again.

7 And in the same house remain, eating and drinking such things as they give: for the labourer is worthy of his hire. Go not from house to house.

8 And into whatsoever city ye enter, and they receive you, eat such things as are set before you:

9 But into whatsoever city ye enter, and they receive you not, go your ways out into the streets of the same, and say,

10 Even the very dust of your city, which cleaveth on us, we do wipe off against you: notwithstanding be ye sure of this, that the kingdom of God is come nigh unto you.

11 But I say unto you, that it shall be more tolerable in that day for Sodom, than for that city.

XXIX. The Feast of the Tabernacles.

NOW the Jews' feast of tabernacles was at hand.

2 His brethren therefore said unto him, Depart hence, and go into Judea, that thy disciples also may see the works that thou doest.

3 For there is no man that doeth any thing in secret and he himself seeketh to be known openly. If thou do these things, shew thyself to the world.

4 For neither did his brethren believe in him.

5 Then Jesus said unto them, My time is not yet come: but your time is alway ready.

6 The world cannot hate you; but me it hateth, because I testify of it, that the works thereof are evil.

7 Go ye up unto this feast: I go not up yet unto this feast; for my time is not yet full come.

8 When he had said these words unto them, he abode still in Galilee.

9 ¶ But when his brethren were gone up, then, went he also up unto the feast, not openly, but as it were in secret.

10 Then the Jews sought him at the feast, and said, Where is he?

11 And there was much murmuring among the people concerning him: for some said, He is a good man: others said, Nay; but he deceiveth the people.

12 Howbeit no man spake openly of him for fear of the Jews.

13 ¶ Now about the midst of the feast Jesus went up into the temple, and taught.

14 And the Jews marveled, saying, How knoweth this man letters, having never learned?

15 Jesus answered them, and said, My doctrine is not mine, but his that sent me.

16 Did not Moses give you the law, and yet none of you keepeth the law? Why go ye about to kill me?

17 The people answered and said, Thou hast a devil: who goeth about to kill thee?

18 Jesus answered and said unto them, I have done one work, and ye all marvel.

19 Moses therefore gave unto you circumcision; (not because it is of Moses, but of the fathers;) and ye on the sabbath day circumcise a man.

20 If a man on the sabbath day receive circumcision, that the law of Moses should not be broken; are ye angry at me, because I have made a man every whit whole en the sabbath day?

21 Judge not according to the appearance, but judge righteous judgment.

22 Then said some of them of Jerusalem, Is not this he, whom they seek to kill?

23 But, lo, he speaketh boldly, and they say nothing unto him. Do the rulers know indeed that this is the very Christ?

24 ¶ The Pharisees heard that the people murmured such things concerning him; and the Pharisees and the chief priests sent officers to take him.

25 So there was a division among the people because of him.

26 And some of them would have taken him; but no man laid hands on him.

27 ¶ Then came the officers to the chief priests and Pharisees; and they said unto them, Why have ye not brought him?

28 The officers answered, Never man spake like this man.

29 Then answered them the Pharisees, Are ye also deceived?

30 Have any of the rulers or of the Pharisees believed on him?

31 But this people who knoweth not the law are cursed.

32 Nicodemus saith unto them, (he that came to Jesus by night, being one of them,)

33 Doth our law judge any man, before it hear him, and know what he doeth?

34 They answered and said unto him, Art thou also of Galilee? Search, and look: for out of Galilee ariseth no prophet.

35 And every man went unto his own house.

XXX. The Woman Taken in Adultery.

JESUS went unto the mount of Olives.

2 And early in the morning he came again into the temple, and all the people came unto him; and he sat down, and taught them.

3 And the scribes and Pharisees brought unto him a woman taken in adultery; and when they had set her in the midst,

4 They say unto him, Master, this woman was taken in adultery, in the very act.

5 Now Moses in the law commanded us, that such should be stoned; but what sayest thou?

6 This they said, tempting him, that they might have to accuse him. But Jesus stooped down, and with his finger wrote on the ground, as though he heard them not.

7 So when they continued asking him, he lifted up himself, and said unto them, He that is without sin among you, let him first cast a stone at her.

8 And again he stooped down, and wrote on the ground.

9 And they which heard it, being convicted by their own conscience, went out one by one beginning at the eldest, even unto the last: and Jesus was left alone, and the woman standing in the midst.

10 When Jesus had lifted up himself, and saw none but the woman, he said unto her, Woman, where are those thine accusers? hath no man condemned thee?

11 She said, No man, Lord. And Jesus said unto her, Neither do I condemn thee; go, and sin no more.

XXXI. To be Born Blind No Proof of Sin.

AND as Jesus passed by, he saw a man which was blind from his birth.

2 And his disciples asked him, saying, Master, who did sin, this man, or his parents, that he was born blind?

3 Jesus answered, Neither hath this man sinned, nor his parents: but that the works of God should be made manifest in him.

XXXII. The Good Shepherd.

VERILY, verily, I say unto you, He that entereth not by the door into the sheepfold, but climbeth up some other way, the same is a thief and a robber.

2 But he that entereth in by the door is the shepherd of the sheep.

3 To him the porter openeth; and the sheep hear his voice: and he calleth his own sheep by name, and leadeth them out.

4 And when he putteth forth his own sheep, he goeth before them, and the sheep follow him; for they know his voice.

5 And a stranger will they not follow, but will flee from him: for they know not the voice of strangers.

6 I am the good shepherd: the good shepherd giveth his life for the sheep.

7 But he that is an hireling, and not the shepherd, whose own the sheep are not, seeth the wolf coming, and leaveth the sheep, and fleeth: and the wolf catcheth them, and scattereth the sheep.

8 The hireling fleeth, because he is an hireling, and careth not for the sheep.

9 I am the good shepherd, and know my sheep, and am known of mine.

10 And other sheep I have, which are not of this fold: them also I must bring, and they shall hear my voice; and there shall be one fold, and one shepherd.

XXXIII. Love God and Thy Neighbour; Parable of the Samaritan.

AND, behold, a certain lawyer stood up, and tempted him, saying, Master, what shall I do to inherit eternal life?

2 He said unto him, What is written in the law? how readest thou?

3 And he answering said, Thou shalt love the Lord thy God with all thy heart, and with all thy soul, and with all thy strength, and with all thy mind; and thy neighbour as thyself.

4 And he said unto him, Thou hast answered right: this do, and thou shalt live.

5 But he, willing to justify himself, said unto Jesus, And who is my neighbour?

6 And Jesus answering said, A certain man went down from Jerusalem to Jericho, and fell among thieves, which stripped him of his raiment, and wounded him, and departed, leaving him half dead.

7 And by chance there came down a certain priest that way: and when he saw him he passed by on the other side.

8 And likewise a Levite, when he was at the place, came and looked on him, and passed by on the other side.

9 But a certain Samaritan, as he journeyed, came where he was: and when he saw him, he had compassion on him,

10 And went to him, and bound up his wounds, pouring in oil and wine, and set him on his own beast, and brought him to an inn, and took care of him.

11 And on the morrow when he departed, he took out two pence, and gave them to the host, and said unto him, Take care of him; and whatsoever thou spendest more, when I come again, I will repay thee.

12 Which now of these three, thinkest thou, was neighbour unto him that fell among the thieves?

13 And he said, He that shewed mercy on him. Then said Jesus unto him, Go, and do thou likewise.

XXXIV. Form of Prayer.

AND it came to pass, that, as he was praying in a certain place, when he ceased, one of his disciples said unto him, Lord, teach us to pray, as John also taught his disciples.

2 And he said unto them, When ye pray, say, Our Father which art in heaven, Hallowed be thy name. Thy kingdom come. Thy will be done, as in heaven, so in earth.

3 Give us day by day our daily bread.

4 And forgive us our sins; for we also forgive every one that is indebted to us. And lead us not into temptation; but deliver us from evil.

5 And he said unto them, Which of you shall have a friend, and shall go unto him at midnight, and say unto him, Friend, lend me three loaves;

6 For a friend of mine in his journey is come to me, and I have nothing to set before him?

7 And he from within shall answer and say, Trouble me not: the door is now shut; and my children are with me in bed; I cannot rise and give thee.

8 I say unto you, Though he will not rise and give him because he is his friend, yet because of his importunity he will rise and give him as many as he needeth.

9 And I say unto you, Ask, and it shall be given you; seek, and ye shall find; knock, and it shall be opened unto you.

10 For every one that asketh receiveth; and be that seeketh findeth; and to him that knocketh it shall be opened.

11 If a son shall ask bread of any of you that is a father, will he give him a stone? or if he ask a fish, will he for a fish give him a serpent?

12 Or if he shall ask an egg, will he offer him a scorpion?

13 If ye then, being evil, know how to give good gifts unto your children: how much more shall your heavenly Father give the Holy Spirit to them that ask him?

XXXV. The Sabbath.

AND it came to pass, as he went into the house of one of the chief Pharisees to eat bread on the sabbath day, that they watched him.

2 And, behold, there was a certain man before him which had the dropsy.

3 And Jesus answering spake unto the lawyers and Pharisees, saying, Is it lawful to heal on the sabbath day?

4 And they held their peace. And he took him, and healed him, and let him go;

5 And answered them, saying, Which of you shall have an ass or an ox fallen into a pit, and will not straightway pull him out on the sabbath day?

6 And they could not answer him again to these things.

XXXVI. The Bidden to a Feast.

AND he put forth a parable to those which were bidden, when he marked how they chose out the chief rooms; saying unto them,

2 When thou art bidden of any man to a wedding, sit not down in the highest room; lest a more honourable man than thou be bidden of him;

3 And he that bade thee and him come and say to thee, Give this man place; and thou begin with shame to take the lowest room.

4 But when thou art bidden, go and sit down in the lowest room; that when he that bade thee cometh, he may say unto thee, Friend, go up higher: then shalt thou have worship in the presence of them that sit at meat with thee.

5 For whosoever exalteth himself shall be abased; and he that humbleth himself shall be exalted.

6 ¶ [Then said he also to him that bade him, When thou makest a dinner or a supper, call not thy friends, nor thy brethren, neither thy kinsmen, nor thy rich neighbours; lest they also bid thee again, and a recompense be made thee.

7 But when thou makest a feast, call the poor, the maimed, the lame, the blind:

8 And thou shalt be blessed; for they cannot recompense thee: for thou shalt be recompensed at the resurrection of the just.

9 ¶ And when one of them that sat at meat with him heard these things, he said unto him, Blessed is he that shall eat bread in the kingdom of God.

10 Then said he unto him, A certain man made a great supper, and bade many:

11 And sent his servant at supper time to say to them that were bidden, Come; for all things are now ready.

12 And they all with one consent began to make excuse. The first said unto him, I have bought a piece of ground, and I must needs go and see it: I pray thee have me excused.

13 And another said, I have bought five yoke of oxen, and I go to prove them: I pray thee have me excused.

14 And another said, I have married a wife, and therefore I cannot come.

15 So that servant came, and shewed his lord these things. Then the master of the house being angry said to his servant, Go out quickly into the streets and lanes of the city, and bring in hither the poor, and the maimed, and the halt, and the blind.

16 And the servant said, Lord it is done as thou hast commanded, and yet there is room.

17 And the lord said unto the servant, Go out into the highways and hedges, and compel them to come in, that my house may be filled.

18 For I say unto you, That none of those men which were bidden shall taste of my supper.

XXXVII. Precepts.

FOR which of you, intending to build a tower, sitteth not down first, and counteth the cost, whether he have sufficient to finish it?

2 Lest haply, after he hath laid the foundation, and is not able to finish it, all that behold it begin to mock him,

3 Saying, This man began to build, and was not able to finish.

4 Or what king, going to make war against another king, sitteth not down first, and consulteth whether he be able with ten thousand to meet him that cometh against him with twenty thousand?

5 Or else, while the other is yet a great way off, he sendeth an ambassage, and desireth conditions of peace.

XXXVIII. Parables of the Lost Sheep and Prodigal Son.

THEN drew near unto him all the publicans and sinners for to hear him.

2 And the Pharisees and scribes murmured, saying, This man receiveth sinners, and eateth with them.

3 And he spake this parable unto them, saying,

4 What man of you, having an hundred sheep, if he lose one of them, doth not leave the ninety and nine in the wilderness, and go after that which is lost, until he find it?

5 And when he hath found it, he layeth it on his shoulders, rejoicing.

6 And when he cometh home, he calleth together his friends and neighbours, saying unto them, Rejoice with me; for I have found my sheep which was lost.

7 I say unto you, that likewise joy shall be in heaven over one sinner that repenteth, more than over ninety and nine just persons, which need no repentance.

8 ¶ Either what woman having ten pieces of silver, if she lose one piece, doth not light a candle, and sweep the house, and seek diligently till she find it?

9 And when she hath found it, she calleth her friends and her neighbours together, saying, Rejoice with me; for I have found the piece which I had lost.

10 Likewise, I say unto you, there is joy in the presence of the angels of God over one sinner that repenteth.

11 ¶ And he said, A certain man had two sons:

12 And the younger of them said to his father, Father, give me the portion of goods that falleth to me. And he divided unto them his living.

13 And not many days after the younger son gathered all together and took his journey into a far country, and there wasted his substance with riotous living.

14 And when he had spent all, there arose a mighty famine in that land; and he began to be in want.

15 And he went and joined himself to a citizen of that country; and he sent him into his fields to feed swine.

16 And he would fain have filled his belly with the husks that the swine did eat: and no man gave unto him.

17 And when he came to himself, he said, How many hired servants of my father's have bread enough and to spare, and I perish with hunger!

18 I will arise and go to my father, and will say unto him, Father, I have sinned against heaven, and before thee,

19 And am no more worthy to be called thy son: make me as one of thy hired servants.

20 And he arose, and came to his father. But when he was yet a great way off, his father saw him, and had compassion, and ran, and fell on his neck, and

kissed him.

21 And the son said unto him, Father, I have sinned against heaven, and in thy sight, and am no more worthy to be called thy son.

22 But the father said to his servants, Bring forth the best robe, and put it on him; and put a ring on his hand, and shoes on his feet:

23 And bring hither the fatted calf, and kill it; and let us eat, and be merry:

24 For this my son was dead, and is alive again; he was lost, and is found. And they began to be merry.

25 Now his elder son was in the field; and as he came and drew nigh to the house, he heard music and dancing.

26 And he called one of the servants, and asked what these things meant.

27 And he said unto him, Thy brother is come; and thy father hath killed the fatted calf, because he hath received him safe and sound.

28 And he was angry, and would not go in: therefore came his father out, and intreated him.

29 And he answering said to his father, Lo, these many years do I serve thee, neither transgressed I at any time thy commandment: and yet thou never gavest me a kid, that I might make merry with my friends:

30 But as soon as this thy son was come, which hath devoured thy living with harlots, thou hast killed for him the fatted calf.

31 And he said unto him, Son, thou art ever with me, and all that I have is thine.

32 It was meet that we should make merry, and be glad; for this thy brother was dead, and is alive again; and was lost, and is found.

XXXIX. Parable of the Unjust Steward.

AND he said also unto his disciples, There was a certain rich man, which had a steward; and the same was accused unto him that he had wasted his goods.

2 And he called him, and said unto him, How is it that I hear this of thee? give an account of thy stewardship; for thou mayest be no longer steward.

3 Then the steward said within himself, What shall I do? for my lord taketh away from me the stewardship: I cannot dig; to beg I am ashamed.

4 I am resolved what to do, that, when I am put out of the stewardship, they may receive me into their houses.

5 So he called every one of his lord's debtors unto him, and said unto the first, How much owest thou unto my lord?

6 And he said, An hundred measures of oil. And he said unto him, Take thy bill, and sit down quickly, and write fifty.

7 Then said he to another, And how much owest thou? And he said, An hundred measures of wheat. And he said unto him, Take thy bill, and write fourscore.

8 And the lord commended the unjust steward, because he had done wisely; for the children of this world are in their generation wiser than the children of light.

9 And I say unto you, Make to yourselves friends of the mammon of unrighteousness; that, when ye fail, they may receive you into everlasting habitations.

10 He that is faithful in that which is least is faithful also in much: and he that is unjust in the least is unjust also in much.

11 If therefore ye have not been faithful in the unrighteous mammon, who will commit to your trust the true riches?

12 And if ye have not been faithful in that which is another man's, who shall give you that which is your own?

13 No servant can serve two masters: for either he will hate the one, and love the other; or else he will hold to the one, and despise the other. Ye cannot serve God and mammon.

14 ¶ And the Pharisees also, who were covetous, heard all these things: and they derided him.

15 And he said unto them, Ye are they which justify yourselves before men; but God knoweth your hearts: for that which is highly esteemed among men is abomination in the sight of God.

XL. Parable of Lazarus.

THERE was a certain rich man, which was clothed in purple and fine linen and fared sumptuously every day:

2 And there was a certain beggar named Lazarus, which was laid at his gate, full of sores,

3 And desiring to be fed with the crumbs which fell from the rich man's table: moreover the dogs came and licked his sores.

4 And it came to pass, that the beggar died, and was carried by the angels into Abraham's bosom: the rich man also died, and was buried;

5 And in hell he lift up his eyes, being in torments and seeth Abraham afar off, and Lazarus in his bosom.

6 And he cried and said, Father Abraham, have mercy on me, and send Lazarus, that he may dip the tip of his finger in water, and cool my tongue; for I am tormented in this flame.

7 But Abraham said, Son, remember that thou in thy lifetime receivedst thy good things, and likewise Lazarus evil things: but now he is comforted, and thou art tormented.

8 And beside all this, between us and you there is a great gulf fixed: so that they which would pass from hence to you cannot; neither can they pass to us, that would come from thence.

9 Then he said, I pray thee therefore, father, that thou wouldest send him to my father's house:

10 For I have five brethren; that he may testify unto them, lest they also come into this place of torment.

11. Abraham saith unto him, They have Moses and the prophets; let them hear them.

12 And he said, Nay, father Abraham: but if one went unto them from the dead, they will repent.

13 And he said unto him, If they hear not Moses and the prophets, neither will they be persuaded, though one rose from the dead.

XLI. Precepts to be Always Ready.

THEN said he unto the disciples, it is impossible but that offences will come: but woe unto him, through whom they come!

2 It were better for him that a millstone were hanged about his neck, and he cast into the sea, than that he should offend one of these little ones.

3 ¶ Take heed to yourselves: If thy brother trespass against thee, rebuke him; and if he repent, forgive him.

4 And if he trespass against thee seven times in a day, and seven times in a day turn again to thee. saying, T repent; thou shalt forgive him.

5 But which of you, having a servant plowing or feeding cattle, will say unto him by and by, when he is come from the field, Go and sit down to meat?

6 And will not rather say unto him, Make ready wherewith I may sup, and gird thyself, and serve me, till I have eaten and drunken; and afterward thou shalt eat and drink?

7 Doth he thank that servant because he did the things that were commanded him? I trow not.

8 So likewise ye, when ye shall have done all those things which are commanded you, say, We are unprofitable servants: we have done that which was our duty to do.

9 ¶ And when he was demanded of the Pharisees, when the kingdom of God should come, he answered them and said, The Kingdom of God cometh not with observation.

10 And as it was in the days of Noe, so shall it be also in the days of the Son of man.

11 They did eat, they drank, they married wives, they were given in marriage, until the day that Noe entered into the ark, and the flood came, and destroyed them all.

12 Likewise also as it was in the days of Lot; they did eat, they drank, they bought, they sold, they planted, they builded;

13 But the same day that Lot went out of Sodom it rained fire and brimstone from heaven, and destroyed them all.

14 Even thus shall it be in the day when the Son of man is revealed.

15 In that day, he which shall be upon the housetop, and his staff in the house, let him not come down to take it away: and he that is in the field, let him likewise not return back.

16 Remember Lot's wife.

17 Whosoever shall seek to save his life shall lose it; and whosoever shall lose his life shall preserve it.

18 I tell you, in that night there shall be two men in one bed; the one shall be taken, and the other shall be left.

19 Two women shall be grinding together; the one shall be taken, and the other left.

20 Two men shall be in the field; the one shall be taken, and the other left.

XLII. Parables of the Widow and Judge, the Pharisee and Publican.

AND he spake a parable unto them to this end, that men ought always to pray, and not to faint;

2 Saying, There was in a city a judge, which feared not God, neither regarded man:

3 And there was a widow in that city; and she came unto him, saying, Avenge me of mine adversary.

4 And he would not for a while: but afterward he said within himself, Though I fear not God, nor regard man,

5 Yet because this widow troubleth me, I will avenge her, lest by her continual coming she weary me.

6 And the Lord said, Hear what the unjust judge saith.

7 And shall not God avenge his own elect, which cry day and night unto him, though he bear long with them?

8 I tell you that he will avenge them speedily. Nevertheless when the Son of man cometh, shall he find faith on the earth?

9 ¶ And he spake this parable unto certain which trusted in themselves that they were righteous, and despised others:

10 Two men went up into the temple to pray; the one a Pharisee, and the other a publican.

11 The Pharisee stood and prayed thus with himself, God, I thank thee that I am not as other men are, extortioners, unjust, adulterers, or even as this publican.

12 I fast twice in the week, I give tithes of all that I possess.

13 And the publican, standing afar off, would not lift up so much as his eyes unto heaven, but smote upon his breast, saying, God be merciful to me a sinner.

14 I tell you, this man went down to his house justified rather than the other: for every one that exalteth himself shall be abased; and he that humbleth himself shall be exalted.

XLIII. Precepts.

NOW it came to pass, as they went, that he entered into a certain village: and a certain woman named Martha received him into her house.

2 And she had a sister called Mary, which also sat at Jesus' feet, and heard his word.

3 But Martha was cumbered about much serving, and came to him, and said, Lord, dost thou not care that my sister hath left me to serve alone? bid her therefore that she help me.

4 And Jesus answered and said unto her, Martha, Martha, thou art careful and troubled about many things:

5 But one thing is needful: and Mary hath chosen that good part, which shall not be taken away from her.

6 And it came to pass, that when Jesus had finished these sayings, he departed from Galilee, and came into the coasts of Judea beyond Jordan;

7 And great multitudes followed him; and he healed them there.

8 The Pharisees also came unto him, tempting him, and saying unto him, Is it lawful for a man to put away his wife for every cause?

9 And he answered and said unto them, Have ye not read, that he which made them at the beginning made them male and female,

10 And said, For this cause shall a man leave father and mother, and shall cleave to his wife: and they twain shall be one flesh?

11 Wherefore they are no more twain, but one flesh. What therefore God hath joined together, let not man put asunder.

12 They say unto him, Why did Moses then command to give a writing of divorcement, and to put her away?

13 He saith unto them, Moses because of the hardness of your hearts suffered you to put away your wives: but from the beginning it was not so.

14 And I say unto you, Whosoever shall put away his wife, except it be for fornication, and shall marry another, committeth adultery: and whoso marrieth her which is put away doth commit adultery.

15 His disciples say unto him, If the case of the man be so with his wife, it is not good to marry.

16 But he said unto them, All men cannot receive this saying, save they to whom it is given.

17 For there are some eunuchs, which were so born from their mother's womb: and there are some eunuchs, which were made eunuchs of men; and there be eunuchs, which have made themselves eunuchs for the kingdom of heaven's sake. He that is able to receive it, let him receive it.

18 Then were there brought unto him little children, that he should put his hands on them, and pray: and the disciples rebuked them.

19 But Jesus said, Suffer little children, and forbid them not, to come unto me: for of such is the kingdom of heaven.

20 And he laid his hands on them, and departed thence.

21 And, behold, one came and said unto him, Good Master, what good thing shall I do, that I may have eternal life?

22 And he said unto him, Why callest thou me good? there is none good but one, that is, God: but if thou wilt enter into life, keep the commandments.

23 He saith unto him, Which? Jesus said, Thou shalt do no murder, Thou shalt not commit adultery, Thou shalt not steal, Thou shalt not bear false witness,

24 Honour thy father and thy mother: and, Thou shalt love thy neighbour as thyself.

25 The young man saith unto him, All these things have I kept from my youth up: what lack I yet?

26 Jesus said unto him, If thou wilt be perfect, go and sell that thou hast, and give to the poor, and thou shalt have treasure in heaven: and come and follow me.

27 But when the young man heard that saying, he went away sorrowful: for he had great possessions.

28 Then said Jesus unto his disciples, Verily I say unto you, That a rich man shall hardly enter into the kingdom of heaven.

29 And again I say unto you, It is easier for a camel to go through the eye of a needle, than for a rich man to enter into the kingdom of God.

30 When his disciples heard it, they were exceedingly amazed, saying, Who then can be saved?

31 But Jesus beheld them, and said unto them, With men this is impossible; but with God all things are possible.

XLIV. Parable of the Labourers in the Vineyard.

FOR the kingdom of heaven is like unto a man that is an householder, which went out early in the morning to hire labourers into his vineyard.

2 And when he had agreed with the labourers for a penny a day, he sent them into his vineyard.

3 And he went out about the third hour, and saw others standing idle in the marketplace,

4 And said unto them: Go ye also into the vineyard, and whatsoever is right I will give you. And they went their way.

5 Again he went out about the sixth and ninth hour, and did likewise.

6 And about the eleventh hour he went out, and found others standing idle, and saith unto them, Why stand ye here all the day idle?

7 They say unto him, Because no man hath hired us. He saith unto them, Go ye also into the vineyard; and whatsoever is right, that shall ye receive.

8 So when even was come, the lord of the vineyard saith unto his steward, Call the labourers, and give them their hire, beginning from the last unto the first.

9 And when they came that were hired about the eleventh hour, they received every man a penny.

10 But when the first came, they supposed that they should have received more; and they likewise received every man a penny.

11 And when they had received it, they murmured against the goodman of the house,

12 Saying, These last have wrought but one hour, and thou hast made them equal unto us, which have borne the burden and heat of the day.

13 But he answered one of them, and said, Friend, I do thee no wrong; didst thou not agree with me for a penny?

14 Take that thine is and go thy way: I will give unto this last, even as unto thee.

15 Is it not lawful for me to do what I will with mine own? Is thine eye evil, because I am good?

16 So the last shall be first, and the first last: for many be called, but few chosen.

XLV. Zacchaeus, and the Parable of the Talents.

AND Jesus entered and passed through Jericho.

2. And, behold, there was a man named Zacchaeus, which was the chief among the publicans, and he was rich.

3 And he sought to see Jesus who he was; and could not for the press, because he was little of stature.

4 And he ran before, and climbed up into a sycamore tree to see him: for he was to pass that way.

5 And when Jesus came to the place, he looked up, and saw him, and said unto him, Zacchaeus, make haste, and come down; for today I must abide at thy house.

6 And he made haste, and came down, and received him joyfully.

7 And when they saw it, they all murmured, saying, That he was gone to be guest with a man that is a sinner.

8 And Zacchaeus stood, and said unto the Lord; Behold, Lord, the half of my goods I give to the poor; and if I have taken anything from any man by false accusation, I restore him fourfold.

9 And Jesus said unto him, This day is salvation come to this house, forsomuch as he also is a son of Abraham.

10 For the Son of man is come to seek and to save that which was lost.

11 ¶ And as they heard these things, he added and spake a parable, because he was nigh to Jerusalem, and because they thought that the kingdom of God should immediately appear.

12 He said therefore, A certain nobleman went into a far country to receive for himself a kingdom, and to return.

13 And he called his ten servants, and delivered them ten pounds, and said unto them, Occupy till I come.

14 But his citizens hated him, and sent a message after him, saying, We will not have this man to reign over us.

15 And it came to pass, that when he was returned, having received the kingdom, then he commanded these servants to be called unto him, to whom he had given the money, that he might know how much every man had gained by trading.

16 Then came the first, saying, Lord, thy pound hath gained ten pounds.

17 And he said unto him, Well, thou good servant: because thou hast been faithful in a very little, have thou authority over ten cities.

18 And the second came, saying, Lord, thy pound hath gained five pounds.

19 And he said likewise to him, Be thou also over five cities.

20 And another came, saying, Lord, behold, here is thy pound, which I have kept laid up in a napkin:

21 For I feared thee, because thou art an austere man: thou takest up that

thou layedst not down, and reapest that thou didst not sow.

22 And he saith unto him, Out of thine own mouth will I judge thee, thou wicked servant. Thou knewest that I was an austere man, taking up that I laid not down, and reaping that I did not sow:

23 Wherefore then gavest not thou my money into the bank, that at my coming I might have required mine own with usury?

24 And he said unto them that stood by, Take from him the pound, and give it to him that hath ten pounds.

25 (And they said unto him, Lord, he hath ten pounds.)

26 For I say unto you, That unto every one which hath shall be given; and from him that hath not, even that he hath shall be taken away from him.

27 But those mine enemies which would not that I should reign over them, bring hither, and slay them before me.

28 And when he had thus spoken, he went before, ascending up to Jerusalem.

XLVI. Goes to Jerusalem and Bethany.

AND when they drew nigh unto Jerusalem, and were come to Bethphage, unto the mount of Olives, then sent Jesus two disciples,

2 Saying unto them, Go into the village over against you, and straightway ye shall find an ass tied, and a colt with her: loose them, and bring them unto me.

3 And if any man say ought unto you, ye shall say, The Lord hath need of them; and straightway he will send them.

4 And the disciples went, and did as Jesus commanded them,

5 And brought the ass, and the colt, and put on them their clothes, and they set him thereon.

6 And a very great multitude spread their garments in the way; others cut down branches from the trees, and strawed them in the way.

7 And when he was come into Jerusalem, all the city was moved, saying, Who is this?

8 The Pharisees therefore said among themselves, Perceive ye how ye prevail nothing? behold, the world is gone after him.

9 And there were certain Greeks among them that came up to worship at the feast:

10 The same came therefore to Philip, which was of Bethsaida of Galilee, and desired him, saying, Sir, we would see Jesus.

11 Philip cometh and telleth Andrew: and again Andrew and Philip tell Jesus.

12 And Jesus answered them, saying, The hour is come, that the Son of man should be glorified.

13 Verily, verily, I say unto you, Except a corn of wheat fall into the ground and die, it abideth alone: but if it die, it bringeth forth much fruit.

14 And he left them, and went out of the city into Bethany; and he lodged there.

XLVII. The Traders Cast Out from the Temple.

AND on the morrow, when they were come from Bethany, he was hungry:

2 And they came to Jerusalem: and Jesus went into the temple, and began to cast out them that sold and bought in the temple, and overthrew the tables of the money changers, and the seats of them that sold doves;

3 And would not suffer that any man should carry any vessel through the temple.

4 And he taught, saying unto them, Is it not written, My house shall be called of all nations the house of prayer? but ye have made it a den of thieves.

5 And the scribes and chief priests heard it, and sought how they might destroy him: for they feared him, because all the people was astonished at his doctrine.

6 And when even was come, he went out of the city.

XLVIII. Parable of the Two Sons.

AND they came again to Jerusalem: and as he was walking in the temple, there came to him the chief priests, and the scribes, and the elders,

2 And they answered Jesus and said, We cannot tell. And he said unto them, Neither tell I you by what authority I do these things.

3 But what think ye? A certain man had two sons; and he came to the first, and said, Son, go work today in my vineyard.

4 He answered and said, I will not: but afterward he repented, and went.

5 And he came to the second, and said likewise. And he answered and said I go, sir: and went not.

6 Whether of them twain did the will of his father? They say unto him, The first. Jesus saith unto them, Verily I say unto you, That the publicans and the harlots go into the kingdom of God before you.

XLIX. Parable of the Vineyard and Husbandmen.

HEAR another parable: There was a certain householder, which planted a vineyard, and hedged it round about, and digged a wine-press in it, and built a tower, and let it out to husbandmen, and went into a far country:

2 And at the season he sent to the husbandmen a servant, that he might receive from the husband-men of the fruit of the vineyard.

3 And they caught him, and beat him, and sent him away empty.

4 And again he sent unto them another servant; and at him they cast stones, and wounded him in the head, and sent him away shamefully handled.

5 And again he sent another; and him they killed, and many others; beating some, and killing some.

6 Having yet therefore one son, his well-beloved, he sent him also last unto them, saying, They will reverence my son.

7 But those husbandmen said among themselves, This is the heir; come, let us kill him, and the inheritance shall be ours.

8 And they took him, and killed him and cast him out of the vineyard.

9 What shall therefore the lord of the vineyard do? he will come and destroy the husbandmen, and will give the vineyard unto others.

10 And when the chief priests and Pharisees had heard his parables, they perceived that he spake of them.

11 But when they sought to lay hands on him, they feared the multitude, because they took him for a prophet.

L. Parable of the King and the Wedding.

AND Jesus answered and spake unto them again by parables, and said,

2 The kingdom of heaven is like unto a certain king, which made a marriage for his son;

3 And sent forth his servants to call them that were bidden to the wedding; and they would not come.

4 Again, he sent forth other servants, saying, Tell them which are bidden, Behold, I have prepared my dinner; my oxen and my fatlings are killed, and all things are ready: come unto the marriage.

5 But they made light of it, and went their ways, one to his farm, another to his merchandise:

6 And the remnant took his servants, and entreated them spitefully, and slew them.

7 But when the king heard thereof, he was wroth: and he sent forth his armies, and destroyed those murderers, and burned up their city.

8 Then saith he to his servants, The wedding is ready, but they which were bidden were not worthy.

9 Go ye therefore into the highways, and as many as ye shall find, bid to the marriage.

10 So those servants went out into the highways, and gathered together all as many as they found, both bad and good; and the wedding was furnished with guests.

11 And when the king came in to see the guests, he saw there a man which had not on a wedding garment:

12 And he saith unto him, Friend, how earnest thou in hither not having a wedding garment? And he was speechless.

13 Then the king said to the servants, Bind him hand and foot, and take him away and cast him into outer darkness: there shall be weeping and gnashing of teeth.

14 For many are called, but few are chosen.

LI. Tribute, Marriage, Resurrection.

THEN went the Pharisees, and took counsel how they might entangle him in his talk.

2 And they sent out unto him their disciples with the Herodians, saying, Master, we know that thou art true, and teachest the way of God in truth, neither carest thou for any man: for thou regardest not the person of men.

3 Tell us therefore, What thinkest thou? Is it lawful to give tribute unto Caesar, or not?

4 But Jesus perceived their wickedness, and said, Why tempt ye me, ye hypocrites?

5 Shew me the tribute money. And they brought unto him a penny.

6 And he saith unto them, Whose is this image and superscription?

7 They say unto him, Caesar's. Then saith he unto them, Render therefore unto Caesar the things which are Caesar's; and unto God the things that are God's.

8 When they had heard these words, they marvelled, and left him and went their way.

9 The same day came to him the Sadducees, which say that there is no resurrection, and asked him,

10 Saying, Master, Moses said, If a man die, having no children, his brother shall marry his wife, and raise up seed unto his brother.

11 Now there were with us seven brethren: and the first, when he had married a wife, deceased, and, having no issue, left his wife unto his brother:

12 Likewise the second also, and the third, unto the seventh.

13 And last of all the woman died also.

14 Therefore in the resurrection whose wife shall she be of the seven? for they all had her.

15 Jesus answered and said unto them, Ye do err, not knowing the scriptures, nor the power of God.

16 For in the resurrection they neither marry, nor are given in marriage, but are as the angels of God in heaven.

17 But as touching the resurrection of the dead, have ye not read that which was spoken unto you by God, saying,

18 I am the God of Abraham, and the God of Isaac and the God of Jacob? God is not the God of the dead, but of the living.

19 And when the multitude heard this, they were astonished at his doctrine.

LII. The Two Commandments.

AND one of the scribes came, and having heard them reasoning together, and perceiving that he had answered them well, asked him, Which is the first commandment of all?

2 And Jesus answered him, The first of all the commandments is, Hear, O Israel; The Lord our God is one Lord:

3 And thou shalt love the Lord thy God with all thy heart, and with all thy soul, and with all thy mind, and with all thy strength: this is the first commandment.

4 And the second is like, namely this, Thou shalt love thy neighbour as thyself. There is none other commandment greater than these.

5 On these two commandments hang all the law and the prophets.

6 And the scribe said unto him, Well, Master, thou hast said the truth: for there is one God; and there is none other but he:

7 And to love him with all the heart, and with all the understanding, and with all the soul, and with all the strength, and to love his neighbour as himself, is more than all whole burnt offerings and sacrifices.

LIII. Precepts, Pride, Hypocrisy, Swearing.

THEN spake Jesus to the multitude, and to his disciples,

2 Saying, The scribes and the Pharisees sit in Moses' seat:

3 All therefore whatsoever they bid you observe, that observe and do; but do not ye after their works: for they say, and do not.

4 For they bind heavy burdens and grievous to be borne, and lay them on men's shoulders; but they themselves will not move them with one of their fingers.

5 But all their works they do for to be seen of men: they make broad their phylacteries, and enlarge the borders of their garments,

6 And love the uppermost rooms at feasts, and the chief seats in the synagogues,

7 And greetings in the markets, and to be called of men, Rabbi, Rabbi.

8 But be not ye called Rabbi: for one is your Master, even Christ; and all ye are brethren.

9 And call no man your father upon the earth; for one is your Father, which is in heaven.

10 Neither be ye called masters: for one is your Master, even Christ.

11 But he that is greatest among you shall be your servant.

12 And whosoever shall exalt himself shall be abased; and he that shall humble himself shall be exalted.

13 ¶ But woe unto you, scribes and Pharisees, hypocrites! for ye shut up the kingdom of heaven against men: for ye neither go in yourselves, neither suffer ye them that are entering to go in.

14 Woe unto you, scribes and Pharisees, hypocrites! for ye devour widows' houses, and for a pretence make long prayer: therefore ye shall receive the greater damnation.

15 Woe unto you, scribes and Pharisees, hypocrites! for ye compass sea and land to make one proselyte, and when he is made, ye make him twofold more the child of hell than yourselves.

16 Woe unto you, ye blind guides, which say, Whosoever shall swear by the temple, it is nothing;
but whosoever shall swear by the gold of the temple, he is a debtor!

17 Ye fools and blind: for whether is greater, the gold, or the temple that sanctifieth the gold?

18 And, Whosoever shall swear by the altar, it is nothing; but whosoever sweareth by the gift that is upon it, he is guilty.

19 Ye fools and blind: for whether is greater, the gift, or the altar that sanctifieth the gift?

20 Whoso therefore shall swear by the altar, sweareth by it, and by all things thereon.

21 And whoso shall swear by the temple, sweareth by it, and by him that

dwelleth therein.

22 And he that shall swear by heaven, sweareth by the throne of God, and by him that sitteth thereon.

23 Woe unto you, scribes and Pharisees, hypocrites! for ye pay tithe of mint and anise and cummin, and have omitted the weightier matters of the law, judgment, mercy, and faith: these ought ye to have done, and not to leave the other undone.

24 Ye blind guides, which strain at a gnat, and swallow a camel.

25 Woe unto you, scribes and Pharisees, hypocrites! for ye make clean the outside of the cup and of the platter, but within they are full of extortion and excess.

26 Thou blind Pharisee, cleanse first that which is within the cup and platter, that the outside of them may be clean also.

27 Woe unto you, scribes and Pharisees, hypocrites! for ye are like unto whited sepulchres, which indeed appear beautiful outward, but are within full of dead men's bones, and of all uncleanness.

28 Even so ye also outwardly appear righteous unto men, but within ye are full of hypocrisy and iniquity.

29 Woe unto you, scribes and Pharisees, hypocrites! because ye build the tombs of the prophets, and garnish the sepulchres of the righteous,

30 And say, If we had been in the days of our fathers, we would not have been partakers with them in the blood of the prophets.

31 Wherefore ye be witnesses unto yourselves, that ye are the children of them which killed the prophets.

32 Fill ye up then the measure of your fathers.

33 Ye serpents, ye generation of vipers, how can ye escape the damnation of hell?

LIV. The Widow's Mite.

AND Jesus sat over against the treasury, and beheld how the people cast money into the treasury: and many that were rich cast in much.

2 And there came a certain poor widow, and she threw in two mites, which make a farthing.

3 And he called unto him his disciples, and saith unto them, Verily I say unto you, That this poor widow hath cast more in, than all they which have cast into the treasury:

4 For all they did cast in of their abundance; but she of her want did cast in all that she had, even all her living.

LV. Jerusalem and the Day of Judgment.

AND ND Jesus went out, and departed from the temple: and his disciples came to him for to shew him the buildings of the temple.

2 And Jesus said unto them, See ye not all these things? verily I say unto you, There shall not be left here one stone upon another, that shall not be thrown down.

3 Then let them which be in Judea flee into the mountains:

4 Let him which is on the housetop not come down to take any thing out of his house:

5 Neither let him which is in the field return back to take his clothes.

6 And woe unto them that are with child, and to them that give suck in those days!

7 But pray ye that your flight be not in the winter, neither on the sabbath day:

8 For then shall be great tribulation, such as was not since the beginning of the world to this time, no, nor ever shall be.

9 ¶ Now learn a parable of the fig tree; When his branch is yet tender, and putteth forth leaves, ye know that summer is nigh:

10 So likewise ye, when ye shall see all these things, know that it is near even at the doors.

11 ¶ But of that day and hour knoweth no man, no, not the angels of heaven, but my Father only.

12 But as the days of Noe were, so shall also the coming of the Son of man be.

13 For as in the days that were before the flood they were eating and drinking, marrying and giving in marriage until the day that Noe entered into the ark,

14 And knew not until the flood came, and took them all away; so shall also the coming of the Son of man be.

15 Then shall two be in the field; the one shall be taken, and the other left.

16 Two women shall be grinding at the mill; the one shall be taken, and the other left.

17 Watch therefore: for ye know not what hour your Lord doth come.

18 But know this, that if the goodman of the house had known in what watch the thief would come, he would have watched, and would not have suffered his house to be broken up.

19 Therefore be ye also ready: for in such an hour as ye think not the Son of man cometh.

LVI. The Faithful and Wise Servant.

WHO then is a faithful and wise servant, whom his lord hath made ruler over his household, to give them meat in due season?

2 Blessed is that servant, whom his lord when he cometh shall find so doing.

3 Verily I say unto you, That he shall make him ruler over all his goods.

4 But and if that evil servant shall say in his heart, My lord delayeth his coming;

5 And shall begin to smite his fellow-servants, and to eat and drink with the drunken;

6 The lord of that servant shall come in a day when he looketh not for him, and in an hour that he is not aware of,

7 And shall cut him asunder, and appoint him his portion with the hypocrites: there shall be weeping and gnashing of teeth.

LVII. Parable of the Ten Virgins.

THEN shall the kingdom of heaven be likened unto ten virgins, which took their lamps, and went forth to meet the bridegroom.

2 And five of them were wise, and five were foolish.

3 They that were foolish took their lamps, and took no oil with them:

4 But the wise took oil in their vessels with their lamps.

5 While the bridegroom tarried, they all slumbered and slept.

6 And at midnight there was a cry made, Behold, the bridegroom cometh; go ye out to meet him.

7 Then all those virgins arose, and trimmed their lamps.

8 And the foolish said unto the wise, Give us of your oil; for our lamps are gone out.

9 But the wise answered, saying, Not so; lest there be not enough for us and you: but go ye rather to them that sell, and buy for yourselves.

10 And while they went to buy, the bridegroom came; and they that were ready went in with him to the marriage: and the door was shut.

11 Afterward came also the other virgins, saying, Lord, Lord, open to us.

12 But he answered and said, Verily I say unto you, I know you not.

13 Watch, therefore, for ye know neither the clay nor the hour wherein the Son of man cometh.

LVIII. Parable of the Talents.

FOR the kingdom of heaven is as a man travelling into a far country, who called his own servants, and delivered unto them his goods.

2 And unto one he gave five talents, to another two, and to another one; to every man according to his several ability; and straightway took his journey.

3 Then he that had received the five talents went and traded with the same, and made them other five talents.

4 And likewise he that had received two, he also gained other two.

5 But he that had received one went and digged in the earth, and hid his lord's money.

6 After a long time the lord of those servants cometh, and reckoneth with them.

7 And so he that had received five talents came and brought other five talents, saying, Lord, thou deliveredst unto me five talents: behold, I have gained beside them five talents more.

8 His lord said unto him, Well done, thou good and faithful servant: thou hast been faithful over a few things, I will make thee ruler over many things: enter thou into the joy of thy lord.

9 He also that had received two talents came and said, Lord, thou deliveredst unto me two talents: behold, I have gained two other talents beside them.

10 His lord said unto him, Well done, good and faithful servant; thou hast been faithful over a few things, I will make thee ruler over many things; enter thou into the joy of thy lord.

11 Then he which had received the one talent came and said, Lord, I knew thee that thou art an
hard man, reaping where thou hast not sown, and gathering where thou hast not strawed:

12 And I was afraid, and went and hid thy talent in the earth: lo, there thou hast that is thine.

13 His lord answered and said unto him, Thou wicked and slothful servant, thou knewest that I reap where I sowed not, and gather where I have not strawed:

14 Thou oughtest therefore to have put my money to the exchangers, and then at my coming I should have received mine own with usury.

15 Take therefore the talent from him, and give it unto him which hath ten talents.

16 For unto every one that hath shall be given, and he shall have abundance: but from him that hath not shall be taken away even that which he hath.

17 And cast ye the unprofitable servant into outer darkness: there shall be weeping and gnashing of teeth.

LIX. The Day of Judgment.

AND take heed to yourselves, lest at any time your hearts be overcharged with surfeiting, and drunkenness, and cares of this life, and so that day come upon you unawares.

2 For as a snare shall it come on all them that dwell on the face of the whole earth.

3 Watch ye therefore, and pray always, that ye may be accounted worthy to escape all these things that shall come to pass, and to stand before the Son of man.

4 When the Son of man shall come in his glory, and all the holy angels with him, then shall he sit upon the throne of his glory:

5 And before him shall be gathered all nations: and he shall separate them one from another, as a shepherd divideth his sheep from the goats:

6 And he shall set the sheep on his right hand, but the goats on the left.

7 Then shall the King say unto them on his right hand, Come, ye blessed of my Father, inherit the kingdom prepared for you from the foundation of the world:

8 For I was an hungred, and ye gave me meat: I was thirsty, and ye gave me drink: I was a stranger, and ye took me in:

9 Naked, and ye clothed me: I was sick, and ye visited me: I was, in prison, and ye came unto me.

10 Then shall the righteous answer him, saying, Lord, when saw we thee an hungred, and fed thee? or thirsty, and gave thee drink?

11 When saw we thee a stranger, and took thee in? or naked, and clothed thee?

12 Or when saw we thee sick, or in prison, and came unto thee?

13 And the King shall answer and say unto them, Verily I say unto you, Inasmuch as ye have done it unto one of the least of these my brethren, ye have done it unto me.

14 Then shall he say also unto them on the left hand, Depart from me, ye cursed, into everlasting fire, prepared for the devil and his angels:

15 For I was an hungred, and ye gave me no meat: I was thirsty, and ye gave me no drink:

16 I was a stranger, and ye took me not in: naked, and ye clothed me not: sick, and in prison, and ye visited me not.

17 Then shall they also answer him, saying, Lord, when saw we thee an hungred, or athirst, or a stranger, or naked, or sick, or in prison, and did not minister unto thee?

18 Then shall he answer them, saying, Verily, I say unto you, Inasmuch as ye did it not to one of the least of these, ye did it not to me.

19 And these shall go away into everlasting punishment: but the righteous into life eternal.

LX. A Woman Anointeth Him.

AFTER two days was the feast of the passover, and of unleavened bread: and the chief priests and the scribes sought how they might take him by craft, and put him to death.

2 But they said, Not on the feast day, lest there be an uproar of the people.

3 ¶ And being in Bethany in the house of Simon the leper, as he sat at meat, there came a woman having an alabaster box of ointment of spikenard very precious; and she brake the box, and poured it on his head.

4 And there were some that had indignation within themselves, and said, Why was this waste of the ointment made?

5 For it might have been sold for more than three hundred pence, and have been given to the poor. And they murmured against her.

6 And Jesus said, Let her alone; why trouble ye her? she hath wrought a good work on me.

7 For ye have the poor with you always, and whensoever ye will ye may do them good: but me ye have not always.

8 She hath done what she could: she is come aforehand to anoint my body to the burying.

LXI. Judas Undertakes to Point Out Jesus.

THEN one of the twelve, called Judas Iscariot, went unto the chief priests,

2 And said unto them, What will ye give me, and I will deliver him unto you? And they covenanted with him for thirty pieces of silver.

3 And from that time he sought opportunity to betray him.

LXII. Precepts to His Disciples, Washes their Feet. Trouble of Mind and Prayer.

NOW the first day of the feast of unleavened bread the disciples came to Jesus, saying unto him, Where wilt thou that we prepare for thee to eat the passover?

2 And he said, Go into the city to such a man, and say unto him, The Master saith, My time is at hand; I will keep the passover at thy house with my disciples.

3 And the disciples did as Jesus had appointed them; and they made ready the passover.

4 Now when the even was come, he sat down with the twelve.

5 And there was also a strife among them, which of them should be accounted the greatest.

6 And he said unto them, The kings of the Gentiles exercised lordship over them; and they that
exercise authority upon them are called benefactors.

7 But ye shall not be so: but he that is greatest among you, let him be as the younger; and he that is chief, as he that Both serve.

8 For whether is greater, he that sitteth at meat, or he that serveth? is not he that sitteth at meat? but I am among you as he that serveth.

9 And supper being ended, the devil having now put into the heart of Judas Iscariot, Simon's son, to betray him;

10 He riseth from supper, and laid aside his garments; and took a towel, and girded himself.

11 After that he poureth water into a bason, and began to wash the disciples' feet, and to wipe them with the towel wherewith he was girded.

12 Then cometh he to Simon Peter; and Peter saith unto him, Lord, dost thou wash my feet?

13 Jesus answered and said unto him, What I do thou knowest not now; but thou shalt know hereafter.

14 Peter saith unto him, Thou shalt never wash my feet. Jesus answered him, If I wash thee not, thou hast no part with me.

15 Simon Peter saith unto him, Lord, not my feet only, but also my hands and my head.

16 Jesus saith to Him, He that is washed needeth not save to wash his feet, but is clean every whit: and ye are clean, but not all.

17 For he knew who should betray him; therefore said he, Ye are not all clean.

18 So after he had washed their feet, and had taken his garments, and was set down again, he said unto them, Know ye what I have done to you?

19 Ye call me Master and Lord: and ye say well; for so I am.

20 If I then, your Lord and Master, have washed your feet; ye also ought to

wash one another's feet.

21 For I have given you an example, that ye should do; as I have done to you.

22 Verily, verily, I shy unto you, The servant is not greater than his lord; neither he that is sent greater than he that sent him.

23 If ye know these things, happy are ye if ye do them.

24 When Jesus had thus said, he was troubled in spirit, and testified, and said, Verily, verily, I say unto you, that one of you shall betray me.

25 Then the disciples looked one on another, doubting of whom he spake.

26 Now there was leaning on Jesus' bosom one of his disciples whom Jesus loved.

27 Simon Peter therefore beckoned to him, that he should ask who it should be of whom he spake.

28 He then lying on Jesus' breast saith unto him, Lord, who is it?

29 Jesus answered, He it is, to whom I shall give a sop, when I have dipped it. And when he had dipped the sop, he gave it to Judas Iscariot, the son of Simon.

30 ¶ Therefore, when he was gone out, Jesus said, Now is the Son of man glorified, and God is glorified in him.

31 A new commandment I give unto you, That ye love one another; as I have loved you, that ye also love one another.

32 By this shall all men know that ye are my disciples, if ye have love one to another.

33 Then said Jesus unto them, All ye shall be offended because of me this night: for it is written,
I will smite the shepherd, and the sheep of the flock shall be scattered abroad.

34 Peter answered and said unto him, Though all men shall be offended because of thee, yet will I never be offended.

35 And he said unto him, Lord, I am ready to go with thee, both into prison, and to death.

36 And he said, I tell thee, Peter, the cock shall not crow this day, before that thou shalt thrice deny that thou knowest me.

37 Peter said unto him, Though I should die with thee, yet will I not deny thee. Likewise also said all the disciples.

38 ¶ Then cometh Jesus with them unto a place called Gethsemane, and said unto the disciples, Sit ye here, while I go and pray yonder.

39 And he took with him Peter and the two. sons of Zebedee, and began to be sorrowful and very heavy.

40 Then saith he unto them, My soul is exceeding sorrowful, even unto death: tarry ye here, and watch with me.

41 And he went a little farther, and fell on his face, and prayed, saying, O my Father, if it be possible, let this cup pass from me: nevertheless not as I will, but as thou wilt.

42 And he cometh unto the disciples, and findeth them asleep, and saith unto Peter, What, could ye not watch with me one hour?

43 Watch and pray, that ye enter not into temptation: the spirit indeed is willing, but the flesh is weak.

44 He went away again the second time, and prayed, saying, O my Father,

if this cup may not pass away from me, except I drink it, thy will be done.

45 And he came and found them asleep again: for their eyes were heavy.

46 And he left them, and went away again, and prayed the third time, saying the same words.

47 Then cometh he to his disciples, and saith unto them, Sleep on now, and take your rest: behold, the hour is at hand, and the Son of man is betrayed into the hands of sinners.

LXIII. Judas Conducts the Officers to Jesus.

WHEN Jesus had spoken these words, he went forth with his disciples over the brook Cedron, where was a garden, into the which he entered, and his disciples.

2 And Judas also, which betrayed him, knew the place: for Jesus ofttimes resorted thither with his disciples.

3 Judas then, having received a band of men and officers from the chief priests and Pharisees, cometh thither with lanterns and torches and weapons.

4 Now he that betrayed him gave them a sign, saying, Whomsoever I shall kiss, that same is he: hold him fast.

5 And forthwith he came to Jesus, and said, Hail, master; and kissed him.

6 And Jesus said unto him, Friend, wherefore art thou come? Then came they, and laid hands on Jesus, and took him.

LXIV. He is Arrested and Carried Before Caiaphas, the High Priest and is Condemned.

JESUS therefore, knowing all things that should come upon him, went forth, and said unto them, Whom seek ye?

2 They answered him, Jesus of Nazareth. Jesus saith unto them, I am he. And Judas also, which betrayed him, stood with them.

3 As soon then as he had said unto them, I am he, they went backward, and fell to the ground.

4 Then asked he them again, Whom seek ye? And they said, Jesus of Nazareth.

5 Jesus answered, I have told you that I am he; if therefore ye seek me, let these go their way:

6 And Jesus said unto him, Friend, wherefore art thou come? Then came they, and laid hands on Jesus, and took him.

7 And, behold, one of them which were with Jesus stretched out his hand, and drew his sword, and struck a servant of the high priest's, and smote off his ear.

8 Then said Jesus unto him, Put up again thy sword into his place: for all they that take the sword shall perish with the sword.

9 In that same hour said Jesus to the multitudes, Are ye come out as against a thief with swords and staves for to take me? I sat daily with you teaching in the temple, and ye laid no hold on me.

10 But all this was done, that the scriptures of the prophets might be fulfilled. Then all the disciples forsook him, and fled.

11 And there followed him a certain young man, having a linen cloth cast about his naked body; and the young men laid hold on him:

12 And he left the linen cloth, and fled from them naked.

13 ¶ And they that had laid hold on Jesus led him away to Caiaphas the high priest, where the scribes and the elders were assembled.

14 And Simon Peter followed Jesus, and so did another disciple: that disciple was known unto the high priest, and went in with Jesus into the palace of the high priest.

15 But Peter stood at the door without. Then went out that other disciple, which was known unto the high priest, and spake unto her that kept the door, and brought in Peter.

16 Then saith the damsel that kept the door, unto Peter, Art not thou also one of this man's disciples? He saith, I am not.

17 And the servants and officers stood there, who had made a fire of coals; for it was cold: and they warmed themselves: and Peter stood with them, and warmed himself.

18 ¶ And Simon Peter stood and warmed himself. They said therefore unto him, Art not thou also one of his disciples? He denied it, and said, I am not.

19 One of the servants of the high priest, being his kinsman whose ear Peter cut off, saith, Did not I see thee in the garden with him?

20 Peter then denied again: and immediately the cock crew.

21 And Peter remembered the word of Jesus, which said unto him, Before the cock crow, thou shalt deny me thrice. And he went out, and wept bitterly.

22 ¶ The high priest then asked Jesus of his disciples, and of his doctrine.

23 Jesus answered him, I spake openly to the world; I ever taught in the synagogue, and in the temple, whither the Jews always resort; and in secret have I said nothing.

24 Why askest thou me? ask them which heard me, what I have said unto them: behold, they know what I said.

25 And when he had thus spoken, one of the officers which stood by struck Jesus with the palm of his hand, saying, Answerest thou the high priest so?

26 Jesus answered him, If I have spoken evil, bear witness of the evil; but if well, why smitest thou me?

27 And the chief priests and all the council sought for witness against Jesus to put him to death; and found none.

28 For many bare false witness against him, but their witness agreed not together.

29 And there arose certain, and bare false witness against him, saying,

30 We heard him say, I will destroy this temple that is made with hands, and within three days I will build another made without hands.

31 But neither so did their witness agree together.

32 And the high priest stood up in the midst, and asked Jesus, saying, Answerest thou nothing? what is it which these witness against thee?

33 But he held his peace, and answered nothing. Again the high priest asked him, and said unto him, Art thou the Christ, the Son of the Blessed?

34 Art thou the Christ? tell us. And he said unto them, If I tell you, ye will not believe:

35 And if I also ask you, ye will not answer me, nor let me go.

36 Then said they all, Art thou then the Son of God? And he said unto them, Ye say that I am.

37 Then the high priest rent his clothes, and saith, What need we any further witnesses?

38 Ye have heard the blasphemy: what think ye? And they all condemned him to be guilty of death.

39 And some began to spit on him, and to cover his face, and to buffet him, and to say unto him, Prophesy: and the servants did strike him with the palms of their hands.

LXV. Is then Carried to Pilate.

THEN led they Jesus from Caiaphas unto the hall of judgment: and it was early; and they themselves went not into the judgment hall, lest they should be defiled; but that they might eat the passover.

2 Pilate then went out unto them, and said, What accusation bring ye against this man?

3 They answered and said unto him, If he were not a malefactor, we would not have delivered him up unto thee.

4 Then said Pilate unto them, Take ye him, and judge him according to your law. The Jews therefore said unto him, It is not lawful for us to put any man to death.

5 Then Pilate entered into the judgment hall again, and called Jesus, and said unto him, Art thou the King of the Jews?

6 Jesus answered him, Sayest thou this thing of thyself, or did others tell it thee of me?

7 Pilate answered, Am I a Jew? Thine own nation and the chief priests have delivered thee unto me: what hast thou done?

8 Jesus answered, My kingdom is not of this world; if my kingdom were of this world, then would my servants fight, that I should not be delivered to the Jews: but now is my kingdom not from hence.

9 Pilate therefore said unto him, Art thou a king then? Jesus answered, Thou sayest that I am a king. To this end was I born, and for this cause came I into the world, that I should bear witness unto the truth. Every one that is of the truth heareth my voice.

10 Pilate saith unto him, What is truth? And when he had said this, he went out again unto the Jews, and saith unto them, I find in him no fault at all.

11 And they were the more fierce, saying, He stirreth up the people, teaching throughout all Jewry, beginning from Galilee to this place.

12 Then said Pilate unto him, Hearest thou not how many things they witness against thee?

LXVI. Who Sends Him to Herod.

WHEN Pilate heard of Galilee, he asked whether the man were a Galilean.

2 And as soon as he knew that he belonged unto Herod's jurisdiction, he sent him to Herod, who himself also was at Jerusalem at that time.

3 ¶ And when Herod saw Jesus, he was exceeding glad: for he was desirous to see him of a long season, because he had heard many things of him; and he hoped to have seen some miracle done by him.

4 Then he questioned with him in many words; but he answered him nothing.

5 And the chief priests and scribes stood and vehemently accused him.

6 And Herod with his men of war set him at naught, and mocked him, and arrayed him in a gorgeous robe, and sent him again to Pilate.

7 And the same day Pilate and Herod were made friends together: for before they were at enmity between themselves.

LXVII. Receives Him Back, Scourges and Delivers Him to Execution.

AND Pilate, when he had called together the chief priests and the rulers and the people,

2 Said unto them, Ye have brought this man unto me, as one that perverteth the people: and, behold, I, having examined him before you, have found no fault in this man touching those things whereof ye accuse him:

3 No, nor yet Herod: for I sent you to him; and, lo, nothing worthy of death is done unto him.

4 I will therefore chastise him, and release him.

5 ¶ Now at that feast the governor was wont to release unto the people a prisoner, whom they would.

6 And they had then a notable prisoner, called Barabbas.

7 Therefore when they were gathered together, Pilate said unto them, Whom will ye that I release unto you? Barabbas, or Jesus which is called Christ?

8 For he knew that for envy they had delivered him.

9 ¶ When he was set down on the judgment seat, his wife sent unto him, saying, Have thou nothing to do with that just man: for I have suffered many things this day in a dream because of him.

10 But the chief priests and elders persuaded the multitude that they should ask Barabbas, and destroy Jesus.

11 The governor answered and said unto them, Whether of the twain will ye that I release unto you? They said, Barabbas.

12 Pilate saith unto them, What shall I do then with Jesus which is called Christ? They all say unto him, Let him be crucified.

13 And the governor said, Why, what evil hath he done? But they cried out the more, saying, Let him be crucified.

14 Then released he Barabbas unto them: and when he had scourged Jesus, he delivered him to be crucified.

LXVIII. His Crucifixion, Death, and Burial.

THEN the soldiers of the governor took Jesus into the common hall, and gathered unto him the whole band of soldiers.

2 And when they had platted a crown of thorns, they put it upon his head, and a reed in his right hand: and they bowed the knee before him, and mocked him, saying, Hail, King of the Jews!

3 And they spit upon him, and took the reed and smote him on the head.

4 And after that they had mocked him, they took the robe off from him, and put his own raiment on him, and led him away to crucify him.

5 ¶j Then Judas, which had betrayed him, when he saw that he was condemned, repented himself, and brought again the thirty pieces of silver to the chief priests and elders,

6 Saying, I have sinned in that. I have betrayed the innocent blood. And they said, What is that to us? see thou to that.

7 And he cast down the pieces of silver in the temple, and departed, and went and hanged himself.

8 And the chief priests took the silver pieces, and said, It is not lawful for to put them into the treasury, because it is the price of blood.

9 And they took counsel, and bought with them the potter's field, to bury strangers in.

10 Wherefore that field was called, The field of blood, unto this day.

11 ¶ And as they led him away, they laid hold upon one Simon, a Cyrenian, coming out of the country, and on him they laid the cross, that he might bear it after Jesus.

12 And there followed him a great company of people, and of women, which also bewailed and lamented him.

13 But Jesus turning unto them said, Daughters of Jerusalem, weep not for me, but weep for yourselves, and for your children.

14 For, behold, the days are coming, in the which they shall say, Blessed are the barren, and the wombs that never bare, and the paps which never gave suck.

15 Then shall they begin to say to the mountains, Fall on us; and to the hills, Cover us.

16 For if they do these things in a green tree, what shall be done in the dry?

17 ¶ And there were also two other, malefactors, led with him to be put to death.

18 And he bearing his cross went forth into a place called the place of a skull, which is called in the Hebrew, Golgotha:

19 Where they crucified him, and two other with him, on either side one, and Jesus in the midst.

20 ¶ And Pilate wrote a title, and put it on the cross. And the writing was, JESUS OF NAZARETH THE KING OF THE JEWS.

21 This title then read many of the Jews: for the place where Jesus was crucified was nigh to the city: and it was written in Hebrew, and Greek, and Latin.

22 Then said the chief priests of the Jews to Pilate, Write not, The King of the Jews; but that he said, I am King of the Jews.

23 Pilate answered, What I have written I have written.

24 ¶ Then the soldiers, when they had crucified Jesus, took his garments, and made four parts, to every soldier a part; and also his coat: now the coat was without seam, woven from the top throughout.

25 They said therefore among themselves, Let us not rend it, but cast lots for it, whose it shall be: that the scripture might be fulfilled, which saith, They parted my raiment among them, and for my vesture they did cast lots. These things therefore the soldiers did.

26 ¶ And they that passed by reviled him, wagging their heads,

27 And saying, Thou that destroyest the temple, and buildest it in three days, save thyself. If thou be the Son of God, come down from the cross.

28 Likewise also the chief priests mocking him, with the scribes and elders, said,

29 He saved others; himself he cannot save. If he be the King of Israel, let him now come down from the cross, add we will believe him.

30 He trusted in God; let him deliver him now, if he will have him: for he said, I am the Son of God.

31 ¶ And one of the malefactors which were hanged railed on him, saying, If thou be Christ, save thyself and us.

32 But the other answering rebuked him, saying, Dost not thou fear God, seeing thou art in the same condemnation?

33 And we indeed justly; for we receive the due reward of our deeds: but this man hath done nothing amiss.

34 Then said Jesus, Father, forgive them; for they know not what they do. And they parted his raiment, and cast lots.

35 ¶ Now there stood by the cross of Jesus his mother, and his mother's sister, Mary the wife of Cleophas, and Mary Magdalene.

36 When Jesus therefore saw his mother, and the disciple standing by, whom he loved, he saith unto his mother, Woman, behold thy son!

37 Then saith he to the disciple, Behold thy mother! And from that hour that disciple took her unto his own home.

38 And about the ninth hour Jesus cried with a loud voice, saying, Eli, Eli, lama sabachthani? that is to say, My God, my God, why hast thou forsaken me?

39 Some of them that stood there, when they heard that, said, This man calleth for Elias.

40 And straightway one of them ran, and took a spunge, and filled it with vinegar, and put it on a reed, and gave him to drink.

41 The rest said, Let be, let us see whether Elias will come to save him.

42 ¶ Jesus, when he had cried again with a loud voice, yielded up the ghost.

43 And many women were there beholding afar off, which followed Jesus from Galilee, ministering unto him:

44 Among which was Mary Magdalene, and Mary the mother of James and Joses, and the mother of Zebedee's children.

LXIX. His Burial.

TIE Jews therefore, because it was the preparation, that the bodies should not remain upon the cross on the sabbath day, (for that sabbath day was an high day,) besought Pilate that their legs might be broken, and that they might be taken away.

2 Then came the soldiers, and brake the legs of the first, and of the other which was crucified with him.

3 But when they came to Jesus, and saw that he was dead already, they brake not his legs:

4 But one of the soldiers with a spear pierced his side, and forthwith came there out blood and water.

5 ¶ And after this Joseph of Arimathaea, being a disciple of Jesus, but secretly for fear of the Jews, besought Pilate that he might take away the body of Jesus: and Pilate gave him leave. He came therefore, and took the body of Jesus.

6 And there came also Nicodemus, which at the first came to Jesus by night, and brought a mixture of myrrh and aloes, about an hundred pound weight.

7 Then took they the body of Jesus, and wound it in linen clothes with the spices, as the manner of the Jews is to bury.

8 Now in the place where he was crucified there was a garden; and in the garden a new sepulchre, wherein never man yet laid.

9 There laid they Jesus: and rolled a great stone to the door of the sepulchre, and departed.

The Complete Sayings of Jesus Christ

Table of Contents

THE COMPILER'S PURPOSE

THE shelves of the libraries and of the bookstores bend beneath the tomes of the sayings, the bare sayings, of all the other great men; but one will not find in library or bookstore, in any published book, the complete sayings of Jesus, the bare sayings in simple sequence, Christ's own words, separate.

¶This compiler's purpose has been to enable any reader, whether confirmed Christian or inquiring pagan, or a frankly detached, to get him a book of CHRIST'S OWN WORDS, "divested," so runs the title page, "of the context, excepting those brief portions of the gospel narratives retained to establish the place, the time, or occasion, or a question the reply to which is the Master's own answer."

Many a reader, arrived at FINIS in the New Testament itself, has but a hazy picture of Christ on his daily walks as a circuit preacher everywhere within walking distance; has but a sketchy outline of the times and occasions—so many biographers!—Matthew, Mark, Luke, John, Paul—each essaying not a biography as such, not the record of the Teacher's sayings as such, but intent upon launching each his own conception of Christ's mission.

¶Christ's sayings complete, brought into a sequence of times and occasions, but lifted out of contexts alien to the present purpose, may prove to be a glowing story new not only to the non-reader, but new even to the whilom New-Testament readers who have not as yet discerned the "continuities."

Devoted readers will not be diverted from the Great Text. Perhaps other readers—the casual New-Testament reader and the non-reader—after enjoying these pages may venture the greater enjoyment: the attentive perusal of all the gospels and all the epistles, perhaps of all the New Testament.

A. H.

LINEAGE OF JESUS—BORN IN BETHLEHEM

Matthew 1, 1-2; 6-7; 11-12; 16-17.

THE book of the generation of Jesus Christ, the son of David, the son of Abraham:

Abraham begat Isaac; and Isaac begat . . . .

. . .. And Jesse begat David the king; and David the king begat Solomon; and Solomon begat . . . .

. . .. And Josias begat Jechonias and his brethren, about the time they were carried away to Babylon; and Jechonias begat . . . .

. . .. And Jacob begat Joseph the husband of Mary, of whom was born Jesus who is called Christ.

So all the generations from Abraham to David are * fourteen generations; and from David until the carrying away into Babylon are fourteen generations; and from the carrying away into Babylon unto Christ are fourteen generations.

Luke 2, 1-12; 16-21.

It came to pass in those days, that there went out a decree from Cesar Augustus, that all the world should be taxed. And all went to be taxed, every one into his own city.

Joseph also went up from Galilee, out of the city of Nazareth, into Judea, unto the city of David which is called Bethlehem (because he was of the house and lineage of David), to be taxed with Mary his espoused wife, being great with child.

So it was, that, while they were there, the days were accomplished that she should be delivered. She brought forth her firstborn son, and wrapped him in swaddling clothes, and laid him in a manger; because there was no room for them in the inn. Dec. B.C. 5. †

¶There were in the same country shepherds abiding in the field, keeping watch over their flock by night. And, lo, the angel of the Lord came upon them, and said, Behold, I bring you good tidings of great joy, which shall be to all people.

For unto you is born this day in the city of David a Savior, which is Christ the Lord. Ye shall find the babe wrapped in swaddling clothes, lying in a manger.

And they came with haste, and found Mary, and Joseph, and the babe lying in a manger.

When eight days were accomplished for the circumcising of the child, his name was called JESUS, which was so named of the angel before he was conceived in the womb.

THE ESCAPE FROM HEROD—AGAIN IN GALILEE AT NAZARETH

B.C. 4

Matthew 2, 1-5; 7-15; 19-23.

NOW when Jesus was born in Bethlehem of Judea in the days of Herod the king, behold, there came wise men from the east to Jerusalem, saying, Where is he that is born King of the Jews? for we have seen his star in the east, and are come to worship him.

When Herod the king had heard these things, he was troubled. And when he had gathered the chief priests and scribes of the people together, he demanded of them where Christ should be born. They said, In Bethlehem of Judea.

Then Herod privily called the wise men, and inquired of them what time the star appeared. He sent them to Bethlehem, and said, Search diligently for the child; and when ye have found him, bring me word, that I may come and worship him also.

The wise men departed; and, lo, the star, which they saw in the east, went before them, till it stood over where the child was. They rejoiced with exceeding great joy.

¶And when they saw the child with Mary his mother, they worshipped him: and they opened their treasures, and presented unto him gifts, gold, and frankincense, and myrrh.

Warned of God in a dream that they should not return to Herod, the wise men departed into their own country another way.

When the wise men were departed, behold, the angel of the Lord appeareth to Joseph in a dream, saying, Arise, take the child and his mother, and flee into Egypt and be thou there until I bring thee word: for Herod will seek the child to destroy him.

Joseph arose, took the child and his mother by night, and departed into Egypt: and was there until the death of Herod.

¶When Herod was dead, behold, an angel of the Lord appeareth in a dream to Joseph in Egypt, saying, Arise, and take the child and his mother, and go into the land of Israel.

But Joseph heard that Archelaus did reign in Judea in the room of his father Herod: he was afraid to go thither: he turned aside into the parts of Galilee: and he came and dwelt in Nazareth.

THE BOY JESUS

A.D. 8. Age 12. Nazareth. Jerusalem

Luke 2, 40-52.

THE child grew, and waxed strong in spirit, filled with wisdom: and the grace of God was upon him.

Now his parents went to Jerusalem every year at the feast of the passover. When Jesus was twelve years old, they went up to Jerusalem after the custom of the feast.

They fulfilled the days, and as they returned, the child Jesus tarried behind in Jerusalem; and Joseph and his mother knew not of it. They, supposing him to have been in the company, went a day's journey and [then] they sought him among their kinsfolk and acquaintance. When they found him not, they turned back to Jerusalem, seeking him.

After three days they found him in the temple, sitting in the midst of the doctors, both hearing them, and asking questions. All that heard him were astonished at his understanding and answers.

His mother said unto him, Son, why hast thou thus dealt with us? behold, thy father and I have sought thee sorrowing. Jesus said unto them,

How is it that ye sought me? wist ye not that I must be about my Father's business?

And they understood not.

He went down with them to Nazareth, and was subject into them: but his mother kept all these sayings in her heart.

And Jesus increased in wisdom and stature, and in favor with God and man. *

JESUS AT THIRTY—BAPTIZED BY JOHN

A.D. 27. Age 30 Judea: Jordan.

Matthew 3, 1-6; 13-17: Mark 1, 10-11; Luke 3, 22-23.

IN those days came John the Baptist, preaching in the wilderness of Judea, saying, Repent ye: for the kingdom of heaven is at hand.

This is he that was spoken of by the prophet Esaias, saying, The voice of one crying in the wilderness, Prepare ye the way of the Lord, make his paths straight.

John had his raiment of camel's hair, and a leathern girdle about his loins; and his meat was locusts and wild honey.

Then went out to him Jerusalem, and all Judea, and all the region round about Jordan, and were baptized of him in Jordan, confessing their sins.

¶Then cometh Jesus from Galilee to Jordan unto John, to be baptized of him. But John forbade him, saying, I have need to be baptized of thee, and comest thou to me?

Jesus answering said unto him,

Suffer it to be so now: for thus it becometh us to fulfill all righteousness.

Then John suffered him. And Jesus, when he was baptized, went up straightway out of the water: and praying, lo, the heavens were opened unto him, and he saw the Spirit of God descending in a bodily shape like a dove, and lighting upon him; and to a voice from heaven, saying, This is my beloved Son, in whom I am well pleased.

And Jesus himself began to be about thirty years of age.

CHRIST'S LONG FAST IN THE WILDERNESS—SATAN'S FUTILE WILES

A.D. 27. Age 30. Judea.

Matthew 4, 1-11: Mark 1, 13: Luke 4, 1-13.

THEN was Jesus led up of the Spirit into the wilderness to be tempted of the devil. He was there in the wilderness forty days, and was with the wild beasts.

In those days he did eat nothing. And when he had fasted forty days and forty nights, he was a hungered.

The tempter came: he said, If thou be the Son of God, command that these stones be made bread. But Jesus answered,

It is written, Man shall not live by bread alone, but by every word that proceedeth out of the mouth of God.

Then, in Jerusalem, the holy city, on a pinnacle of the temple, the devil saith unto Jesus, If thou be the Son of God, cast thyself down from hence: for it is written, He shall give his angels charge concerning thee, to keep thee: and in their hands they shall bear thee up, lest at any time thou dash they foot against a stone.

Jesus answering said,

It is written again, Thou shalt not tempt the Lord thy God.

Again, up an exceeding high mountain, the devil sheweth him, in a moment of time, all the kingdoms of the world, and the glory of them, and saith unto Jesus, All these things will I give thee; all this power, and the glory of them: if thou wilt fall down and worship me, all shall be thine.

And Jesus answered,

Get thee behind me, Satan; get thee hence: for it is written, Thou shalt worship the Lord thy God, and him only shalt thou serve.

Then the devil leaveth him.

JOHN ANSWERS THE PRIESTS

A.D. 27 Age 30. Bethabara

John, 1, 19-20 . . . 22-29 . . . 37-51.

JOHN, when the Jews sent priests and Levites from Jerusalem to ask him, Who art thou? confessed, I am not the Christ. I am the voice of one crying in the wilderness, Make straight the way of the Lord.

They asked him, Why baptizest thou then, if thou be not that Christ?

John answered, I baptize with water: but there standeth one among you, whom ye know not; he it is, who coming after me is preferred before me, whose shoe's latchet I am not worthy to unloose.

These things were done in Bethabara beyond Jordan, where John was baptizing.

¶The next day after, John stood, and two of his disciples; and looking upon Jesus as he walked, he saith, Behold the Lamb of God, which taketh away the sin of the world.

The two disciples heard John speak, and they followed Jesus. He saw them following, and saith,

What seek ye?

They answered, Rabbi (which is to say, Master), where dwellest thou? Jesus saith,

Come and see.

They came and saw where he dwelt, and they abode with him that day. One of the two was Andrew, Simon Peter's brother. He first findeth Simon, and saith unto him, We have found the Messias. *

Andrew brought Simon to Jesus. And when Jesus beheld Simon, he said,

Thou art Simon the son of Jona: thou shalt be called Cephas.

Cephas is, by interpretation, A stone. †

¶The day following, Jesus would go forth into Galilee, and findeth Philip: he was of Bethsaida, the city of Andrew and Simon Peter. And Jesus saith unto

Philip,

Follow me.

Philip findeth Nathanael, and saith unto him, We have found him of whom Moses did write, Jesus of Nazareth, the son of Joseph. And Nathanael said, Can there any good thing come out of Nazareth? Philip said, Come and see.

Jesus saw Nathanael coming, and saith of him,

Behold an Israelite indeed, in whom is no guile!

Nathanael saith, Whence knowest thou me? Jesus answered,

Before that Philip called thee, when thou wart under the fig tree, I saw thee.

Nathanael answered, Master, thou art the Son of God; thou art the King of Israel. Jesus said,

Because I said unto thee, I saw thee under the fig tree, believest thou? thou shalt see greater things than these. Verily, verily, I say unto you, Hereafter ye shall see heaven open, and the angels of God ascending and descending upon the Son of man.

JESUS' MOTHER AND THE WATER CHANGED TO WINE

A.D. 27. Age 30. Cana. Jerusalem.

John 2, 1-9; 12-16; 18-21.

THE third day, there was a marriage in Cana of Galilee. Both Jesus was called, and his disciples, to the marriage; and the mother of Jesus was there.

When they wanted wine, his mother saith unto Jesus, They have no wine. Jesus saith,

Woman, what have I to do with thee? mine hour is not yet come.

His mother saith unto the servants, Whatsoever he saith, do it.

There were set there six waterpots of stone containing two or three firkins apiece. Jesus saith,

Fill the waterpots with water.

They filled them to the brim. And he saith,

Draw out now, and bear unto the governor of the feast.

And they bare it. The ruler of the feast tasted. The water was made wine.

¶After this he went to Capernaum, Jesus, and his mother, and his brethren, and his disciples; and they continued there not many days.

¶The Jews' passover was at hand: Jesus went up to Jerusalem.

¶ *He found in the temple those that sold oxen and sheep and doves; and the changers of money sitting: and when he had made a scourge of small cords, he drove them all out of the temple, and the sheep, and the oxen; and poured out the changers' money, and overthrew the tables; and said unto them that sold doves,

Take these things hence, make not my Father's house a house of merchandise.

¶Then the Jews said unto Jesus, What sign shewest thou unto us, seeing that thou doest these things? He answered,

Destroy this temple, and in three days I will raise it up. †

Then said the Jews, Forty and six years was this temple in building, and wilt thou rear it up in three days?

But Jesus spake of the temple of his body.

NIGHTTIME VISIT OF NICODEMUS—CHRIST ENLIGHTENS HIM

April, A.D. 27 Age 30. Jerusalem.

John 3, 1-21.

A MAN of the Pharisees, named Nicodemus, a ruler of the Jews, came to Jesus by night, and said unto him, Master, we know that thou art a teacher come from God: for no man can do these miracles that thou doest, except God be with him. Jesus answered,

Verily, verily, I say unto thee, Except a man be born again, he cannot see the kingdom of God.

Nicodemus saith unto him, How can a man be born when he is old? Jesus answered,

Verily, verily, I say unto thee, Except a man be born of water and of the Spirit, he cannot enter into the kingdom of God. That which is born of the flesh is flesh: and that which is born of the Spirit is spirit.

Marvel not that I said unto thee, Ye must be born again. The wind bloweth where it listeth, and thou hearest the sound thereof, but canst not tell whence it cometh, and whither it goeth: so is every one that is born of the Spirit.

Nicodemus said, How can these things be? Jesus answered,

Art thou a master of Israel, and knowest not these things? Verily, verily, I say unto thee, We speak that we do know, and testify that we have seen; and ye receive not our witness.

If I have told you earthly things, and ye believe not, how shall ye believe, if I tell you of heavenly things? And no man hath ascended up to heaven, but he that came down from heaven, even the Son of man which is in heaven.

¶And as Moses lifted up the serpent in the wilderness, even so must the Son of man be lifted up: that whosoever believeth in him should not perish, but have eternal life.

¶For God so loved the world, that he gave his only begotten Son, that whosoever believeth in him should not perish, but have everlasting life. For God sent not his Son into the world to condemn the world; but that the world through him might be saved.

¶He that believeth on him is not condemned; but he that believeth not is condemned already, because he hath not believed in the name of the only begotten Son of God.

And this is the condemnation, that light has come into the world, and men loved darkness rather than light, because their deeds were evil. For every one that doeth evil hateth the light, neither cometh to the light, lest his deeds should be reproved. But he that doeth truth cometh to the light, that his deeds may be made manifest, that they are wrought in God. *

JOHN EXTOLS JESUS

A.D. 27. Age 30. Samaria: Sychar.

John 3, 22 . . . 28; 1-40.

AFTER these things came Jesus and his disciples into the land of Judea. John was baptizing in Enon near to Salim. For John was not yet cast into prison.

¶There arose a question between some of John's disciples and the Jews. They came unto John, saying, Rabbi, he that was with thee beyond Jordan, to whom thou barest witness, behold, the same baptizeth, and all men come to him.

John said, Ye yourselves bear me witness, that I said, I am not the Christ, but that I am sent before him.

¶When Jesus knew how the Pharisees had heard that he made and baptized more disciples than John (though Jesus himself baptized not, but his disciples), he left Judea, and departed again into Galilee. And he must needs go through Samaria.

Then cometh he to a city of Samaria called Sychar, near to the parcel of ground that Jacob gave to his son Joseph.

Now Jacob's well was there. Jesus being wearied with his journey, sat on the well.

There cometh a woman of Samaria to draw water: Jesus saith unto her,

Give me to drink.

The woman saith, How is it that thou, being a Jew, asketh drink of me, a woman of Samaria? for the Jews have no dealings with the Samarians. Jesus answered,

If thou knewest the gift of God, and who it is that saith to thee, Give me to drink; thou wouldest have asked of him, and he would have given thee living water.

The woman saith, Sir, thou hast nothing to draw with, and the well is deep: from whence then hast thou that living water? Art thou greater than our father

Jacob, which gave us the well, and drank thereof himself, and his children, and his cattle? Jesus said,

Whosoever drinketh of this water shall thirst again; but whosoever drinketh of the water that I shall give him shall never thirst; but the water that I shall give him shall be in him a well of water springing up into everlasting life.

The woman answered, Sir, give me this water, that I thirst not, neither come hither to draw. Jesus saith,

Go, call thy husband, and come hither.

The woman answered, I have no husband. Jesus said,

Thou hast well said, I have no husband: for thou hast had five husbands; and he whom thou now hast is not thy husband: in that saidst thou truly.

The woman saith, Sir, I perceive that thou art a prophet. Our fathers worshipped in this mountain; and ye say, that in Jerusalem is the place where men ought to worship. Jesus saith,

Woman, believe me, the hour cometh, when ye shall neither in this mountain, nor yet at Jerusalem, worship the Father. Ye worship ye know not what: we know what we worship; for salvation is of the Jews.

But the hour cometh, and now is, when the true worshippers shall worship the Father in spirit and in truth: for the Father seeketh such to worship him.

God is a Spirit: and they that worship him must worship him in spirit and in truth.

The woman saith, I know that Messias cometh, which is called Christ: when he is come, he will tell us all things. Jesus saith,

I that speak unto thee am he.

The woman went her way into the city, and saith to the men, Come, see a man, which told me all things that ever I did: is not this the Christ?

¶In the mean while his disciples prayed him, saying, Master, eat. But he said,

I have meat to eat that ye know not of.

Therefore said the disciples one to another, Hath any man brought him aught to eat? Jesus saith unto them,

My meat is to do the will of him that sent me, and to finish his work.

Say not ye, There are yet four months, and then cometh harvest? Behold, I say unto you, Lift up your eyes, and look on the fields; for they are white already to harvest. And he that reapeth receiveth wages, and gathereth fruit unto life eternal: that both he that soweth and he that reapeth may rejoice together.

And herein is that saying true, One soweth, and another reapeth.

I sent you to reap that whereon ye bestowed no labor: other men labored, and ye are entered into their labor.

¶Many of the Samaritans of that city believed on him for the saying of the woman, which testified, He told me all that ever I did.

So they besought Jesus that he would tarry with them: and he abode there two days.

CHRIST IN CANA CURES NOBLEMAN'S SON AT CAPERNAUM

A.D. 27. Age 30. Galilee: Cana (again).

John 4, 43-53.

AFTER two days Jesus went into Galilee: for Jesus himself testified, that a prophet hath no honor in his own country.

The Galileans received him, having seen all the things that he did at Jerusalem at the feast: for they also went unto the feast.

So Jesus came again into Cana of Galilee, where he [had] made the water wine.

And there was a certain nobleman, whose son was sick at Capernaum. He went unto Jesus, and besought him that he would come down, and heal his son: for he was at the point of death. Then said Jesus unto him,

Except ye see signs and wonders, ye will not believe.

The nobleman saith, Sir, come down ere my child die. Jesus answered,

Go thy way: thy son liveth.

The man believed, and went his way. And going down, his servants met him, and told him, Thy son liveth.

Then inquired he of them the hour when the child began to amend. They said, Yesterday at the seventh hour the fever left him.

So the father knew that it was at the same hour, in the which Jesus said unto him, Thy son liveth.

AT THE POOL OF BETHESDA

A.D. 27. Age 30. Jerusalem: Pool of Bethesda.

John 5, 1-47.

AFTER this there was a feast of the Jews; and Jesus went up to Jerusalem.

At Jerusalem there is a pool, called Bethesda, having five porches. In these lay impotent folk: blind, halt, withered, waiting for the moving of the water. For an angel went down at a certain season into the pool, and troubled the water: whosoever then first after the troubling of the water stepped in was made whole of whatever disease he had.

A certain man was there, which had an infirmity thirty and eight years. When Jesus saw him lie, and knew that he had been now a long time in that case, he saith unto him,

Wilt thou be made whole?

The impotent man answered, Sir, I have no man, when the water is troubled, to put me into the pool: but while I am coming, another steppeth down before me. Jesus saith unto him,

Rise, take up thy bed, and walk.

Immediately the man was made whole, and took up his bed, and walked: and on the same day was the sabbath.

¶The Jews therefore said unto him that was cured, It is the sabbath day: it is not lawful for thee to carry thy bed.

He answered, He that made me whole, the same said unto me, Take up thy bed, and walk.

Then they asked him, What man is that? And he that was healed wist not who it was: for Jesus had conveyed himself away, a multitude being in that place.

Afterward Jesus findeth him in the temple, and said unto him,

Behold, thou art made whole: sin no more, lest a worse thing come unto thee.

The man departed, and told the Jews that it was Jesus, which had made him whole. And the Jews sought to slay Jesus, because he had done these things on the sabbath day.

¶But Jesus answered them,

My Father worketh hitherto, and I work.

The Jews sought the more to kill him, because he not only had broken the sabbath, but said also that God was his Father, making himself equal with God. Then Jesus said unto them,

Verily, verily, I say unto you, The Son can do nothing of himself, but what he seeth the Father do: for what things soever he doeth, these also doeth the Son likewise. For the Father loveth the Son, and sheweth him all things that himself doeth: and he will shew him greater works than these, that ye may marvel.

For as the Father raiseth up the dead, and quickeneth them; even so the Son quickeneth whom he will.

For the Father judgeth no man, but hath committed all judgment unto the Son; that all men should honor the Son, even as they honor the Father. He that honoreth not the Son honoreth not the Father which hath sent him.

Verily, verily, I say unto you, He that heareth my word, and believeth on him that sent me, hath everlasting life, and shall not come into condemnation; but is passed from death unto life.

Verily, verily, I say unto you. The hour is coming, and now is, when the dead shall hear the voice of the Son of God: and they that hear shall live. For as the Father hath life in himself; so hath he given to the Son to have life in himself; and hath given him authority to execute judgment also because he is the Son of man. Marvel not at this: for the hour is coming, in the which all that are in the graves shall hear his voice, and shall come forth; they that have done good, unto the resurrection of life; and they that have done evil, unto the resurrection of damnation.

I can of mine own self do nothing: as I hear, I judge: and my judgment is just; because I seek not mine own will, but the will of the Father which hath sent me. If I bear witness of myself, my witness is not true.

¶There is another that beareth witness of me; and I know that the witness which he witnesseth of me is true.

Ye sent unto John, and he bare witness unto the truth. But I receive not testimony from man: but these things I say, that ye might be saved. He was a burning and a shining light: and we were willing for a season to rejoice in his light.

¶But I have greater witness than that of John: for the works which the Father hath given me to finish, the same works that I do, bear witness of me, that the

Father hath sent me. And the Father himself, which hath sent me, hath borne witness of me. Ye have neither heard his voice at any time, nor seen his shape. And ye have not his word abiding in you: for whom he hath sent, him ye believe not.

¶Search the Scriptures; for in them ye think ye have eternal life: and they are they which testify of me. And ye will not come to me, that ye might have life.

I receive not honor from men. But I know you, that ye have not the love of God in you. I am come in my Father's name, and ye receive me not: if another shall come in his own name, him ye will receive. How can ye believe, which receive honor one of another, and seek not the honor that cometh from God only?

Do not think that I will accuse you to the Father: there is one that accuseth you, even Moses, in whom ye trust. For had ye believed Moses, ye would have believed me: for he wrote of me. But if ye believe not his writings, how shall ye believe my words?

CHRIST READS IN SYNAGOGUE AT NAZARETH

A.D. 28. Age 31. Nazareth. Capernaum.

Luke 4, 16-31; Mark 1, 15; Matthew 4, 17.

JESUS came to Nazareth, where he had been brought up: and, as his custom was, he went into the synagogue on the sabbath day, and stood up for to read. When he had opened the book, he found the place where it was written,

*The Spirit of the Lord is upon me, because he hath anointed me to preach the gospel to the poor; he hath sent me to heal the brokenhearted, to preach deliverance to the captives, and recovering of sight to the blind, to set at liberty them that are bruised, to preach the acceptable year of the Lord.

He closed the book, gave it again to the minister, and sat down. The eyes of all them that were in the synagogue were fastened on him: and he began to say unto them,

This day is this Scripture fulfilled in your ears.

And all bare witness, and wondered at the gracious words which pro-ceded out of his mouth. They said, Is not this Joseph's son? And Jesus said,

Ye will surely say unto me this proverb, Physician, heal thyself: whatsoever we have heard done in Capernaum, do also here in thy country.

And he said,

Verily I say unto you, No prophet is accepted in his own country.

But I tell you of a truth, many widows were in Israel in the days of Elias, when the heaven was shut up three years and six months, when great famine was throughout all the land; but unto none of them was Elias sent, save unto Sarepta, a city of Sidom, unto a woman that was a widow.

And many lepers were in Israel in the time of Eliseus the prophet: and none of them was cleansed, saving Naaman the Syrian.

They in the synagogue, when they heard these things, were filled with wrath, and rose up, and thrust Jesus out, and led him unto the brow of the hill wheron their city was built, that they might cast him down headlong.

¶Now Jesus had heard that John was cast into prison; and, passing through the midst of them, he went his way: and leaving Nazareth, he departed into Galilee: he came to Capernaum.

Jesus dwelt in Capernaum, preaching the gospel of the kingdom of God, and saying,

The time is fulfilled, and the kingdom of heaven is at hand: repent ye, and believe the gospel. Repent: for the kingdom of God is at hand.

From that time Jesus began to preach; and he taught them on the sabbath days.

BY THE SEA

A.D. 28. Age 31. Galilee: Capernaum.

Mark 1, 16-26; Luke 4, 31 ... 38 ... 44; Matthew 4, 17 ... 25.

NOW as Jesus walked by the sea of Galilee, he saw Simon Peter and Andrew his brother casting a net into the sea: for they were fishers. He said unto them,

Come ye after me, and I will make you to become fishers of men. Follow me.

Straightway they forsook their nets, and followed him.

When he had gone a little further thence, he saw James the son of Zebedee, and John his brother, who were in a ship with their father, mending their nets. He called them: and they left their father in the ship with the hired servants, and followed Jesus.

¶They went into Capernaum; and on the sabbath day Jesus entered into the synagogue, and taught. They were astonished: for his word was with power: he taught them as one that had authority, and not as the scribes.

There was in their synagogue a man with an unclean spirit; and he cried out, Let us alone, thou Jesus of Nazareth. Art thou come to destroy us? I know who thou art: the Holy One of God.

Jesus rebuked him, saying,

Hold thy peace, and come out of him.

When the unclean spirit had thrown the man in the midst, he came out of him, and hurt him not.

¶Jesus arose, and, when they were come out of the synagogue, entered the house of Peter and Andrew, with James and John.

¶In the morning, rising up a great while before day, Jesus went out into a solitary place, and there prayed.

The people sought him, and came unto him, and stayed him, that he should not depart. He said,

I must preach the kingdom of God to other cities also: for therefore am I sent.

Simon and they that were with him followed after Jesus, and when they had found him, they said unto him, *All men seek for thee. He answered,

Let us go into the next towns, that I may preach there also: for therefore came I forth.

¶And Jesus went about all Galilee, teaching in their synagogues, and preaching the gospel of the kingdom. His fame went throughout Syria. And there followed him multitudes from Galilee, and Decapolis; * from Jerusalem, and Judea; and from beyond Jordan.

THE SERMON ON THE MOUNT

A.D. 28, Age 31 Near Capernaum.

Matthew 5, 1-48.

SEEING the multitudes, Jesus went up into a mountain: and when he was set, his disciples came unto him: and he opened his mouth, and taught them, saying,

Blessed are the poor in spirit: for theirs is the kingdom of heaven.

Blessed are they that mourn: for they shall be comforted.

Blessed are the meek: for they shall inherit the earth.

Blessed are they which do hunger and thirst after righteousness: for they shall be filled.

Blessed are the merciful: for they shall obtain mercy.

Blessed are the pure in heart: for they shall see God.

Blessed are the peacemakers: for they shall be called the children of God.

Blessed are they which are persecuted for righteousness' sake: for theirs is the kingdom of heaven.

Blessed are ye, when men shall revile you, and persecute you, and shall say all manner of evil against you falsely, for my sake.

Rejoice, and be exceeding glad: for great is your reward in heaven: for so persecuted they the prophets which were before you.

¶Ye are the salt of the earth; but if the salt have lost his savor, wherewith shall it be salted? it is thenceforth good for nothing, but to be cast out, and to be trodden under foot of men.

Ye are the light of the world. A city that is set on a hill cannot be hid. Neither do men light a candle, and put it under a bushel, but on a candlestick; and it giveth light unto all that are in the house. Let your light so shine before men, that they may see your good works, and glorify your Father which is in heaven.

¶Think not that I am come to destroy the law, or the prophets: I am not come to destroy, but to fulfil. For verily I say unto you, Till heaven and earth pass, one jot or one tittle shall in no wise pass from the law, till all be fulfilled.

Whosoever therefore shall break one of these least commandments, and shall teach men so, he shall be called the least in the kingdom of heaven: but whosoever shall do and teach them, the same shall be called great in the kingdom of heaven. For I say unto you, That except your righteousness shall exceed the righteousness of the scribes and Pharisees, ye shall in no case enter into the kingdom of heaven.

¶Ye have heard that it was said by them of old time, Thou shalt not kill; and whosoever shall kill shall be in danger of the judgment: but I say unto you, That whosoever is angry with his brother without a cause shall be in danger of the judgment: and whosoever shall say to his brother, Raca, shall be in danger of the council: but whosoever shall say, Thou fool, shall be in danger of hell fire.

Therefore if thou bring thy gift to the altar, and there rememberest that thy brother hath aught against thee; leave there thy gift before the altar, and go thy way; first be reconciled to thy brother, and then come and offer thy gift.

Agree with thine adversary quickly, while thou art in the way with him; lest at any time the adversary deliver thee to the judge, and the judge deliver thee to the officer, and thou be cast into prison. Verily I say unto thee, Thou shalt by no means come out thence, till thou hast paid the uttermost farthing.

¶Ye have heard that it was said by them of old time, Thou shalt not commit adultery: but I say unto you, That whosoever looketh on a woman to lust after her hath committed adultery with her already in his heart.

And if thy right eye offend thee, pluck it out, and cast it from thee: for it is profitable for thee that one of thy members should perish, and not that thy whole body should be cast into hell.

And if thy right hand offend thee, cut it off, and cast it from thee, for it is profitable for thee that one of thy members should perish, and not that thy whole body should be cast into hell.

It hath been said, Whosoever shall put away his wife, let him give her a writing of divorcement: but I say unto you, That whosoever shall put away his wife, saving for the cause of fornication, causeth her to commit adultery: and whosoever shall marry her that is divorced cornmitteth adultery. *

¶Again, ye have heard that it hath been said by them of old time, Thou shalt not forswear thyself, but shalt perform unto the Lord thine oaths: but I say unto you, Swear not at all; neither by heaven; for it is God's throne: nor by the earth; for it is his footstool: neither by Jerusalem; for it is the city of the great King. Neither shalt thou swear by thy head, because thou canst not make one hair white or black. But let your communication be, Yea, yea; Nay, nay: for whatsoever is more than these cometh of evil.

¶Ye have heard that it hath been said, An eye for an eye, and a tooth for a tooth: but I say unto you, That ye resist not evil: but whosoever shall smite thee on thy right cheek, turn to him the other also. And if any man will sue thee at the law, and take away thy coat, let him have thy cloak also. And whosoever shall compel thee to go a mile, go with him twain. Give to him that asketh thee, and from him that would borrow of thee turn not thou away.

¶Ye have heard that it hath been said, Thou shalt love thy neighbor, and hate thine enemy: but I say unto you,

†Love your enemies, bless them that curse you, do good to them that hate you, and pray for them which despitefully use you, and persecute you; that ye may be the children of your Father which is in heaven: for he maketh his sun to rise on the evil and on the good, and sendeth rain on the just and on the unjust.

For if ye love them which love you, what reward have ye? do not even the publicans the same? And if ye salute your brethren only, what do ye more than others? do not even the publicans so?

Be ye therefore perfect, even as your Father, which is in heaven is perfect.

THE SERMON ON THE MOUNT (CONTINUED)

A.D. 28, Age 31 Near Capernaum.

Matthew 6, 1-34.

TAKE heed that ye do not your alms before men, to be seen of them; otherwise ye have no reward of your Father which is in heaven. Therefore when thou doest thine alms, do not sound a trumpet before thee, as the hypocrites do in the synagogues and in the streets, that they may have glory of men. Verily I say unto you, They have their reward. But when thou doest alms, let not thy left hand know what thy right hand doeth: that thine alms may be in secret: and thy Father which seeth in secret himself shall reward thee openly.

¶And when thou prayest, thou shalt not be as the hyprocites are: for they love to pray standing in the synagogues and in the corners of the streets, that they may be seen of men. Verily I say unto you, They have their reward. But thou, when thou prayest, enter into thy closet, and when thou hast shut thy door, pray to thy Father which is in secret; and thy Father which seeth in secret shall reward thee openly.

But when ye pray, use not vain repetitions, as the heathen do: for they think that they shall be heard for their much speaking. Be not ye therefore like unto them: for your Father knoweth what things ye have need of, before ye ask him.

After this manner therefore pray ye:

Our Father which art in heaven, Hallowed be thy name. Thy kingdom come. Thy will be done in earth, as it is in heaven.

Give us this day our daily bread. And forgive us our debts, as we forgive our debtors.

And lead us not into temptation, but deliver us from evil:

For thine is the kingdom, and the power, and the glory, for ever. Amen.

For if ye forgive men their trespasses, your heavenly Father will also forgive you: but if ye forgive not men their trespasses, neither will your Father forgive your trespasses.

¶Moreover when ye fast, be not, as the hypocrites, of a sad countenance: for they disfigure their faces, that they may appear unto men to fast. Verily I say unto you, They have their reward. But thou, when thou fastest, anoint thy head, and wash thy face; that thou appear not unto men to fast, but unto thy Father which is in secret: and thy Father, which seeth in secret, shall reward thee openly.

¶Lay not up for yourselves treasures upon earth, where moth and rust doth corrupt, and where thieves break through and steal: but lay up for yourselves treasures in heaven, where neither moth nor rust doth corrupt, and where thieves do not break through nor steal. For where your treasure is, there will your heart be also.

The light of the body is the eye: if therefore thine eye be single, thy whole body shall be full of light. But if thine eye be evil, thy whole body shall be full of darkness. If therefore the light that is in thee be darkness, how great is that darkness!

¶No man can serve two masters: for either he will hate the one, and love the other: or else he will hold to the one, and despise the other. Ye cannot serve God and mammon.

Therefore I say unto you, Take no thought for your life, what ye shall eat, or what ye shall drink; nor yet for your body, what ye shall put on. Is not the life more than meat, and the body than raiment? Behold the fowls of the air: for they sow not, neither do they reap, nor gather into barns; yet your heavenly Father feedeth them. Are ye not much better than they?

Which of you by taking thought can add one cubic unto his stature? And why take ye thought for raiment? Consider the lilies of the field, how they grow; they toil not, neither do they spin; and yet I say unto you, That even Solomon in all his glory was not arrayed like one of these. Wherefore, if God so clothe the grass of the field, which to day is, and to morrow is cast into the oven, shall he not much more clothe you, O ye of little faith?

Therefore take no thought, saying, What shall we eat? or, What shall we drink? or, Wherewithal shall we be clothed? (for after all these things do the Gentiles seek) for your heavenly Father knoweth that ye have need of all these things.

But seek ye first the kingdom of God, and his righteousness; and all these things shall be added unto you. Take therefore no thought for the morrow: for the morrow shall take thought for the things of itself. Sufficient unto the day is the evil thereof.

THE SERMON ON THE MOUNT (CONCLUDED)

A.D. 28, Age 31 Near Capernaum.

Matthew 7, 1-29.

JUDGE not, that ye be not judged. For with what judgment ye judge, ye shall be judged: and with what measure ye mete, it shall be measured to you again.

And why beholdest thou the mote that is in thy brother's eye, but considerest not the beam that is in thine own eye? Or how wilt thou say to thy brother, Let me pull out the mote out of thine eye; and, behold, a beam is in thine own eye? Thou hypocrite, first cast out the beam out of thine own eye; and then shalt thou see clearly to cast out the mote out of thy brother's eye.

¶Give not that which is holy unto the dogs, neither cast ye your pearls before swine, lest they trample them under their feet, and turn again and rend you.

¶Ask, and it shall be given you; seek, and ye shall find; knock, and it shall be opened unto you: for every one that asketh receiveth; and he that seeketh findeth; and to him that knocketh it shall be opened.

Or what man is there of you, whom if his son ask bread, will he give him a stone? Or if he asks a fish, will he give him a serpent? If ye then, being evil, know how to give good gifts unto your children, how
much more shall your Father which is in heaven give good things to them that ask him?

¶ *Therefore all things whatsoever ye would that men should do to you, do ye even so to them: for this is the law and the prophets.

Enter ye in at the strait gate: for wide is the gate, and broad is the way, that leadeth to destruction, and many there be which go in thereat: because strait is the gate, and narrow is the way, which leadeth unto life, and few there be that find it.

¶Beware of false prophets, which come to you in sheep's clothing, but inwardly they are ravening wolves. Ye shall know them by their fruits. Do men gather grapes of thorns, or figs of thistles? Even so every good tree bringeth forth good fruit; but a corrupt tree bringeth forth evil fruit. A good tree cannot bring forth evil fruit, neither can a corrupt tree bring forth good fruit. Every tree that bringeth not forth good fruit is hewn down, and cast into the fire. Wherefore by their fruits ye shall know them.

¶Not every one that saith unto me, Lord, Lord, shall enter into the kingdom of heaven; but he that doeth the will of my Father which is in heaven. Many will say to me in that day, Lord, Lord, have we not prophesied in thy name? and in thy name have cast out devils? and in thy name done many wonderful works? And then will I profess unto them, I never knew you: depart from me, ye that work iniquity.

¶Therefore whosoever heareth these sayings of mine, and doeth them, I will liken him unto a wise man, which built his house upon a rock: and the rain descended, and the floods came, and the winds blew, and beat upon that house: and it fell not: for it was founded upon a rock.

And every one that heareth these sayings of mine, and doeth them not, shall be likened unto a foolish man, which built his house upon the sand: and the rain descended, and the floods came, and the winds blew, and beat upon that house; and it fell: and great was the fall of it.

When Jesus had ended these sayings, † the people were astonished at his doctrine: for he taught them as one having authority, and not as the scribes.

A LEPER CLEANSED

A.D. 28. Age 31. By Lake Gennesaret. Capernaum.

Matthew 8, 1-4; 9, 2-7; Mark 1, 40-45; 2, 1-12; Luke 5, 1-15; and 18-25.

WHEN Jesus was come down from the mountain, multitudes followed him. And, behold, there came a leper, who, seeing Jesus, besought him, saying, Lord, if thou wilt, thou canst make me clean.

Jesus, moved with compassion, put forth his hand, and touched him, saying,

I will; be thou clean.

And immediately his leprosy was cleansed. Jesus straitly charged him,

See thou tell no man; but go thy way: say nothing to any man. Shew thyself to the priest, and offer the gift for thy cleansing, those things which Moses commanded, for a testimony unto them.

But he began to blaze abroad the matter; and so much the more went there a fame abroad of Jesus.

¶It came to pass, that, as the people pressed upon Jesus to hear the word of God, he stood by the lake of Gennesaret, and saw two ships. He entered into one, which was Simon's, and prayed him that he would thrust out a little from the land. And he sat down, and taught the people out of the ship.

Now when he had left speaking, he said unto Simon,

Launch out into the deep, and let down your nets for a draught.

Simon answering said, Master we have toiled all the night, and have taken nothing: nevertheless at thy word I will let down the net.

When they had this done, they inclosed a multitude of fishes: and their net brake. They beckoned unto their partners, which were in the other ship, that they should come and help them. They came, and filled both the ships, so that they began to sink.

When Simon Peter saw it, he fell down at Jesus' knees, saying, Depart from me; for I am a sinful man, O Lord.

For he was astonished at the draught of the fishes: and so was also James, and John, which were partners with Simon.

Jesus said unto Simon,

Fear not; from henceforth thou shalt catch men.

They brought their ships to land, forsook all, and followed Jesus.

¶Again Jesus entered into Capernaum after some days; and it was noised that he was in the house. Straightway many were gathered together, insomuch that there was no room to receive them, no, not so much as about the door: and he preached the word unto them.

¶And, behold, men brought one sick of the palsy, lying on a bed borne by four. They could not come nigh unto Jesus for the press: and when they could not find by what way they might bring him in, they went upon the housetop, and uncovered the roof, and let him down through the tiling with his couch into the midst before Jesus.

Jesus seeing their faith said unto the sick of the palsy,

Son, be of good cheer; thy sins be forgiven thee. *

Certain of the scribes sitting there, and reasoning in their hearts, said within themselves, This man blasphemeth: who can forgive sins, but God alone? Jesus knowing their thoughts said,

What reason ye in your hearts? Why reason ye these things? Wherefore think ye evil? Whether is it easier to say to the sick of the palsy, Thy sins be forgiven thee; or to say, Arise, and take up thy bed, and walk? But that ye may know that the Son of man hath power on earth to forgive sins,

He saith to the sick of the palsy,

I say unto thee, Arise, and take up thy couch, and go thy way into thine house.

And he arose, took up his bed, and departed to his house.

MATTHEW (LEVI) CALLED

A.D. 28, Age 31. Capernaum.

Luke 5, 27-39; Matthew 9, 9-17; Mark 2, 13-22.

JESUS went forth again by the sea side; and the multitudes resorted unto him, and he taught them.

¶As he passed forth from thence, he saw a man, named Matthew (Levi, a publican *), sitting at the receipt of custom: he said unto him,

Follow me.

And he rose up, left all, and followed Jesus.

¶Levi made him a great feast † in his own house: and, behold, many publicans and others sat at meat with Jesus and his disciples.

But their scribes and Pharisees murmured against his disciples, saying, Why do ye eat with publicans and sinners? Why eateth your master with publicans and sinners?

When Jesus heard that, he saith unto them,

They that be whole need not a physician, but they that are sick. But go ye and learn what that meaneth. I will have mercy, and not sacrifice: ‡ for I am not come to call the righteous, but sinners to repentance.

¶The disciples of John used to fast often: and they come and say unto Jesus, Why do thy disciples fast not? Jesus said unto them,

Can ye make the children of the bridechamber fast, while the bridegroom is with them? as long as they have the bridegroom with them, they cannot fast. But the days will come, when the bridegroom shall be taken away from them, and then shall they fast in those days.

¶And he spake also a parable unto them,

No man also seweth a piece of new cloth upon an old garment; else the new piece that filleth it up agreeth not with the old: it taketh away from the old, and the rent is made worse.

Another parable put he forth.

And no man putteth new wine into old bottles: *else the bottles will be marred: the new wine will burst the bottles, and be spilled, and the bottles shall perish. But new wine must be put into new bottles; and both are preserved.

No man also having drunk old wine straightway desireth new; for he saith, The old is better.

IN THE CORNFIELD ON THE SABBATH

A.D. 28. Age 31. Capernaum.

Matthew 12, 1-16: Mark 2, 23-28; 3, 1-15; 22-29: Luke 6, 1-13; 11, 24-26.

AT that time Jesus went on the sabbath day through the cornfields; and his disciples were a hungered, and began, as they went, to pluck the ears of corn, and to eat, rubbing them with their hands.

But certain of the Pharisees said unto Jesus, Behold, why do thy disciples on the sabbath day that which is not lawful? Jesus said unto them,

Have ye never read so much as this: what David did, when himself was a hungered, and had need, he, and they which were with him: how he went into the house of God in the days of Abiathar the high priest, and did take and eat the shewbread, and gave also to them which were with him, which was not lawful for him to eat, neither for them which were with him, but for the priests alone?

Or have ye not read in the law, how that on the sabbath days the priests in the temple profane the sabbath, and are blameless?

But I say unto you, That in this place is one greater than the temple. But if ye had known what this meaneth, I will have mercy, and not sacrifice, ye would not have condemned the guiltless.

The sabbath was made for man, and not man for the sabbath: therefore the Son of man is Lord even of the sabbath day.

¶On another sabbath, Jesus entered into the synagogue and taught.

There was a man there whose right hand was withered. The scribes and Pharisees watched Jesus, whether he would heal on the sabbath day. But he knew their thoughts, and he said to the man,

Rise up, and stand forth in the midst.

He arose and stood forth. Then said Jesus unto them,

I will ask you one thing: Is it lawful on the sabbath days to do good, or to do evil? to save life, or to kill? to save life, or to destroy it?

But thy held their peace. And Jesus said,

What man shall there be among you, that shall have one sheep, and if it fall into a pit on the sabbath day, will he not lay hold on it, and lift it out? How much then is a man better than a sheep? Wherefore it is lawful to do well on the sabbath days.

When Jesus had looked round about on them with anger, being grieved for the hardness of their hearts, he saith unto the man,

Stretch forth thine hand.

He did so: and his hand was restored whole, like as the other.

¶The Pharisees were filled with madness; they went forth, and straightaway took counsel with the Herodians what they might do to Jesus.

Jesus knew it: he withdrew himself with his disciples to the sea. And he straitly charged them that they should not make him known.

¶Jesus goeth up into a mountain, and calleth unto him whom he would: and they came. He ordained twelve, whom also he named apostles, that they should be with him, and that he might send them forth to preach, and to have power to heal sicknesses, and to cast out devils.

¶The scribes said, He hath Beelzebub, and by the prince of devils casteth he out devils. Jesus said unto them in parables, *

How can Satan cast out Satan?

And if a kingdom be divided against itself, that kingdom cannot stand. And if a house be divided against itself, that house cannot stand. And if Satan rise up against himself, and be divided, he cannot stand, but hath an end.

No man can enter into a strong man's house, and spoil his goods, except he will first bind the strong man; and then he will spoil his house.

Verily I say unto you, All sins shall be forgiven unto the sons of men, and blasphemies wherewith soever they shall blaspheme: but he that shall blaspheme against the Holy Ghost hath never forgiveness, but is in danger of eternal damnation.

Because they said, he hath an unclean spirit.

*When the unclean spirit is gone out of a man, he walketh through dry places, seeking rest: and finding none, he saith, I will return unto my house whence I came out. And when he cometh, he findeth it swept and garnished. Then goeth he, and taketh to him seven other spirits more wicked than himself; and the last

state of that man is worse than the first.

THE TWELVE BY NAME—THE SERMON IN THE PLAIN

A.D. 28. Age 31. Near Capernaum.

Matthew 10, 2-4: Mark 3, 16-19: Luke 6, 14-38.

IN those days Jesus went out into a mountain, and continued all night in prayer to God. When it was day, he called unto him his twelve disciples.

Now the names of the twelve apostles are these: †Simon [whom he also surnamed Peter], and Andrew his brother; James the son of Zebedee, and John his brother; James the son of Alpheus, and Thomas; and Lebbeus whose surname was Thaddeus [Jude]; Philip, Bartholomew [Nathanael]; and Matthew the publican [Levi]; and Simon called Zelotes, the Canaanite; and Judas Iscariot, who also was the traitor, and betrayed Jesus.

¶Jesus came down with them, and stood in the plain; and the company of the disciples stood with them. A multitude of people out of all Judea and Jerusalem, and from the sea coast of Tyre and Sidon came to hear him, and to be healed.

¶Jesus lifted up his eyes on his disciples, and said,

Blessed be ye poor: for yours is the kingdom of God.

Blessed are ye that hunger now: for ye shall be filled.

Blessed are ye that weep now: for ye shall laugh.

Blessed are ye, when men shall have you, and when they shall separate you from their company, and shall reproach you, and cast out your name as evil, for the Son of man's sake.

Before ye in that day, and leap for joy: for, behold, your reward is great in heaven: for in the like manner did their fathers unto the prophets.

But woe unto you that are rich! for ye have received your consolation.

Woe unto you that are full! for ye shall hunger.

Woe unto you that laugh now! for ye shall mourn and weep.

Woe unto you, when all men shall speak well of you! for so did their fathers to the false prophets.

¶But I say unto you which hear,

Love your enemies, do good to them which hate you, bless them that curse you, and pray for them which despitefully use you.

And unto him that smiteth thee on the one cheek offer also the other; and him that taketh away by cloak forbid not to take thy coat also.

Give to every man that asketh of thee; and of him that taketh away thy goods ask them not again.

*And as ye would that men should do to you, do ye also to them likewise.

For if ye love them which love you, what thank have ye? for sinners also love those that love them. And if ye do good to them which do good to you, what thank have ye? for sinners also do even the same. And if ye lend to them of whom ye hope to receive, what thank have ye? for sinners also lend to sinners, to receive as much again.

But love ye your enemies, and do good, and lend, hoping for nothing again; and your reward shall be great, and ye shall be the children of the Highest: for he is kind unto the unthankful and to the evil. Be ye therefore merciful, as your Father also is merciful.

Judge not, and ye shall not be judged: condemn not, and ye shall not be condemned: forgive, and ye shall be forgiven:

Give, and it shall be given unto you; good measure, pressed down, and shaken together, and running over, shall men give into your bosom. For with the same measure that ye mete withal it shall be measured to you again.

THE SERMON IN THE PLAIN (CONCLUDED)

A.D. 28. Age 31. Near Capernaum.

Luke 6, 39-49.

AND he spake a parable unto them,

Can the blind lead the blind? shall they not both fall into the ditch? The disciple is not above his master: but every one that is perfect shall be as his master.

And why beholdest thou the mote that is in thy brother's eye, but perceivest not the beam that is in thine own eye? Either how canst thou say to thy brother, Brother, let me pull out the mote that is in thine eye, when thou thyself beholdest not the beam that is in thine own eye? Thou hypocrite, cast out first the beam out of thine own eye, and then shalt thou see clearly to pull out the mote that is in thy brother's eye.

For a good tree bringeth not forth corrupt fruit; neither doth a corrupt tree bring forth good fruit. For every tree is known by his own fruit. For of thorns men do not gather figs, nor of a bramble bush gather they grapes.

A good man out of the good treasure of his heart bringeth forth that which is good; and an evil man out of the evil treasure of his heart bringeth forth that which is evil: for of the abundance of the heart his mouth speaketh.

¶And why call ye me, Lord, Lord, and do not the things which I say? Whosoever cometh to me, and heareth my sayings, and doeth them, I will shew you to whom he is like:

He is like a man which built a house, and digged deep, and laid the foundation on a rock: and when the flood arose, the stream beat vehemently upon that house, and could not shake it: for it was founded upon a rock. But he that heareth, and doeth not, is like a man that without a foundation built a house upon the earth; against which the stream did beat vehemently, and immediately it fell; and the ruin of that house was great.

THE CENTURION'S SERVANT HEALED

A.D. 28. Age 31. Capernaum. Nain.

Matthew 8, 5-13: Luke 7, 11-18.

WHEN Jesus was entered into Capernaum, there came unto him a centurion beseeching him, saying, Lord, my servant lieth at home sick of the palsy, grievously tormented.

The elders of the Jews came, saying, That he was worthy: for he loveth our nation, and hath built us a synagogue.

And Jesus saith unto the centurion,

I will come and heal him.

The centurion answered, Lord, I am not worthy that thou shouldest come under my roof: but speak the word only, and my servant shall be healed. Jesus marvelled, and turned and said to the people that followed him,

Verily I say unto you, I have not found so great faith, no, not in Israel. And I say unto you, That many shall come from the east and west, and shall sit down with Abraham, and Isaac, and Jacob, in the kingdom of heaven: but the children of the kingdom shall be cast out into outer darkness: there shall be weeping and gnashing of teeth.

And Jesus said unto the centurion,

Go thy way; and as thou hast believed, so be it done unto thee.

His servant was healed in the selfsame hour. *

¶The day after, Jesus went into a city called Nain: many of his disciples, and much people went with him.

Now when he came nigh to the gate of the city, behold, there was a dead man carried out, the only son of a widow: much people of the city was with her. The Lord had compassion on her, and said,

Weep not.

He touched the bier, and they that bare him stood still. Jesus said,

Young man, I say unto thee, Arise.

And he that was dead sat up, and began to speak.

There came a fear on all: they glorified God, saying, A great prophet is risen among us.

This rumor of Jesus went forth throughout all Judea and the region round about. And the disciples of John shewed him [John the Baptist] of all these things.

JOHN, FROM PRISON, SENDS MESSENGERS

A.D. 28 . Age 31. Galilee, near Cana.

Matthew 11, 2-15; 16-19: Luke 7, 24-35.

NOW when John had heard in the prison the works of Christ, he sent two of his disciples to Jesus. Unto him they said, John Baptist hath sent us unto thee, saying, Art thou he that should come? or do we look for another?

And in that same hour Jesus cured many of their infirmities; and unto many that were blind he gave sight.

Then said Jesus unto the two disciples [of John],

Go your way, and tell John again what things ye have seen and heard: how that the blind receive their sight, and the lane walk, the lepers are cleansed, and the deaf hear, the dead are raised up, and the poor have the gospel preached to them. And blessed is he, whosoever shall not be offended † in me.

¶When the messengers of John were departed, Jesus began to speak unto the people concerning John, ‡

What went ye out into the wilderness for to see? A reed shaken with the wind? But what went ye out for to see? A man clothed in soft raiment? Behold, they that wear soft clothing, they which are gorgeously apparelled, and live delicately, are in kings' courts, in kings' houses.

But what went ye out for to see? A prophet? Yea, I say unto you, and much more than a prophet. For this is he of whom it is written, Behold, I send my messenger before thy face, which shall prepare thy way before thee.

Verily, I say unto you, Among them that are born of women there hath not risen a greater prophet than John the Baptist: notwithstanding, he that is least in the kingdom of God is greater than he.

And from the days of John the Baptist until now the kingdom of heaven suffereth violence, and the violent take it by force. For all the prophets and the law prophesied until John. And if ye will receive it, this is Elias, which was for to come.

He that hath ears to hear, let him hear.

The people that heard him, and the publicans, justified God, being baptized with the baptism of John. But the Pharisees and lawyers rejected the counsel of God against themselves, being not baptized of him. Jesus said,

¶But whereunto then shall I liken the men of this generation? and to what are they like? They are like unto children sitting in the marketplace, and calling unto their fellows, one to another, and saying, We have piped unto you, and ye have not danced; we have mourned unto you, and ye have not lamented: ye have not wept.

For John the Baptist came neither eating bread nor drinking wine; and they say, He hath a devil. The Son of man is come eating and drinking; and they say, Behold a man gluttonous and a winebibber, a friend of publicans and sinners!

But wisdom is justified of all her children.

WOE UNTO CHORAZIN, BETHSAIDA, CAPERNAUM

A.D. 28. Age 31. Capernaum?

Matthew 11, 20-30: Luke 10, 13-15.

THEN began he to upbraid the cities wherein most of his mighty works were done, because they repented not: *

Woe unto thee, Chorazin! woe unto thee, Bethsaida! for if the mighty works, which were done in you, had been done in Tyre and Sidon, they would have repented long ago in sackcloth and ashes. But I say unto you, It shall be more tolerable for Tyre and Sidon at the day of judgment, than for you.

And thou, Capernaum, which are exalted unto heaven, shall be brought down to hell: for if the mighty works, which have been done in thee, had been done in Sodom, it would have remained until this day. But I say unto you, That it shall be more tolerable for the land of Sodom in the day of judgment, than for thee.

¶At that time Jesus said,

I thank thee, O Father, Lord of heaven and earth, because thou hast hid these things from the wise and prudent, and hast revealed them unto babes. Even so, Father: for so it seemed good in thy sight.

All things are delivered unto me of my Father, and no man knoweth the Son, but the Father; neither knoweth any man the Father, save the Son, and he to whomsoever the Son will reveal him.

¶Come unto me, all ye that labor and are heavy laden, and I will give you rest.

Take my yoke upon you, and learn of me; for I am meek and lowly in heart: and ye shall find rest unto your souls. For my yoke is easy, and my burden is light.

THE WOMAN WITH THE ALABASTER BOX

A.D. 28. Age 31 Galilee (Capernaum?).

Luke 7, 36-50.

ONE of the Pharisees [Simon] desired him that he would eat with him. And Jesus went into the Pharisee's house, and sat down to meat.

And, behold, a woman in the city, which was a sinner, brought an alabaster box of ointment, and stood weeping; and began to wash Jesus' feet, and did wipe them with the hairs of her head, and kissed his feet, and anointed them with the ointment. *

Now the Pharisee [Simon, the leper] spake within himself, saying, This man, if he were a prophet, would have known what manner of woman this is; for she is a sinner. Jesus said unto him,

Simon, I have somewhat to say unto thee:

There was a certain creditor which had two debtors; the one owed five hundred pence, and the other fifty. And when they had nothing to pay, he frankly forgave them both.

Tell me therefore, which of them will love him most?

Simon answered, I suppose that he to whom he forgave most. Jesus said,

Thou hast rightly judged.

He turned to the woman, and said unto Simon,

Seest thou this woman?

I entered into thine house, thou gavest me no water for my feet: but she hath washed my feet with tears, and wiped them with the hairs of her head.

Thou gavest me no kiss: but this woman, since the time I came in, hath not ceased to kiss my feet.

My head with oil thou didst not anoint: but this woman hath anointed my feet with ointment.

Wherefore I say unto thee, Her sins, which are many, are forgiven; for she loveth much: but to whom little is forgiven, the same loveth little.

And he said unto her,

Thy sins are forgiven.

They that sat at meat with him began to say within themselves, Who is this that forgiveth sins also? Jesus said to the woman,

Thy faith hath saved thee; go in peace.

THE MAN BLIND, MUTE, AND BEDEVILED

A.D. 28. Age 31. Capernaum.

Matthew 12, 22-37: Luke 11, 17-23: Mark 3, 22-29.

UNTO Jesus was brought one possessed with a devil, blind, and dumb; and he healed him, insomuch that the blind and dumb both spake and saw.

The people were amazed, and said, Is not this the son of David? But the Pharisees said, This fellow doth not cast out devils, but by Beelzebub the prince of the devils.

Jesus knew their thoughts, and said unto them,

*Every kingdom divided against itself is brought to desolation; and every city or house divided against itself falleth: it shall not stand: and if Satan cast out Satan, he is divided against himself; how shall then his kingdom stand? because ye say that I cast out devils through Beelzebub.

And if I by Beelzebub cast out devils, by whom do your children cast them out? therefore they shall be your judges.

But if I with the finger of God cast out devils by the Spirit of God,

no doubt then the kingdom of God is come unto you.

Or else, how can one enter into a strong man's house, and spoil his goods, except he first bind the strong man? and then he will spoil his house.

When a strong man armed keepeth his palace, his goods are in peace: but when a stronger than he shall come upon him, and overcome him, he taketh from him all his armor wherein he trusted, and divideth the spoils.

He that is not with me is against me; and he that gathereth not with me scattereth abroad.

¶Wherefore I say unto you, All manner of sin and blasphemy shall be forgiven unto the sons of men: but the blasphemy against the Holy Ghost shall not be forgiven unto men.

And whosoever speaketh a word against the Son of man, it shall be forgiven him: but whosoever speaketh against the Holy Ghost is in danger of eternal damnation: it shall not be forgiven him, neither in this world, neither in the world to come.

Either make the tree good, and his fruit good; or else make the tree corrupt: for the tree is known by his fruit.

O generation of vipers, how can ye, being evil, speak good things? for out of the abundance of the heart the mouth speaketh. A good man out of the good treasure of the heart bringeth forth good things: and an evil man out of the evil treasure bringeth forth evil things.

But I say unto you, That every idle word that men shall speak, they shall give account thereof in the day of judgment.

For by thy words thou shalt be justified, and by thy words thou shalt be condemned.

DOUBTERS SEEK A SIGN

A.D. 28. Age 31. Capernaum.

Matthew 12, 38-45.

CERTAIN of the scribes and of the Pharisees answered Jesus, saying, Master, we would see a sign from thee. But he said unto them,

An evil and adulterous generation seeketh after a sign; and there shall no sign be given to it, but the sign of the prophet Jonas: for as Jonas was three days and three nights in the whale's belly; so shall the Son of man be three days and three nights in the heart of the earth.

The men of Nineveh shall rise in judgment with this generation, and shall condemn it: because they repented at the preaching of Jonas; and, behold, a greater than Jonas is here.

The queen of the south shall rise up in the judgment with this generation, and shall condemn it: for she came from the uttermost parts of the earth to hear the wisdom of Solomon; and, behold, a greater than Solomon is here.

When the unclean spirit is gone out of a man, he walketh through dry places, seeking rest, and findeth none. Then he saith, I will return into my house from whence I came out; and when he is come, he findeth it empty, swept, and garnished. Then goeth he, and taketh with himself seven other spirits more wicked than himself, and they enter in and dwell there: and the last state of that man is worse than the first. Even so shall it be also unto this wicked generation. *

HIS MOTHER AND BRETHREN WOULD SPEAK WITH JESUS

A.D. 28, Age 31, Capernaum: Sea of Galilee.

Matt. 12, 46-50; 13, 1-30; Mark 3, 31-35; 4, 1-29: Luke 8, 4-18; 19-21.

WHILE Jesus yet talked, behold, there came his mother and his brethren, desiring to speak with him, and could not come at him for the press. Then one said unto him, Thy mother and thy brethren without seek for thee. But Jesus answered him that told him,

Who is my mother? and who are my brethren?

He looked on them which sat about him, stretched forth his hand toward his disciples, and said,

Behold my mother and my brethren! My mother and my brethren are these which hear the word of God, and do it. For whosoever shall do the will of God my Father which is in heaven, the same is my brother, and my sister, and mother.

¶The same day went Jesus out of the house, and sat by the sea side. Much people were come to him out of every city; so that he entered into a ship, and sat. The multitude stood on the shore. And Jesus spake many things unto them in parables, saying, †

Hearken: Behold, a sower went forth to sow his seed: and it came to pass, as he sowed, some fell by the way side, and it was trodden down, and the fowls of the air came and devoured it up.

Some seed fell on stony ground where it had not much earth: and immediately it sprang up, because it had not much deepness of earth:

but when the sun was up, because it had no depth of earth, it was scorched; and because it had no root, it withered away.

And some fell upon a rock: as soon as it was sprung up, it withered away, because it lacked moisture.

And some fell among thorns, and the thorns grew up with it, and choked it, and it yielded no fruit.

But other fell into good ground, and did yield fruit that sprang up, and increased; and bare fruit, some a hundredfold, some sixtyfold, and some thirtyfold.

He that hath ears to hear, let him hear.

When he was alone, his disciples came and said unto Jesus, Why speakest thou in parables? He answered,

Because it is given unto you to know the mysteries of the kingdom of heaven, but to them it is not given but in parables: unto them that are without, all these things are done in parables.

*For whosoever hath, to him shall be given, and he shall have more abundance: but whosoever hath not, from him shall be taken away even that he hath.

Therefore speak I to them in parables: because they seeing see not; and hearing they hear not, neither do they understand.

And in them is fulfilled the prophecy of Esaias, † which saith, By hearing ye shall hear, and shall not understand; and seeing ye shall see, and shall not perceive: for this people's heart is waxed gross, and their ears are dull of hearing, and their eyes they have closed; lest at any time they should see with their eyes, and hear with their ears, and should understand with their heart, and should be converted, and I should heal them, and their sins should be forgiven them.

‡But blessed are your eyes, for they see: and your ears, for they hear. For verily I say unto you, That many prophets and righteous men have desired to see those things which ye see, and have not seen them; and to hear those things which ye hear, and have not heard them.

And he said unto them,

Know ye not this parable? And how then will ye know all parables?

¶Hear ye therefore the parable of the sower. Now the parable is this:

The seed is the word of God. The sower soweth the word. When any one heareth the word of the kingdom, and understandeth it not, then cometh immediately Satan the wicked one, and catcheth away that word, which was sown in his heart: the devil taketh away the word out of their hearts, lest they should believe and be saved. This is he which received seed by the way side, where the word is sown.

They on the rock received seed into stony places: these are they who when they have heard the word, anon with joy receive it, and for a while believe; yet have no root in themselves, and so endure but for a time; and in time of temptation fall away: for afterward, when affliction or tribulation or persecution ariseth for the word's sake, immediately they are offended. *

And they which received the seed among thorns, are they, which, when they have heard the word, go forth, and are choked with the cares of this world and the deceitfulness of riches and the pleasures of this life; and bring no fruit to perfection: the lusts of other things entering in, choke the word, and it becometh unfruitful.

But he that received the seed into the good ground is he that in an honest and good heart, having heard the word, understandeth it, and keepeth it, and beareth fruit with patience, and bringeth forth, some a hundredfold, some sixty, some thirty.

Another parable put he forth unto them, saying,

The kingdom of heaven is likened unto a man which sowed good seed in his field: but while men slept, his enemy came and sowed tares among the wheat, and went his way. But when the blade was sprung up, and brought forth fruit, then appeared the tares also.

So the servants of the householder came and said unto him, Sir, didst not thou sow good seed in thy field? from whence then hath it tares?

¶He said unto them, An enemy hath done this.

The servants said unto him, Wilt thou then that we go and gather them up?

But he said, Nay; lest while ye gather up the tares, ye root up also the wheat with them. Let both grow together until the harvest: and in the time of harvest I will say to the reapers, Gather ye together first the tares, and bind them in bundles to burn them: but gather the wheat into my barn.

¶And he said unto them,

Is a candle brought to be put under a bushel, or under a bed? and not to be set on a candlestick?

No man, when he hath lighted a candle, covereth it with a vessel, or putteth it under a bed; but setteth it on a candlestick, that they which enter in may see the light.

For there is nothing hid, neither was anything kept secret, which shall not be manifested; but that it should be known and come abroad. If any man have ears to hear, let him hear.

Take heed what ye hear. With what measure ye mete, it shall be measured to you; and unto you that hear shall more be given: for he that hath, to him shall be given; and he that hath not, from him shall be taken even that which he hath. *

¶And he said,

So is the kingdom of God, as if a man should cast seed into the ground; and should sleep, and rise night and day, and the seed should spring and grow up, he knoweth not how. For the earth bringeth forth fruit of herself; first the blade, then the ear, after that the full corn in the ear. But when the fruit is brought forth, immediately he putteth in the sickle, because the harvest is come.

PARABLES: THE MUSTARD SEED, THE LEAVEN, THE MERCHANTMAN, THE NET

A.D. 28. Age 31. Capernaum: Sea of Galilee.

Mk. 4, 30-34; 35-41: Matt. 13, 31-34; 36-52: Lk. 13, 18-21; 8, 22-25.

ANOTHER parable put he forth unto them, saying,

†Whereunto shall we liken the kingdom of God? or with what comparison shall we compare it? A grain of mustard seed is the least of all seeds: is indeed less than all the seeds that be in the earth; but when it is sown in the earth, it groweth up: it becometh greater than all herbs; it shooteth out great branches, and becometh a tree, so that the fowls of the air come and lodge in the branches thereof.

Then said he,

Unto what is the kingdom of God like? and whereunto shall I resemble it? The kingdom of heaven is like unto a grain of mustard seed, which a man took and cast into a garden in his field; and it grew, and waxed a great tree, and the birds of the air lodged in the branches thereof, in the shadow of it.

¶Again Jesus said,

Whereunto shall I liken the kingdom of God?

And another parable spake he unto them,

The kingdom of heaven is like unto leaven, which a woman took, and hid in three measures of meal, till the whole was leavened.

All these things spake Jesus unto the multitude in parables.

Then he sent the multitude away, and went into the house: and his disciples came, saying, Declare unto us the parable of the tares of the field. He answered,

He that soweth the good seed is the Son of man; the field is the world; the good seed are the children of the kingdom; but the tares are the children of the wicked one; the enemy that sowed them is the devil; the harvest is the end of the world; and the reapers are the angels.

As therefore the tares are gathered and burned in the fire; so shall it be in the end of this world. The Son of man shall send forth his angels, and they shall gather out of his kingdom all things that offend, and them which do iniquity; and shall cast them into a furnace of fire: there shall be wailing and gnashing of teeth.

Then shall the righteous shine forth as the sun in the kingdom of their Father.

Who hath ears to hear, let him hear.

¶Again, the kingdom of heaven is like unto a treasure hid in a field; the which when a man hath found, he hideth, and for joy thereof goeth and selleth all that he hath, and buyeth that field.

¶Again, the kingdom of heaven is like unto a merchantman, seeking goodly pearls: who, when he had found one pearl of great price, went and sold all that he had, and bought it.

¶Again, the kingdom of heaven is like unto a net, that was cast into the sea, and gathered of every kind: which, when it was full, they drew to shore, and sat down, and gathered the good into vessels, but cast the bad away.

So shall it be at the end of the world: the angels shall come forth, and sever the wicked from the just, and shall cast them into the furnace of fire: there shall be wailing and gnashing of teeth.

Jesus saith unto them,

Have ye understood all these things?

They say, Yea, Lord. Then said he unto them,

Therefore every scribe which is instructed unto the kingdom of heaven, is like unto a man that is a householder, which bringeth forth out of his treasure things new and old.

And with many such parables spake Jesus the word unto them, as they were able to hear it. But without a parable spake he not unto them: and when they were alone, he expounded all things to his disciples.

The same day, when even was come, Jesus entered into a ship. His disciples followed, and he said unto them,

Let us pass over unto the other side of the lake.

They took him even as he was in the ship. And they launched forth.

As they sailed, behold, there came down a storm of wind: the waves beat into the ship, insomuch that the ship was covered with the waves.

Jesus was in the hinder part of the ship, asleep on a pillow: and his disciples awoke him, saying, Lord, save us: we perish. He said unto them,

Why are ye fearful, O ye of little faith?

Then he arose and rebuked the winds, and the raging of the water: he said unto the sea,

Peace, be still.

The wind ceased: there was a great calm, and Jesus said unto his disciples,

Why are ye fearful? where is your faith? how is it that ye have no faith?

But the men marvelled, saying, What manner of man is this, that even the winds and the sea obey him?

THE MADMAN AND THE SWINE

A.D. 28. Age 31. Sea of Galilee. Decapolis.

Mark 5, 1-20: Luke 8, 26-40: Matthew 8, 28-34.

THEY came over unto the other side of the sea, and arrived at the country of the Gadarenes, over against Galilee.

And when Jesus was come out of the ship, immediately there met him out of the tombs a man * with an unclean spirit, who ware no clothes, neither abode in any house, but among the tombs: he had devils long time, and no man could bind him, no not with chains.

Jesus said,

Come out of the man, thou unclean spirit.

He fell down before Jesus, and cried out, What have I to do with thee, Jesus, thou Son of God most high? I beseech thee, torment me not. And Jesus asked him,

What is thy name?

He answered, Legion: for we are many.

Now there was a good way off from them a herd of swine feeding. And the devils besought Jesus, saying, If thou cast us out, suffer us to go away into the herd of swine.

Jesus gave them leave: he said,

Go.

The unclean spirits went out, and entered into the swine; and the herd ran violently down a steep place into the sea, and perished in the waters. They were about two thousand.

They that fed the swine went and told it in the city. And, behold, the whole city came out: they come to Jesus, and see him that had the legion, sitting at the feet of Jesus, clothed, and in his right mind: they were afraid. And the Gadarenes round about besought Jesus to depart out of their coasts.

Jesus went up into the ship.

Now the man, out of whom the devils were departed, besought Jesus that he might be with him: but Jesus sent him away, saying,

Return to thine own house. Go home to thy friends; tell them how the Lord had compassion on thee, and shew them how great things God hath done unto thee.

Jesus passed over by ship unto the other side, and came into his own city. Much people gladly received him.

JAIRUS' DAUGHTER HEALED

A.D. 28. Age 31. Capernaum.

Luke 9, 41-42; 49-56; 43-48: Mark 5, 22-24; 35-43; 25-34: Matthew 9, 18-19; 23-26; 27-30.

AND, behold, there came one of the rulers of the synagogue, a man named Jairus. He fell at Jesus' feet: and he besought Jesus that he would come to his house, saying, My little daughter lieth at the point of death: I pray thee, come and lay thy hands on her: and she shall live.

He had one only daughter; she was of the age of twelve years.

Jesus arose and followed him, and so did his disciples: much people thronged him.

There cometh one from the ruler's house, saying to Jairus, Thy daughter is dead: why troublest thou the Master further? Jesus heard. He said,

Be not afraid, only believe. Fear not, believe only, and she shall be made whole.

Jesus came to Jairus' house, and saw the tumult: the minstrels making a noise, and them that wept.

He suffered no man to go in, save Peter, and James, and John, and the father and the mother of the maiden. All wept, and bewailed her. When Jesus was come in, he saith unto them,

Why make ye this ado, and weep? Weep not. Give place. The damsel is not dead, but sleepeth.

They laughed him to scorn, knowing that she was dead. He put them all out.

Jesus, and the father and mother of the damsel, and they that were with them, entered in where the maiden was lying. He took her by the hand, saying,

Maid, arise.

She arose straightway, and walked. Jesus commanded that something be given her to eat.

¶Behold, a certain woman, which was diseased twelve years, and had suffered many things from many physicians, and had spent all that she had, and was nothing bettered, but rather grew worse: she came in the press behind, and touched the hem of Jesus' garment: for she said within herself, If I may but touch his clothes, I shall be whole.

Straightway she felt in her body that she was healed.

Jesus, knowing that virtue had gone out of him, turned him about in the press, and said,

Who touched me?

When all denied, Peter said, Master, the multitude throng thee and press thee, and sayest thou, Who touched me? Jesus said,

Somebody hath touched me: for I perceive that virtue is gone out of me. Who touched my clothes?

He looked about to see her that had done this thing. The woman fearing and trembling, knowing what was done in her, came and told him the truth, before all the people: for what cause she had touched him, and how she was healed immediately. Jesus said unto her,

Daughter, be of good comfort; thy faith hath made thee whole. Go in peace, and be whole of thy plague.

¶When Jesus departed thence, two blind men followed him, crying Thou Son of David, have mercy on us.

When he was come into the house, the blind men came to him: and Jesus saith unto them,

Believe ye that I am able to do this?

They said, Yea, Lord. Then touched he their eyes, saying,

According to your faith be it unto you.

And their eyes were opened. Jesus straitly charged them,

See that no man know it.

But they spread abroad his fame in all that country.

HOME AGAIN: A PROPHET WITHOUT HONOR

A.D. 29. Age 32. Nazareth. Capernaum.

Mark 6, 1-6, 7-13: Matthew 13, 54-58; 9, 35-38; 10, 5-42: Luke 9, 1-6.

JESUS went out from thence, and came into his own country. When the sabbath day was come, he began to teach in the synagogue: and many hearing him were astonished, saying, What wisdom is this which is given unto him? Is not this the carpenter, the son of Joseph? Is not his mother called Mary? and his brethren, James, and Joses, and Simon, and Judas? and his sisters, are they not all here? Whence then has this man all these things and they were offended in him. But Jesus said unto them,

A prophet is not without honor, save in his own country, and among his own kin, and in his own house.

And he did not many works, there, because of their unbelief.

¶Jesus went about the cities and villages, teaching in synagogues, and preaching the gospel of the kingdom, and healing sickness among the people.

But when he saw the multitudes, he was moved with compassion, because they fainted and were scattered abroad, as sheep having no shepherd. Then saith he to his disciples,

The harvest truly is plenteous, but the laborers are few; pray ye therefore the Lord of the harvest, that he will send forth laborers into his harvest.

¶Jesus called unto him the twelve, * and began to send them forth by two and two; and gave them power over unclean spirits, and to cure diseases.

These twelve Jesus sent forth to preach the gospel of the kingdom; and he commanded them:

Go not into the way of the Gentiles, and into any city of the Samaritans enter ye not: but go rather to the lost sheep of the house of Israel. And as ye go, preach, saying, The kingdom of heaven is at hand.

Heal the sick, cleanse the lepers, raise the dead, cast out devils: freely ye have received, freely give.

Take nothing for your journey, neither staves * nor bread; provide neither gold, nor silver, nor brass in your purses, nor scrip for your journey, neither two coats apiece; nor yet shoes, but be shod with sandals; for the workman is worthy of his meat.

And into whatsoever city or town ye shall enter, in what place soever ye enter into a house, inquire who in it is worthy; and there abide till ye go, and thence depart. And when ye come into a house, salute it. † And if the house be worthy, let your peace come upon it: but if it be not worthy, let your peace return to you. And whosoever shall not receive you, nor hear your words, when ye depart out of that house or city, shake off the very dust from your feet for a testimony against them. Verily I say unto you, It shall be more tolerable for the land of Sodom and Gomorrah in the day of judgment, than for that city.

¶Behold, I send you forth as sheep in the midst of wolves: be ye therefore wise as serpents, and harmless as doves.

But beware of men: for they will deliver you up to the councils, and they will scourge you in their synagogues; and ye shall be brought before governors and kings for my sake, for a testimony against them and the Gentiles.

But when they deliver you up, take no thought how or what ye shall speak: for it shall be given you in that same hour what ye shall speak. For it is not ye that speak, but the Spirit of your Father which speaketh in you.

And the brother shall deliver up the brother to death, and the father the child: and the children shall rise up against their parents, and cause them to be put to death.

And ye shall be hated of all men for my name's sake: but he that endureth to the end shall be saved. But when they persecute you in this city, flee ye into another: for verily I say unto you, Ye shall not have gone over the cities of Israel, till the Son of man be come.

The disciple is not above his master, nor the servant above his lord. It is enough for the disciple that he be as his master, and the servant as his lord. If they have called the master of the house Beelzebub, how much more shall they call them of his household?

Fear them not therefore: for there is nothing covered that shall not be revealed; and hid that shall not be known. What I tell you in darkness that speak ye in light: and what ye hear in the ear, that preach ye upon the housetops. And fear not them which kill the body, but are not able to kill the soul: but rather fear him which is able to destroy both soul and body in hell.

Are not two sparrows sold for a farthing? and one of them shall not fall on the ground without your Father. But the very hairs of your head are all numbered. Fear ye not therefore, ye are of more value than many sparrows.

Whosoever therefore shall confess me before men, him will I confess also before my Father which is in heaven. But whosoever shall deny me before men, him will I also deny before my Father which is in heaven.

Think not that I am come to send peace on earth: I came not to send peace, but a sword. For I am come to set a man at variance against his father, and the daughter against her mother, and the daughter in law against her mother in law. And a man's foes shall be they of his own household. He that loveth father or mother more than me is not worthy of me: and he that loveth son or daughter more than me is not worthy of me. And he that taketh not his cross, and followeth after me, is not worthy of me. He that findeth his life shall lose it; and he that loseth his life for my sake shall find it.

¶He that receiveth you receiveth me, and he that receiveth me receiveth him that sent me. He that receiveth a prophet in the name of a prophet shall receive a prophet's reward; and he that receiveth a righteous man in the name of a righteous man shall receive a righteous man's reward.

And whosoever shall give to drink unto one of these little ones a cup of cold water only in the name of a disciple, verily I say unto you, he shall in no wise lose his reward.

They went out through the towns, and preached that men should repent. Healing every where, they anointed with oil many that were sick, and cast out many unclean spirits.

HEROD DESIRES TO SEE CHRIST

A D. 29. Age 32. Decapolis: Bethsaida.

Matthew 14, 1-4; 13-14: Luke 9, 7-11: Mark 6, 17-18; 30-33: John 6, 1-3.

NOW Herod the tetrarch heard of the fame of Jesus: and he was perplexed, because it was said of some, that John was risen from the dead. Herod himself had laid hold upon John, and bound him in prison for Herodias' sake, his brother Philip's wife: for John had said unto Herod, It is not lawful for thee to have thy brother's wife.

And Herod had married her: and sent an executioner, and beheaded John in the prison. Herod said, John have I beheaded; but who is this of whom I hear such things?

And he desired to see Jesus. Jesus' disciples went and told him [Jesus]. And he went over the sea of Galilee, by ship.

¶When the apostles were returned, and were gathered unto Jesus, they told all things, both what they had done, and what they had taught. Jesus said unto them.

Come ye yourselves apart into a desert place, and rest a while.

He took his disciples, and went privately into a desert place belonging to the city called Bethsaida. He went up into a mountain, and there he sat with his disciples.

The people saw them departing, and many knew him, and ran afoot and outwent them, and came together unto him.

FIVE THOUSAND FED

A.D. 29. Age 32. Bethsaida.

John 6, 5-13: Matthew 14, 15-21: Mark 6, 35-44: Luke 9, 12-17.

WHEN Jesus saw a great company come unto him, he saith unto Philip,

Whence shall we buy bread, that these may eat?

This he said to prove Philip, for he himself knew what he would do. Jesus' disciples said, Shall we go and buy two hundred pennyworth of bread, and give them to eat?

Philip answered, Two hundred pennyworth of bread is not sufficient.

¶When the day began to wear away, then came the twelve and said, This is a desert place: send the multitude away, that they may go into the towns and villages round about, and lodge, and buy themselves victuals: for they have nothing to eat. Jesus answered,

They need not depart; give ye them to eat. How many loaves have ye? Go and see.

Andrew, Simon Peter's brother, saith, A lad here hath five barley loaves, and two small fishes: but what are they among so many? Jesus said,

Bring them hither to me. Make the men sit down by fifties in a company.

Now there was much green grass in the place. So the men sat down, in ranks, by hundreds, and by fifties.

Jesus took the loaves, and when, looking up to heaven, he had given thanks, he blessed and brake, and distributed to the disciples, and the disciples to them that were set down; and likewise of the fishes.

They did all eat. And when they were filled, Jesus said unto his disciples,

Gather up the fragments that remain, that nothing be lost.

They filled twelve baskets. They that had eaten were about five thousand men, beside women and children.

JESUS WOULD NOT BE MADE KING

A.D. 29. Age 32. Sea of Galilee. Gennesaret.

Matthew 14, 22-32: Mark 6, 45-53: John 6, 15-21.

WHEN Jesus perceived that they would take him by force, to make him a king, he constrained his disciples to get into a ship, and to go before him unto the other side, while he sent the multitude away.

If He went up into a mountain apart, to pray: when the evening was come, he was there alone.

His disciples went over the sea toward Capernaum. The sea arose by reason of a great wind that blew. It was now dark, and the ship in the midst of the sea, tossed with the waves, and Jesus on the land, alone.

He saw them toiling in rowing; and about the fourth watch of the night, they see Jesus walking on the sea, and drawing nigh unto the ship. They cried out for fear, saying, It is a spirit.

But straightway Jesus spake,

Be of good cheer; it is I: be not afraid.

Peter answered, Lord, if it be thou, bid me come unto thee on the water. Jesus said,

Come.

And Peter walked on the water, to go to Jesus. But he was afraid; and beginning to sink, he cried, Lord, save me.

Jesus stretched forth his hand, and caught him, and said,

O thou of little faith, wherefore didst thou doubt?

When they were come into the ship, the wind ceased. They came into the land of Gennesaret.

"I AM THE BREAD OF LIFE"

A.D. 29. Age 32. Capernaum.

John 6, 22-71.

THE day following, the people which stood on the other side of the sea, where they did eat bread, when they saw that Jesus was not there, neither his disciples, took shipping, and came to Capernaum, seeking him. And When they had found him, they said unto him, Master when camest thou hither? Jesus answered,

Verily, verily, I say unto you, ye seek me, not because ye saw the miracles, but because ye did eat of the loaves, and were filled. Labor not for the meat which perisheth, but for the meat which endureth unto everlasting life, which the Son of man shall give unto you: for him hath God the Father sealed.

Then said they, What shall we do, that we might work the works of God? Jesus answered,

This is the work of God, that ye believe on him whom he hath sent.

They said, What sign shewest thou then, that we may see and believe thee? Our fathers did eat manna in the desert; as it is written, He gave them bread from heaven. Then said Jesus,

Verily, verily, I say unto you, Moses gave you not that bread from heaven; but my Father giveth you the true bread from heaven. For the bread of God is he which cometh down from heaven, and giveth life unto the world.

Then said they, Lord, evermore give us this bread. And Jesus said,

I am the bread of life: he that cometh to me shall never hunger; and he that believeth on me shall never thirst. But I said unto you, That ye also have seen me, and believe not.

All that the Father giveth me shall come to me; and him that cometh to me I will in no wise cast out.

For I came down from heaven, not to do mine own will, but the will of him that sent me. And this is the Father's will which hath sent me, that of all which he hath given me I should lose nothing, but should raise it up again at the last day. And this is the will of him that sent me, that every one which seeth the Son, and believeth on him, may have everlasting life: and I will raise him up at the last day.

The Jews then murmured because he said, I am the bread which came down from heaven. And they said, Is not this Jesus, the son of Joseph, whose father and mother we know? How is it then that he saith, I came down from heaven? Jesus answered,

Murmur not among yourselves. No man can come to me, except the Father which hath sent me draw him: and I will raise him up at the last day. It is written in the prophets, And they shall be all taught of God.

Every man therefore that hath heard, and hath learned of the Father, cometh unto me. Not that any man hath seen the Father, save he which is of God, he hath seen the Father.

Verily, verily, I say unto you, He that believeth on me hath everlasting life.

I am that bread of life.

Your fathers did eat manna in the wilderness, and are dead. This is the bread which cometh down from heaven, that a man may eat thereof, and not die. I am the living bread which came down from heaven: if any man eat of this bread, he shall live forever: and the bread that I will give is my flesh, which I will give for the life of the world.

The Jews therefore strove among themselves saying, How can this man give us his flesh to eat? Then said Jesus, *

Verily, verily, I say unto you, Except ye eat the flesh of the Son of man, and drink his blood, ye have no life in you. Whoso eateth my flesh, and drinketh my blood, hath eternal life; and I will raise him up at the last day. For my flesh is meat indeed, and my blood is drink indeed. He that eateth my flesh, and drinketh my blood, dwelleth in me, and I in him. As the living Father hath sent me, and I live by the Father, so he that eateth me, even he shall live by me. This is that bread which came down from heaven: not as your fathers did eat manna, and are dead: he that eateth of this bread shall live for ever. *

These things said Jesus in the synagogue in Capernaum. Many of his disciples said, This is a hard saying; who can hear it?

When Jesus knew in himself that his disciples murmured, he said unto them,

Doth this offend you?

What and if ye shall see the Son of man ascend up where he was before?

It is the Spirit that quickeneth; the flesh profiteth nothing: the words that I speak unto you, they are spirit, and they are life.

But there are some of you that believe not.

For Jesus knew from the beginning who they were that believed not, and who should betray him. And he said,

Therefore said I unto you, that no man can come unto me, except it were given unto him of my Father.

¶From that time many of his disciples walked not with him. Then said Jesus unto the twelve,

Will ye also go away?

Simon Peter answered, Lord, to whom shall we go? thou hast the words of eternal life. And we are sure that thou art that Christ, the Son of the living God. Jesus answered,

Have I not chosen you twelve, and one of you is a devil?

He spake of Judas Iscariot; for he it was that should betray Jesus, being one of the twelve.

PHARISEES QUERULOUS

A.D. 29. Age 32. Capernaum.

Mark 7, 1-23: Matthew 15, 1-20.

*CERTAIN of the scribes saw some of Jesus' disciples eat bread with unwashen hands. They found fault: for the Pharisees, and all the Jews, except they wash their hands oft, eat not, holding the tradition of the elders. And many other things there be, which they have received to hold, as the washing of cups, and pots, brazen vessels, and of tables.

The Pharisees and scribes asked Jesus, Why walk not thy disciples according to the tradition of the elders, but eat bread with unwashen hands? Why do thy disciples transgress?

But Jesus answered,

Why do ye also transgress the commandment of God by your tradition? Full well ye reject the commandment of God, that ye may keep your tradition. For God commanded, saying (Moses said), Honor thy father and thy mother: and, Whoso curseth father or mother, let him die the death.

But ye say, If a man shall say (Whosoever shall say) to his father or his mother, It is Corban, that is to say, a gift, by whatsoever thou mightest be profited by me; and honor not his father or his mother: he shall be free. And ye suffer him no more to do aught for his father or his mother; making the word of God of none effect through your tradition, which ye have delivered; and many such like things do ye. Thus have ye made the commandment of God of none effect by your tradition.

Well hath Elias prophesied of you hypocrites, as it is written, This people draweth night unto me with their mouth, this people honoreth me with their lips; but their heart is far from me. Howbeit in vain do they worship me, teaching for doctrines the commandments of men.

Ye hypocrites! For, laying aside the commandment of God, ye hold the tradition of men, as the washing of pots and cups: and many other like things ye do.

¶And he called the multitude, and said unto them,

Hearken unto me every one of you. Hear, and understand. Not that which goeth into the mouth defileth a man. There is nothing from without a man, that entering into him can defile him; but the things which come out of him, those are they that defile the man.

If any man have ears to hear, let him hear.

His disciples, when he was entered into the house from the people, asked Jesus concerning the parable. Jesus said,

Are ye also yet so without understanding? Do not ye yet perceive that whatsoever thing from without entereth into a man, entereth in at the mouth, goeth into the belly, and is cast out into the draught, purging all meats? It entereth not into his heart; it cannot defile him.

But those things which proceed out of the mouth come forth from the heart; and they defile the man: for from within, out of the heart of men, proceed evil thoughts, adulteries, fornications, murders, thefts, covetousness, wickedness, false witness, deceit, lasciviousness, an evil eye, blasphemies, pride, foolishness: all these evil things come from within, and these are the things which defile the man; but to eat with unwashen hands defileth not a man.

Then his disciples said unto Jesus, Knowest thou that the Pharisees were offended, after they heard this saying? But he answered,

Every plant which my heavenly Father hath not planted, shall be rooted up. Let them alone: they be blind leaders of the blind. And if the blind lead the blind, both shall fall into the ditch.

THE WOMAN OF CANAAN

A.D. 29. Age 32. Phenicia. Decapolis.

Matthew 15, 21-28: Mark 7, 24-36.

FROM thence Jesus went into the borders of Tyre and Sidon.

And, behold, a woman of Canaan came out of the same coasts, and cried unto him, saying, Have mercy on me, O Lord, thou Son of David: my daughter is grievously vexed with an unclean spirit.

The woman was a Greek, a Syrophenician by nation.

Jesus answered her not a word. And his disciples came, saying, Send her away. Jesus said,

I am not sent but unto the lost sheep of the house of Israel.

He entered into a house, and would have no man know it: but he could not be hid. For then came she whose young daughter had an unclean spirit, saying, Lord, help me.

But Jesus said unto her,

Let the children first be filled: for it is not meet to take the children's bread, and to cast it unto the dogs.

She said, Yes, Lord: yet the dogs under the table eat of the children's crumbs which fall from their masters' table. Jesus answered,

O woman, great is thy faith: be it unto thee even as thou wilt. For this saying go thy way; the devil is gone out of thy daughter.

Her daughter was made whole from that very hour.

¶Departing from the coasts of Tyre and Sidon, Jesus came unto the sea of Galilee, through the midst of the coasts of Decapolis.

They bring unto him one that was deaf, and had an impediment in his speech. Jesus took him aside, and put his fingers into his ears, and touched his tongue; and looking up to heaven, he sighed, and saith,

Be opened.

Straightway his ears were opened, and the string of his tongue was loosed, and he spake plain.

Jesus charged them that they should tell no man: but the more he charged them, so much the more a great deal they published it.

"SEVEN LOAVES AND A FEW LITTLE FISHES"

A.D. 29. Age 32. Decapolis. Dalmanutha. Bethsaida.

Mark 8, 1-26: Matthew 15, 32-39; John 6, 1-12.

IN those days the multitude being great, and having nothing to eat, Jesus called his disciples, and saith,

I have compassion on the multitude, because they have now been with me three days, and have nothing to eat: and if I send them away fasting to their own houses, they will faint by the way.

For divers of them came from far.

His disciples say, From whence can a man satisfy these men with bread here in the wilderness? Jesus saith,

I will not send them away fasting, lest they faint in the way. How many loaves have ye?

They said, Seven, and a few little fishes.

He commanded the people to sit on the ground: and he took the seven loaves, and gave thanks, and brake, and gave to his disciples to set before the people. The few small fishes he blessed, and commanded to set them also before them.

So they did all eat, and were filled. They took up of the broken meat that was left seven baskets full. And they that had eaten were about four thousand, beside women and children. He sent them away.

¶Straightway Jesus entered into a ship with his disciples, and came into the coasts of Magdala, into the parts of Dalmanutha.

The Pharisees with the Sadducees came forth to question with him,

seeking of him a sign from heaven, tempting him. He sighed deeply in his spirit, and saith,

Why doth this generation seek after a sign? verily I say unto you, There shall no sign be given unto this generation.

When it is evening, ye say, It will be fair weather: for the sky is red.

And in the morning, It will be foul weather to day: for the sky is red and lowering.

O ye hypocrites, ye can discern the face of the sky; but can ye not discern the signs of the times? A wicked and adulterous generation seeketh after a sign; and there shall no sign be given unto it, but the sign of the prophet Jonas.

Entering into the ship again, Jesus departed to the other side.

¶Now the disciples had forgotten to take bread; neither had they in the ship with them more than one loaf. Then Jesus charged them,

Take heed and beware of the leaven of the Pharisees and of the Sadducees, and of the leaven of Herod.

They reasoned among themselves, saying, It is because we have taken no bread. Which when Jesus perceived, he said unto them,

O ye of little faith, why reason ye among yourselves, because ye have brought no bread? Perceive ye not yet, neither understand? Have ye your heart yet hardened? Having eyes, see ye not? and having ears, hear ye not? and do ye not remember?

Do ye not understand, neither remember the five loaves of the five thousand, and how many baskets ye took up? Neither the seven loaves of the four thousand, and how many baskets ye took up?

When I brake the five loaves among the five thousand, how many baskets full of fragments took ye up?

They answer, Twelve.

And when the seven among four thousand, how many baskets full of fragments took ye up?

They said, seven. And Jesus said,

How is it that ye do not understand that I spake it not to you concerning bread, that ye should beware of the leaven of the Pharisees and of the Sadducees?

Then understood they how that he bade them not beware of the leaven of bread, but of the doctrine of the Pharisees and of the Sadducees. *

¶Jesus cometh to Bethsaida; and they bring a blind man unto him. He took the man by the hand, and led him out of the town; and when Jesus had put his hands upon his eyes, he asked him if he saw aught. The man looked up, and said, I see men as trees, walking.

Jesus again put his hands upon his eyes, and made him look up: and he was restored, and saw every man clearly. Jesus sent him away, saying,

Neither go into the town, nor tell it to any in the town.

"UPON THIS ROCK I WILL BUILD MY CHURCH"

A.D. 29. Age 32. Cesarea Philippi.

Matthew 16, 13-28: Mark 8, 27-38; 9, 1: Luke 9, 18-27. *

JESUS, and his disciples, came into the towns of Cesarea Philippi. And by the way he asked them, *

Whom do men say that I, the Son of man, am? Whom say the people that I am?

They answering said, John the Baptist; but some say, Elias; and others, Jeremias, or, that one of the old prophets is risen again. Jesus said,

But whom say ye that I am?

Simon Peter answering said, The Christ of God. † Jesus saith unto Peter,

Blessed art thou, Simon Bar-jona: for flesh and blood hath not revealed it unto thee, but my Father which is in heaven.

And I say unto thee, That thou art Peter, ‡ and upon this rock I will build my church; and the gates of hell shall not prevail against it.

And I will give unto thee the keys of the kingdom of heaven: and whatsoever thou shalt bind on earth, shall be bound in heaven; and whatsoever thou shalt loose on earth shall be loosed in heaven.

And he straitly charged them that they should tell no man of him: that he was Jesus the Christ.

¶From that time forth began Jesus to shew unto his disciples, how that he, the Son of man, must go unto Jerusalem, and be killed, saying,

The Son of man must suffer many things, and be rejected of the elders and chief priests and scribes, and be slain, and be raised the third day.

He spake that saying openly. Then Peter began to rebuke him, saying, Be it far from thee, Lord: this shall not be unto thee.

When Jesus had turned and looked on his disciples, he rebuked Peter, saying,

Get thee behind me, Satan: thou are an offence * unto me: for thou savorest not the things that be of God, but the things that be of men.

¶When he had called the people unto him, with his disciples also, he said unto them,

If any man will come after me, whosoever will, let him deny himself, and take up his cross daily, and follow me.

For whosoever will save his life shall lose it: but whosoever will lose his life for my sake and the gospel's, the same shall save it. For what shall it profit a man, what is a man advantaged, if he gain the whole world, and lose himself, lose his own soul? or be cast away? Or what shall a man give in exchange for his soul? For the Son of man shall come in the glory of his Father with his angels; and then he shall reward every man according to his works.

Whosoever therefore shall be ashamed of me and of my words, in this adulterous and sinful generation, of him also shall the Son of man be ashamed, when he shall come in his own glory: and cometh in the glory of his Father with his holy angels.

And he said,

But I tell you of a truth, there be some standing here which shall not taste of death, till they have seen the kingdom of God come with power, the Son of man coming in his kingdom.

THE TRANSFIGURATION

A.D. 29 Age 32. On, and near, Mt. Hermon.

Luke 9, 28-42: Matthew 17, 1-21: Mark 9, 2-29.

IT came to pass, about an eight † days after these sayings, Jesus taketh Peter, John, and James his brother, and went up into a high mountain apart to pray: and Jesus was transfigured before them.

As he prayed, the fashion of his countenance was altered: his face did shine as the sun, and his raiment was white as the light, and glistering, shining as snow, exceeding white, so as no fuller on earth can white them. And, behold, two men, Moses and Elias: who appeared in glory: talking with Jesus [they] spake of his decease which he should accomplish at Jerusalem.

Peter and they that were with Jesus saw his glory, and the two men with Jesus.

There came a bright cloud, and overshadowed them: and a voice out of the cloud, saying, This is my beloved Son, in whom I am well pleased; hear ye him.

The disciples fell on their face, and were sore afraid. Jesus came and touched them, and said,

Arise, and be not afraid.

Suddenly, when they had lifted up their eyes, they saw no man any more, save Jesus only. And he charged them,

Tell the vision to no man, until the Son of man be risen again from the dead.

¶Questioning with one another what the rising from the dead should mean, his disciples asked Jesus, Why say the scribes that Elias must first come? Jesus told them,

Elias verily cometh first, and restoreth all things; and how it is written of the Son of man, that he must suffer many things, and be set at nought.

But I say unto you, That Elias is indeed come already, and they knew him not; and they have done unto him whatsoever they listed, as it is written of him.

Likewise shall also the Son of man suffer of them.

The disciples understood that he spake of John the Baptist. They kept it close, and told no man in those days any of the things which they had seen.

¶When Jesus saw a multitude about his disciples, and the scribes questioning with them, he asked the scribes,

What question ye with them?

One of the multitude answered, Master, I have brought unto thee my son: Lord, have mercy; for he is lunatic, and sore vexed: ofttimes he falleth into the fire, and oft into the water. A spirit teareth him that he foameth again, and gnasheth his teeth, and pineth away. I brought him to thy disciples, and they could not cure him. He is mine only child.

Then Jesus said,

O faithless and perverse generation, how long shall I be with you? How long shall I suffer you?

Bring thy son hither to me.

They brought him: and as he was yet a coming, the spirit tare him; and he fell, and wallowed foaming. Jesus asked his father,

How long is it ago since this came unto him?

He said, Of a child. Have compassion on us. Jesus said,

If thou canst believe, all things are possible to him that believeth.

Straightway the father said with tears, Lord, I believe; help thou my unbelief.

Jesus rebuked the foul spirit, saying,

Thou dumb and deaf spirit, I charge thee, come out of him, and enter no more into him.

The child was cured from that very hour.

¶When Jesus was come into the house, his disciples asked him privately, Why could not we cast him out? Jesus answered,

Because of your unbelief: for verily I say unto you, If ye have faith as a grain of mustard seed, ye shall say unto this mountain, Remove hence; and it shall remove; and nothing shall be impossible unto you. Howbeit this kind goeth not out, can come forth, by nothing, but by prayer and fasting.

JESUS FORETELLS HIS DEATH AND RESURRECTION

A.D. 29. Age 32. Galilee. Capernaum.

Mark 9, 30-37: Luke 9, 44-48: Matthew 17, 22-27.

JESUS departed thence, and passed through Galilee. While in Galilee, all wondered at the things which Jesus did. But while they wondered, Jesus said unto his disciples,

Let these sayings sink down into your ears: for the Son of man shall be betrayed, and delivered into the hands of men: and they shall kill him; and the third day after that he is killed, he shall be raised again.

But they understood not.

¶There arose a reasoning among the disciples: for by the way [to Capernaum] they had disputed amongst themselves which of them should be the greatest. In the house Jesus asked,

What was it that ye disputed among yourselves by the way?

But they held their peace: and Jesus, perceiving the thought of their heart, saith,

If any man desire to be first, the same shall be last of all.

He took a child in his arms, and said,

Whosoever shall receive this child in my name, receiveth me; whosoever shall receive one of such children in my name, receiveth me: and whosoever shall receive me, receiveth me not, but him that sent me: for he that is least among you all, the same shall be great.

When they were come to Capernaum, they that received tribute money came to Peter, and said, Doth not your master pay tribute?

Peter saith, Yes. And when he was come into the house, Jesus prevented * him, saying,

What thinkest thou, Simon? Of whom do the kings of the earth take custom or tribute? of their own children, or of strangers?

Peter saith, of strangers. Jesus answered,

Then are the children free.

Notwithstanding, lest we should offend them, go thou to the sea, and cast a hook, and take up the fish that first cometh up; and when thou has opened his mouth, thou shalt find a piece of money: that take, and give unto them for me and thee. †

JOHN ANSWERED: "FORBID HIM NOT"

A.D. 29. Age 32 Capernaum.

Mark 9, 38-50: Luke 9, 49-50.

JOHN ‡ said, Master, we saw one casting out devils in thy name: and we forbade him, because he followeth not with us. But Jesus said,

Forbid him not: for there is no man which shall do a miracle in my name, that can lightly speak evil of me. For he that is not against us is for us, is on our part.

For whosoever shall give you a cup of water to drink in my name, because ye belong to Christ, verily I say unto you, he shall not lose his reward.

And whosoever shall offend one of these little ones that believe in me, it is better for him that a millstone were hanged about his neck, and he were cast into the sea.

And if thy hand offend thee, cut it off: it is better for thee to enter into life maimed, than having two hands to go into hell, into the fire that never shall be quenched: where their worm dieth not, and the fire is not quenched.

And if thy foot offend thee, cut it off: it is better for thee to enter halt into life, than having two feet to be cast into hell, into the fire that never shall be quenched: where their worm dieth not, and the fire is not quenched.

And if thine eye offend thee, pluck it out: it is better for thee to enter into the kingdom of God with one eye, than having two eyes to be cast into hell fire: where their worm dieth not, and the fire is not quenched.

For every one shall be salted with fire, and every sacrifice shall be salted with salt. Salt is good: but if the salt have lost his saltness, wherewith will ye season it? Have salt in yourselves, and have peace one with another.

"EXCEPT YE BECOME AS LITTLE CHILDREN"

A.D. 29. Age 32. Capernaum.

Matthew 18, 1-35.

AT the same time came the disciples unto Jesus, saying, Who is the greatest in the kingdom of heaven? And Jesus called a little child unto him, set him in the midst of them, and said, *

Verily I say unto you, Except ye be converted, and become as little children, ye shall not enter into the kingdom of heaven.

Whosoever therefore shall humble himself as this little child, the same is greatest in the kingdom of heaven. And whoso shall receive one such little child in my name receiveth me.

But whoso shall offend one of these little ones which believe in me, it were better for him that a millstone were hanged about his neck, and that he were drowned in the depth of the sea.

¶Woe unto the world because of offences! for it must needs be that offences come; but woe to that man by whom the offence cometh!

Wherefore, if thy hand or thy foot offend thee, cut them off, and cast them from thee: it is better for thee to enter into life halt or maimed, rather than having' two hands or two feet to be cast into everlasting fire.

And if thine eye offend thee, pluck it out, and cast it from thee: it is better for thee to enter into life with one eye, rather than having two eyes to be cast into hell fire.

Take heed that ye despise not one of these little ones; for I say unto you, That in heaven their angels do always behold the face of my Father which is in heaven. For the Son of man is come to save that which was lost.

 * How think ye? if a man have a hundred sheep, and one of them be gone astray, doth he not leave the ninety and nine, and goeth into the mountains, and seeketh that which is gone astray? And if so be that he find it, verily I say unto you, he rejoiceth more of that sheep, than of the ninety and nine which went not astray. Even so it is not the will of your Father which is in heaven, that one of these little ones should perish.

¶Moreover if thy brother shall trespass against thee, go and tell him his fault between thee and him alone: if he shall hear thee, thou hast gained thy brother. But if he will not hear thee, then take with thee one or two more, that in the mouth of two or three witnesses every word may be established. And if he shall neglect to hear them, tell it unto the church: but if he neglect to hear the church, let him be unto thee as a heathen man and a publican.

Verily I say unto you, Whatsoever ye shall bind on earth shall be bound in heaven: and whatsoever ye shall loose on earth shall be loosed in heaven. †

Again I say unto you, That if two of you shall agree on earth as touching any thing that they shall ask, it shall be done for them of my Father which is in heaven. For where two or three are gathered together in my name, there am I in the midst of them.

¶Then Peter said, Lord, how oft shall my brother sin against me, and I forgive him? till seven times? Jesus saith,

I say not unto thee, Until seven times: but, Until seventy times seven. Therefore is the kingdom of heaven likened unto a certain king, which would take account of his servants. And when he had begun to reckon, one was brought unto him, which owed him ten thousand talents. But forasmuch as he had not to pay, his lord commanded him to be sold, and his wife, and children, and all that he had, and payment to be made. The servant therefore fell down, and worshipped him, saying, Lord, have patience with me, and I will pay thee all. Then the lord of that servant was moved with compassion and loosed him, and forgave him the debt.

But the same servant went out, and found one of his fellow servants, which owed him a hundred pence: and he laid hands on him, and took him by the throat, saying, Pay me that thou owest. And his fellow servant fell down at his feet, and besought him, saying, Have patience with me, and I will pay thee all. And he would not: but went and cast him into prison, till he should pay the debt.

So when his fellow servants saw what was done, they were very sorry, and came and told unto their lord all that was done. Then his lord, after that he had called him, said unto him, O thou wicked servant, I forgave thee all that debt, because thou desiredst me; shouldest not thou also have had compassion on thy fellow servant, even as I had pity on thee?

And his lord was wroth, and delivered him to the tormentors, till he should pay all that was due unto him. So likewise shall my heavenly Father do also unto you, if ye from your hearts forgive not every one his brother their trespasses.

AT THE FEAST OF THE TABERNACLE

A.D. 29. Age 32. Jerusalem. Galilee.

John 7, 1-46, 53; 8, 1.

AFTER these things, Jesus * walked in Galilee: for he would not walk in Jewry, because the Jews sought to kill him.

Now the Jews' feast of the tabernacles was at hand. Jesus' brethren therefore said unto him, Go into Judea, that thy disciples also may see the works that thou doest. For there is no man that doeth anything in secret, and he himself seeketh to be known openly. If thou do these things, shew thyself to the world.

For neither did his brethren believe in him.

Then Jesus said,

My time is not yet come: but your time is always ready. The world cannot hate you; but me it hateth, because I testify of it, that the works thereof are evil. Go ye up unto this feast: for my time is not yet full come.

¶Jesus abode still in Galilee.

But when his brethren were gone up, then went he also up unto the feast, not openly, but as it were in secret.

There was much murmuring among the people concerning him: for some said, He is a good man: others said, Nay; but he deceiveth the people. Howbeit no man spake openly of him for fear of the Jews. The Jews sought him at the feast.

¶Now about the midst of the feast Jesus went up into the temple and taught. The Jews marvelled, saying, How knoweth this man letters, having never learned? Jesus answered,

My doctrine is not mine, but his that sent me. If any man will do his will, he shall know of the doctrine, whether it be of God, or whether I speak of myself. He that speaketh of himself seeketh his own glory: but he that seeketh his glory that sent him, the same is true, and no unrighteousness is in him.

Did not Moses give you the law, and yet none of you keepeth the law? Why go ye about to kill me?

The people answered, Who goeth about to kill thee? Thou hast a devil. Jesus answered,

I have done one work, and ye all marvel.

Moses therefore gave unto you circumcision (not because it is of Moses, but of the fathers); and ye on the sabbath day circumcise a man. If a man on the sabbath day receive circumcision, that the law of Moses should not be broken; are ye angry at me, because I have made a man every whit whole on the sabbath day?

Judge not according to the appearance, but judge righteous judgment.

Then said some of them of Jerusalem, Is not this he, whom they seek to kill? But, lo, he speaketh boldly, and they say nothing unto him. Do the rulers know indeed that this is the very Christ? Howbeit we know this man whence he is, but when Christ cometh, no man knoweth whence he is.

Then cried Jesus in the temple as he taught, saying,

Ye both know me, and ye know whence I am: and I am not come of myself, but he that sent me is true, whom ye know not. But I know him; for I am from him, and he hath sent me.

Then they sought to take him: but his hour was not yet come.

Many believed on Jesus, and said, When Christ cometh, will he do more miracles than those which this man hath done?

¶The Pharisees and chief priests heard that the people murmured such things concerning Jesus, and sent officers to take him. Then said Jesus,

Yet a little while am I with you, and then I go unto him that sent me. Ye shall seek me, and shall not find me: and where I am, thither ye cannot come.

Then said the Jews among themselves, What manner of saying is this that he said, Ye shall seek me, and shall not find me: and where I am, thither ye cannot come?

¶In the last day, that great day of the feast, Jesus stood and cried,

If any man thirst, let him come unto me, and drink. He that believeth on me, as the Scripture hath said, out of his belly shall flow rivers of living water.

 * (But this spake he of the Spirit, which they that believe on him should receive.)

¶Many of the people, when they heard this saying, said, Of a truth this is the

Prophet. Others said, This is the Christ. But some said, Shall Christ come out of Galilee?

So there was a division among the people because of him. And some of them would have taken him; but no man laid hands upon him.

¶Then came the officers to the chief priests and Pharisees. They said, Why have ye not brought him? The officers answered, Never man spake like this man.

And every man went unto his own home. Jesus went unto the mount of Olives.

THE WOMAN TAKEN IN ADULTERY

A.D. 29. Age 32. Jerusalem.

John 8, 2-59.

EARLY in the morning Jesus came again into the temple. The people came; and he sat down, and taught them.

¶The scribes and Pharisees brought a woman taken in adultery. † They say unto Jesus, Master, Moses in the law commanded us, that such should be stoned: but what sayest thou?

This they said, tempting him, that they might have to accuse him.

But Jesus stooped, and with his finger wrote on the ground, as though he heard them not. So when they continued asking him, he lifted up himself, and said unto them,

He that is without sin among you, let him first cast a stone at her.

Again Jesus stooped, and wrote on the ground. And they, being convicted by their own conscience, went out one by one, beginning at the eldest: Jesus was left alone, and the woman standing in the midst.

When he had lifited up himself, and saw none but the woman, he said,

Woman, where are those thine accusers? hath no man condemned thee?

She said, No man, Lord. And Jesus said unto her,

Neither do I condemn thee: go, and sin no more.

¶Jesus spake again unto the people, saying,

I am the light of the world: he that followeth me shall not walk in darkness, but shall have the light of life.

The Pharisees therefore said, Thou bearest record of thyself; thy record is not true. Jesus answered,

Though I bear record of myself, yet my record is true: for I know whence I came, and whither I go; but ye cannot tell whence I come, and whither I go.

Ye judge after the flesh; I judge no man. And yet if I judge, my judgment is true: for I am not alone, but I and the Father that sent me.

It is also written in your law, that the testimony of two men is true. I am one that bear witness of myself, and the Father that sent me beareth witness of me.

Then said they, Where is thy father? Jesus answered,

Ye neither know me, nor my Father: if ye had known me, ye should have known my Father also.

These words spake Jesus in the treasury, as he taught in the temple: and no man laid hands on him; for his hour was not yet come. Then said Jesus again,

I go my way, and ye shall seek me, and shall die in your sins: whither I go, ye cannot come.

Then said the Jews, Will he kill himself? because he saith, Whither I go, ye cannot come. And he said,

Ye are from beneath; I am from above: ye are of this world; I am not of this world. I said therefore unto you that ye shall die in your sins: for if ye believe not that I am he, ye shall die in your sins.

Then said they, Who art thou? And Jesus answered,

Even the same that I said unto you from the beginning.

I have many things to say and to judge of you: but he that sent me is true; and I speak to the world those things which I have heard of him.

They understood not that he spake to them of the Father. Then said Jesus,

When ye have lifted up the Son of man, then shall ye know that I am he, and that I do nothing of myself; but as my Father hath taught me, I speak these things. And he that sent me is with me: the Father hath not left me alone; for I do always those things that please him.

As he spake these words, many believed. Then said Jesus to those Jews which believed on him,

If ye continue in my word, then are ye my disciples indeed; and ye shall know the truth, and the truth shall make you free.

¶They answered, We be Abraham's seed, and were never in bondage to any man: how sayest thou, Ye shall be made free? Jesus answered,

Verily, verily, I say unto you, Whosoever committeth sin is the servant of sin.

And the servant abideth not in the house for ever: but the Son abideth ever. If the Son therefore shall make you free, ye shall be free indeed.

I know that ye are Abraham's seed; but ye seek to kill me, because my word hath no place in you. I speak that which I have seen with my Father: and ye do that which ye have seen with your father.

They answered, Abraham is our father. Jesus saith,

If ye were Abraham's children, ye would do the works of Abraham. But now ye seek to kill me, a man that hath told you the truth, which I have heard of God: this did not Abraham. Ye do the deeds of your father.

Then they said, We be not born of fornication; we have one Father, even God. Jesus answered,

If God were your Father, ye would love me: for I proceeded forth and came from God; neither came I of myself, but he sent me.

Why do ye not understand my speech? even because ye cannot hear my word. Ye are of your father the devil, and the lusts of your father ye will do: he was a murderer from the beginning, and abode not in the truth, because there is no truth in him. When he speaketh a lie, he speaketh of his own: for he is a liar, and the father of it.

And because I tell you the truth, ye believe me not. Which of you convinceth me of sin? And if I say the truth, why do ye not believe me? He that is of God heareth God's words: ye therefore hear them not, because ye are not of God.

Then answered the Jews, Say we not well that thou art a Samaritan, and hast a devil? Jesus answered,

I have not a devil; but I honor my Father, and ye do dishonor me. And I seek not mine own glory: there is one that seeketh and judgeth.

Verily, verily, I say unto you, if a man keep my saying, he shall never see death.

Then said the Jews, Now we know that thou hast a devil. Abraham is dead, and the prophets, and thou sayest, If a man keep my saying, he shall never taste of death. Art thou greater than our father Abraham, which is dead? and the prophets are dead: who makest thou thyself? Jesus answered,

If I honor myself, my honor is nothing: it is my Father that honoreth me; of whom ye say, that he is your God: yet ye have not known him: but I know him: and if I should say, I know him not, I shall be a liar like unto you; but I know him, and keep his saying. Your father Abraham rejoiced to see my day; and he saw it, and was glad.

Then said the Jews, Thou art not yet fifty years old, and hast thou seen Abraham? Jesus answered,

Verily, verily I say unto you, Before Abraham was, I am.

They took up stones to cast at him: but Jesus hid himself, and went out of the temple, going through the midst of them, and so passed by.

"I AM THE LIGHT OF THE WORLD"

A.D. 29. Age 32. Jerusalem.

John 9, 1-41; 10, 1-18; 22-40.

AS JESUS passed by, he saw a man which was blind from his birth. His disciples asked, Master, who did sin, this man, or his parents, that he was born blind? Jesus answered,

Neither hath this man sinned, nor his parents: but that the works of God should be made manifest in him.

I must work the works of him that sent me, while it is day: the night cometh, when no man can work. As long as I am in the world, I am the light of the world.

When he had thus spoken, he anointed the eyes of the blind man with clay, and said unto him,

Go, wash in the pool of Siloam.

He went, and washed, and came seeing.

¶The neighbors said, Is not this he that sat and begged? He answered, I am he.

Therefore, said they, how were thine eyes opened?

He said, A man called Jesus made clay, and anointed mine eyes, and said unto me, Go to the pool of Siloam, and wash: and I went and washed, and I received sight.

It was the sabbath day when Jesus opened his eyes. Therefore said some of the Pharisees, This man [Jesus] is not of God, because he keepeth not the sabbath day. Others said, How can a man that is a sinner do such miracles? And there was a division among them.

The Jews called the parents, and asked them, Is this your son, who ye say was born blind? how then doth he now see?

His parents answered, We know that this is our son, and that he was born blind: but by what means he now seeth, we know not; he is of age; ask him.

His parents feared the Jews: for the Jews had agreed already, that if any man did confess that Jesus was Christ, he should be put out of the synagogue.

Again the Jews called the man that was blind, and said unto him, Give God the praise: we know that this man [Jesus] is a sinner: we know not from whence he is.

The man answered, Why herein is a marvellous thing, that ye know not from whence he is, and yet he hath opened mine eyes. Now we know that God heareth not sinners: but if any man be a worshipper of God, and doeth his will, him he heareth. If this man were not of God, he could do nothing.

They answered, Thou wast altogether born in sins, and dost thou teach us? And they cast him out.

Jesus heard that they had cast him out; and when he had found him, he said unto him,

Dost thou believe on the Son of God?

He answered, Who is he, Lord, that I might believe on him? Jesus said,

Thou hast both seen him, and it is he that talketh with thee.

And he said, Lord, I believe.

¶Jesus said,

For judgment I am come into this world, that they which see not might see; and that they which see might be made blind.

Some of the Pharisees heard these words, and said, Are we blind also? Jesus answered,

If ye were blind, ye should have no sin: but now ye say, We see; therefore your sin remaineth.

¶This parable spake Jesus unto them,

Verily, verily, I say unto you, He that entereth not by the door into the sheepfold, but climbeth up some other way, the same is a thief and a robber. But he that entereth in by the door is the shepherd of the sheep. To him the porter openeth; and the sheep hear his voice: and he calleth his own sheep by name, and leadeth them out.

And when he putteth forth his own sheep, he goeth before them, and the sheep follow him: for they know his voice. And a stranger will they not follow, but will flee from him: for they know not the voice of strangers.

But they understood not. Then said Jesus,

Verily, verily, I say unto you, I am the door of the sheep. All that ever came before me are thieves and robbers: but the sheep did not hear them.

I am the door: by me if any man enter in, he shall be saved, and shall go in and out, and find pasture.

The thief cometh not, but for to steal, and to kill, and to destroy: I am come that they might have life, and that they might have it more abundantly.

I am the good shepherd: the good shepherd giveth his life for the sheep. But he that is a hireling, and not the shepherd, whose own the sheep are not, seeth the wolf coming, and leaveth the sheep, and fleeth: and the wolf catcheth them, and scattereth the sheep. The hireling fleeth, because he is a hireling, and careth not for the sheep.

I am the good shepherd, and know my sheep, and am known of mine. As the Father knoweth me, even so know I the Father: and I lay down my life for the sheep.

And other sheep I have, which are not of this fold: them also I must bring, and they shall hear my voice; and there shall be one fold, and one shepherd.

Therefore doth my Father love me, because I lay down my life, that I might take it again. No man taketh it from me, but I lay it down of myself. I have power to lay it down, and I have power to take it again. This commandment have I received of my Father.

¶At Jerusalem it was the feast of the dedication. It was winter. Jesus walked in the temple in Solomon's porch.

Then came the Jews round about him, and said, How long dost thou make us to doubt? If thou be the Christ, tell us plainly. Jesus answered,

I told you, and ye believed not: the works that I do in my Father's name, they bear witness of me. But ye believe not, because ye are not of my sheep, as I said unto you. My sheep hear my voice, and I know them, and they follow me: and I give unto them eternal life; and they shall never perish, neither shall any man pluck them out of my hand.

My Father, which gave them me, is greater than all; and no man is able to pluck them out of my Father's hand.

I and my Father are one.

The Jews took up stones again to stone him, Jesus answered,

Many good works have I shewed you from my Father; for which of those works do ye stone me?

The Jews answered, For a good work we stone thee not; but for blasphemy; and because that thou, being a man, makest thyself God. Jesus answered,

Is it not written in your law, I said, Ye are gods?

If he called them gods, unto whom the word of God came, and the Scripture cannot be broken; say ye of him, whom the Father hath sanctified and sent into the world, Thou blasphemest; because I said, I am the Son of God?

If I do not the works of my Father, believe me not. But if I do, though ye believe not me, believe the works; that ye may know, and believe, that the Father is in me, and I in him.

Therefore they sought again to take him: but he escaped out of their hand, and went away again beyond Jordan into the place where John at first baptized; and there he abode.

"HATH NOT WHERE TO LAY HIS HEAD"

A.D. 29, Age 32. Leaving Galilee. Samaria. Perea.

Luke 9, 51-62; 10, 1-24

WHEN the time was come that Jesus should be received up, he steadfastly set his face to go to Jerusalem, and sent messengers before: they entered into a village of the Samaritans.

They did not receive him; and his disciples James and John said, Lord wilt thou that we command fire to come down and consume them, as Elias did? But he rebuked them, saying,

Ye know not what manner of spirit ye are of. For the Son of man is not come to destroy men's lives, but to save them.

They went to another village. In the way, a certain man said unto Jesus, Lord, I will follow thee whithersoever thou goest. Jesus said unto him,

Foxes have holes, and birds of the air have nests; but the Son of man hath not where to lay his head.

And he said unto another,

Follow me.

But he said, Lord, suffer me first to go and bury my father. Jesus said unto him,

Let the dead bury their dead: but go thou and preach the kingdom of God.

Another said, Lord, I will follow thee; but let me first go bid them farewell, which are at home at my house. Jesus said unto him,

No man, having put his hand to the plough, and looking back, is fit for the kingdom of God.

¶After these things the Lord appointed other seventy also, and sent them two and two before his face into every city and place, whither he himself would come. Therefore said he unto them,

The harvest truly is great, but the laborers are few: pray ye therefore the Lord of the harvest, that he would send forth laborers into his harvest.

*Go your ways: behold, I send you forth as lambs among wolves. Carry neither purse, nor scrip, nor shoes: and salute no man by the way.

And into whatsoever house ye enter, first say, Peace be to this house. And if the son of peace be there, your peace shall rest upon it: if not, it shall turn to you again.

And in the same house remain, eating and drinking such things as they give: for the laborer is worthy of his hire. Go not from house to house.

And into whatsoever city ye enter, and they receive you, eat such things as are set before you: and heal the sick that are therein, and say unto them, The kingdom of God is come nigh unto you.

But into whatsoever city ye enter, and they receive you not, go your ways out into the streets of the same, and say, Even the very dust of your city, which cleaveth on us, we do wipe off against you: notwithstanding, be ye sure of this, that the kingdom of God is come nigh unto you.

But I say unto you, that it shall be more tolerable in that day for Sodom, than for that city.

†Woe unto thee, Chorazin! woe unto thee, Bethsaida! for if the mighty works had been done in Tyre and Sidon, which have been done in you, they had a great while ago repented, sitting in sackcloth and ashes. But it shall be more tolerable for Tyre and Sidon at the judgment, than for you.

And thou, Capernaum, which art exalted to heaven, shalt be thrust down to hell.

He that heareth you heareth me; and he that despiseth you despiseth me; and he that despiseth me despiseth him that sent me.

¶The seventy returned with joy, saying, Lord, even the devils are subject unto us through thy name. Jesus said unto them,

I beheld Satan as lightning fall from heaven. Behold, I give unto you power to tread on serpents and scorpions, and over all the power of the enemy; and nothing shall by any means hurt you. Notwithstanding, in this rejoice not, that the spirits are subject unto you; but rather rejoice, because your names are written in heaven.

¶In that hour Jesus rejoiced in spirit, and said,

I thank thee, O Father, Lord of heaven and earth, that thou hast hid these things from the wise and prudent, and has revealed them unto babes: even so, Father; for so it seemed good in thy sight.

All things are delivered to me of my Father: and no man knoweth who the Son is, but the Father; and who the Father is, but the Son, and he to whom the Son will reveal him.

¶He turned him unto his disciples, and said privately,

*Blessed are the eyes which see the things that ye see: for I tell you, that many prophets and kings have desired to see those things which ye see, and have not seen them; and to hear those things which ye hear, and have not heard them.

THE GOOD SAMARITAN

A.D. 29, Age 32. Perea.

Luke 10, 25-37.

A CERTAIN lawyer stood up, and tempted Jesus, saying, Master, what shall I do to inherit eternal life? Jesus said,

What is written in the law? how readest thou?

He answering said, Thou shalt love the Lord thy God with all thy heart, and with all thy soul, and with all thy strength, and with all thy mind; and thy neighbor as thyself. Jesus said unto him,

Thou hast answered right: this do, and thou shalt live.

But he, willing to justify himself, said, And who is my neighbor? Jesus answering said,

A certain man went down from Jerusalem to Jericho, and fell among thieves, which stripped him of his raiment, and wounded him, and departed, leaving him half dead.

And by chance there came down a certain priest that way: and when he saw him, he passed by on the other side.

And like wise a Levite, when he was at the place, came and looked on him, and passed by on the other side.

But a certain Samaritan, as he journeyed, came where he was: and when he saw him, he had compassion on him, and went to him, and bound up his wounds, pouring in oil and wine, and set him on his own beast, and brought him to an inn, and took care of him. And on the morrow when he departed, he took out two pence, and gave them to the host, and said unto him, Take care of him: and whatsoever thou spendest more, when I come again, I will repay thee.

Which now of these three, thinkest thou, was neighbor unto him that fell among the thieves?

He said, He that shewed mercy on him. Then said Jesus unto him,

Go, and do thou likewise.

THE LORD'S PRAYER

A.D. 29. Age 32. Perea.

Luke 11, 1-13; 27-54.

AS Jesus was praying in a certain place, when he ceased, one of his disciples said unto him, Lord, teach us to pray, as John also taught his disciples. Jesus said unto them,

*When ye pray, say, Our Father which art in heaven, Hallowed be thy name. Thy kingdom come. Thy will be done, as in heaven, so in earth.

Give us day by day our daily bread.

And forgive us our sins; for we also forgive every one that is indebted to us.

And lead us not into temptation; but deliver us from evil.

And he said unto them,

Which of you shall have a friend, and shall go unto him at midnight, and say unto him, Friend, lend me three loaves; for a friend of mine in his journey is come to me, and I have nothing to set before him?

And he from within shall answer and say, Trouble me not: the door is now shut, and my children are with me in bed; I cannot rise and give thee.

I say unto you, Though he will not rise and give him, because he is his friend, yet because of his importunity he will rise and give him as many as he needeth.

And I say unto you, Ask, and it shall be given you: seek, and ye shall find; knock, and it shall be opened unto you. For every one that asketh receiveth; and he that seeketh findeth; and to him that knocketh it shall be opened.

If a son shall ask bread of any of you that is a father, will he give him a stone? or if he ask a fish, will he for a fish give him a serpent? Or, if he shall ask an egg, will he offer him a scorpion?

If ye then, being evil, know how to give good gifts unto your children; how much more shall your heavenly Father give the Holy Spirit to them that ask him?

And it came to pass, as he spake these things, a certain woman of the company lifted up her voice, and said, Blessed is the womb that bare thee, and the paps which thou hast sucked. But Jesus said,

Yea rather, blessed are they that hear the word of God, and keep it.

¶When the people were gathered thick together, he began to say,

 *This is an evil generation: they seek a sign; and there shall no sign be given it, but the sign of Jonas the prophet. For as Jonas was a sign unto the Ninevites, so shall also the Son of man be to this generation.

The queen of the south shall rise up in the judgment with the men of this generation, and condemn them: for she came from the utmost parts of the earth to hear the wisdom of Solomon; and, behold, a greater than Solomon is here.

The men of Nineveh shall rise up in the judgment with this generation, and shall condemn it: for they repented at the preaching of Jonas; and, behold, a greater than Jonas is here.

No man, when he hath lighted a candle, putteth it in a secret place, neither under a bushel, but on a candlestick, that they which come in may see the light. The light of the body is the eye: therefore when thine eye is single, thy whole body also is full of light; but when thine eye is evil, thy body also is full of darkness. Take heed therefore that the light which is in thee be not darkness. If thy whole body therefore be full of light, having no part dark, the whole shall be full of light, as when the bright shining of a candle doth give thee light.

As Jesus spake, a certain Pharisee besought him to dine with him: he went in, and sat down to meat. The Pharisee marvelled that Jesus had not washed before dinner. The Lord said unto him,

Now do ye Pharisees make clean the outside of the cup and the platter; but your inward part is full of ravening and wickedness. Ye fools, did not he that made that which is without, make that which is within also? But rather give alms of such things as ye have; and, behold, all things are clean unto you.

But woe unto you, Pharisees! for ye tithe mint and rue and all manner of herbs, and pass over judgment and the love of God: these ought ye to have done, and not to leave the other undone.

Woe unto you, Pharisees! for ye love the uppermost seats in the synagogues, and greetings in the markets.

Woe unto you, scribes and Pharisees, hypocrites! for ye are as graves which appear not, and the men that walk over them are not aware of them.

¶Then answered one of the lawyers, Master, thus saying thou reproachest us also. Jesus said,

Woe unto you also, ye lawyers! for ye lade men with burdens grievous to be borne, and ye yourselves touch not the burdens with one of your fingers.

Woe unto you! for we build the sepulchres of the prophets, and your fathers killed them. Truly ye bear witness that ye allow the deeds of your fathers: for they indeed killed them, and ye build their sepulchres.

Therefore also said the wisdom of God, I will send them prophets and apostles, and some of them they shall slay and persecute: that the blood of all the prophets, which was shed from the foundation of the world, may be required of this generation; from the blood of Abel unto the blood of Zacharias, which perished between the altar and the temple: verily I say unto you, It shall be required of this generation.

Woe unto you, lawyers! for ye have taken away the key of knowledge: ye entered not in yourselves, and them that were entering in ye hindered.

As he said these things, the scribes and the Pharisees began to provoke him to speak of many things: laying wait for him, to catch something out of his mouth, that they might accuse him.

SERMON TO THE INNUMERABLE MULTITUDES

A.D. 29. Age 32. Perea.

Luke 12, 1-40.

IN the mean time, when there were gathered together an innumerable multitude of people, insomuch that they trode one upon another, Jesus began to say unto his disciples first of all,

Beware ye of the leaven of the Pharisees, which is hypocrisy. For there is nothing covered, that shall not be revealed; neither hid, that shall not be known. Therefore, whatsoever ye have spoken in darkness shall be heard in the light; and that which ye have spoken in the ear in closets shall be proclaimed upon the housetops.

And I say unto you my friend, Be not afraid of them that kill the body, and after that have no more that they can do. But I will forewarn you whom ye shall fear: Fear him, which after he hath killed hath power to cast into hell; yea, I say unto you, Fear him.

Are not five sparrows sold for two farthings, and not one of them is forgotten before God? But even the very hairs on your head are all numbered. Fear not therefore; ye are of more value than many sparrows.

Also I say unto you, Whosoever shall confess me before men, him shall the Son of man also confess before the angels of God: but he that denieth me before men shall be denied before the angels of God. And whosoever shall speak a word against the Son of man, it shall be forgiven him: but unto him that blasphemeth against the Holy Ghost it shall not be forgiven.

And when they bring you unto the synagogues, and unto magistrates, and powers, take ye no thought how or what thing ye shall answer, or what ye shall say: for the Holy Ghost shall teach you in the same hour what ye ought to say.

¶One of the company said, Master, speak to my brother, that he divide the inheritance with me. Jesus answered,

Man, who made me a judge or a divider over you?

And he said unto them,

Take heed, and beware of covetousness: for a man's life consisteth not in the abundance of the things which he possesseth.

And he spake a parable:

The ground of a certain rich man brought forth plentifully: and he thought within himself, saying, What shall I do, because I have no room where to bestow my fruits.

And he said, This will I do: I will pull down my barns, and build greater and there will I bestow all my fruits and my goods. And I will say to my soul, Soul, thou hast much goods laid up for many years; take thine ease, eat, drink, and be merry.

But God said unto him, Thou fool, this night thy soul shall be required of thee: then whose shall those things be, which thou hast provided?

So is he that layeth up treasure for himself, and is not rich toward God.

¶Jesus said unto his disciples,

Therefore I say unto you, Take no thought for your life, what ye shall eat, neither for the body, what ye shall put on. The life is more than meat, and the body is more than raiment.

Consider the ravens: for they neither sow nor reap; which neither have storehouse nor barn; and God feedeth them: how much more are ye better than the fowls?

And which of you with taking thought can add to his stature one cubit? If ye then be not able to do that thing which is least, why take ye thought for the rest?

Consider the lilies how they grow: they toil not, they spin not; and yet I say unto you, that Solomon in all his glory was not arrayed like one of these. If then God so clothe the grass, which is to day in the field, and to morrow is cast into the oven; how much more will he clothe you, O ye of little faith?

And seek not ye what ye shall eat, or what ye shall drink, neither be ye of doubtful mind. For all these things do the nations of the world seek after; and your Father knoweth that ye have need of these things.

¶But rather seek ye the kingdom of God; and all these things shall be added unto you.

Fear not, little flock; for it is your Father's good pleasure to give you the kingdom. Sell that ye have, and give alms; provide yourselves bags which wax not old, a treasure in the heavens that faileth not, where no thief approacheth, neither moth corrupteth. For where your treasure is, there will your heart be also.

Let your loins be girded about, and your lights burning; and ye yourselves like unto men that wait for their lord, when he will return from the wedding; that when he cometh and knocketh, they may open unto him immediately.

Blessed are those servants, whom the lord when he cometh shall find watching: verily I say unto you, that he shall gird himself, and make them to sit down to meat, and will come forth and serve them. And if he shall come in the second watch, or come in the third watch, and find them so, blessed are those servants. *And this know, that if the goodman of the house had known what hour the thief would come, he would have watched, and not have suffered his house to be broken through. Be ye therefore ready also; for the Son of man cometh at an hour when ye think not.

SERMON TO THE INUMERABLE MULTITUDE CONTINUED

A.D. 29. Age 32. Perea.

Luke 12, 41-59; 13, 1-9.

THEN Peter said, Lord, speakest thou this parable unto us, or even to all? and the Lord said,

*Who then is that faithful and wise steward, whom his lord shall make ruler over his household, to give them their portion of meat in due season?

Blessed is that servant, whom his lord when he cometh shall find so doing. Of a truth I say unto you, that he will make him ruler over all that he hath.

But if that servant say in his heart, My lord delayeth his coming; and shall begin to beat the menservants and maidens, and to eat and drink, and to be drunken; the lord of that servant will come in a day when he looketh not for him, and at an hour when he is not aware, and will cut him in sunder, and will appoint him his portion with the unbelievers.

And that servant, which knew his lord's will, and prepared not himself, neither did according to his will, shall be beaten with many stripes. But he that knew not, and did commit things worthy of stripes, shall be beaten with few stripes. For unto whomsoever much is given, of him shall be much required; and to whom men have committeth much, of him they will ask more.

¶I am come to send fire on the earth; and what will I, if it be already kindled? But I have a baptism to be baptized with; and how am I straitened till it be accomplished!

Suppose ye that I am come to give peace on earth? I tell you, Nay; but rather division: for from henceforth there shall be five in one house divided, three against two, and two against three. The father shall be divided against the son, and the son against the father; the mother against the daughter, and the daughter against the mother; the mother in law against her daughter in law, and the daughter in law against her mother in law.

¶He said also to the people,

When ye see a cloud rise out of the west, straightway ye say, There cometh a shower; and so it is. And when ye see the south wind blow, ye say, There will be heat; and it cometh to pass. Ye hypocrites, ye can discern the face of the sky and of the earth: but how is it that ye do not discern this time? Yea, and why even of yourselves judge ye not what is right?

¶When thou goest with thine adversary to the magistrate, as thou art in the way, give diligence that thou mayest be delivered from him; lest he hale thee to the judge, and the judge deliver thee to the officer, and the officer cast thee into prison. I tell thee, thou shalt not depart thence, till thou hast paid the very last mite.

¶There were present at that season some that told him of the Galileans, whose blood Pilate had mingled with their sacrifices. Jesus said unto them,

Suppose ye that these Galileans were sinners above all Galileans, because they suffered such things? I tell you, Nay: but, except ye repent, ye shall all likewise perish.

Or those eighteen, upon whom the tower in Siloam fell, and slew them, think ye that they were sinners above all men that dwelt in Jerusalem? I tell you, Nay: but, except ye repent, ye shall all likewise perish.

¶He spake also this parable:

A certain man had a fig tree planted in his vineyard; and he came and sought fruit thereon, and found none. Then said he unto the dresser of his vineyard, Behold, these three years I come seeking fruit on this fig tree, and find none: cut it down; why cumbereth it the ground?

And he answering said unto him, Lord, let it alone this year also, till I shall dig about it, and dung it: and if it bear fruit, well: and if not, then after that thou shalt cut it down.

SABBATH CURE OF CRIPPLED WOMAN

A.D. 29. Age 32. Perea.

Luke 13, 10-21.

JESUS was teaching in one of the synagogues on the sabbath. And, behold, there was a woman which had a spirit of infirmity eighteen years, and was bowed together, and could in no wise lift up herself. Jesus saw her, and said unto her,

Woman, thou are loosed from thine infirmity.

He laid his hands on her: and immediately she was made straight.

The ruler of the synagogue, because that Jesus had healed on the sabbath day, said with indignation unto the people, There are six days in which men ought to work: in them therefore come and be healed, and not on the Sabbath day.

The Lord answered,

Thou hypocrite, doth not each one of you on the sabbath loose his ox or his ass from the stall, and lead him away to watering? And ought not this woman, being a daughter of Abraham, who Satan hath bound, lo, these eighteen years, be loosed from this bond on the sabbath day?

His adversaries were ashamed: and the people rejoiced for the glorious things that were done by him. Then said he,

*Unto what is the kingdom of God like? and whereunto shall I resemble it? It is like a grain of mustard seed, which a man took, and cast into his garden; and it grew, and waxed a great tree; and the fowls of the air lodged in the branches of it.

And again he said,

Whereunto shall I liken the kingdom of God? It is like leaven, which a woman took and hid in three measures of meal, till the whole was leavened.

"O JERUSALEM, JERUSALEM!"

A.D. 29. Age 32. Perea. Bethany.

Luke 13, 22-35; 10, 38-42: John 10, 39-40.

JESUS went through the cities and villages, teaching, and journeying toward Jerusalem.

One said unto him, Lord, are there few that be saved? And he said,

Strive to enter in at the strait gate: for many, I say unto you, will seek to enter in, and shall not be able.

When once the master of the house is risen up, and hath shut the door, and ye being to stand without, and to knock at the door, saying, Lord, Lord, open unto us: and he shall answer and say unto you, I know you not whence ye are: Then shall ye begin to say, We have eaten and drunk in thy presence, and thou hast taught in our streets.

But he shall say, I tell you, I know you not whence ye are; depart from me, all ye workers of iniquity.

There shall be weeping and gnashing of teeth, when ye shall see Abraham, and Isaac, and Jacob, and all the prophets, in the kingdom of God, and you yourselves thrust out.

And they shall come from the east, and from the west, and from the north, and from the south, and shall sit down in the kingdom of God.

And, behold, there are last which shall be first; and there are first which shall be last.

¶The same day there came Pharisees saying unto Jesus, Depart hence; for Herod will kill thee. And he said unto them,

Go ye, and tell that fox, Behold, I cast out devils, and I do cures to day and to morrow, and the third day I shall be perfected. Nevertheless I must walk to day, and to morrow, and the day following: for it cannot be that a prophet perish out of Jerusalem.

O Jerusalem, Jerusalem, which killest the prophets, and stonest them that are sent unto thee; how often would I have gathered thy children together, as a hen doth gather her brood under her wings, and ye would not! Behold, your house is left unto you desolate: and verily I say unto you, Ye shall not see me, until the time come when ye shall say, Blessed is he that cometh in the name of the Lord.

Now it came to pass, as they went, that Jesus entered into a certain village: * and a woman named Martha received him into her house. She had a sister, Mary, which sat at Jesus' feet, and heard his word.

But Martha, cumbered about much serving, said, Lord, dost thou not care that my sister hath left me to serve alone? Bid her that she help me.

Jesus answered,

Martha, Martha, thou are careful and troubled about many things: but one thing is needful; and Mary hath chosen that good part, which shall not be taken away from her.

¶The Jews sought again to take Jesus: but he went away beyond Jordan into the place where John at first baptized; and he abode there.

SERMON IN PARABLES

A.D. 29. Age 32. Perea.

Luke 14, 1-35.

ON a sabbath day, as Jesus went into the house of one of the chief Pharisees to eat bread, they watched him. And, behold, there was a man which had the dropsy. And Jesus spake unto the lawyers and Pharisees, saying,

Is it lawful to heal on the sabbath day?

They held their peace. Jesus healed the man, and let him go, saying unto them,

Which of you shall have an ass or an ox fallen into a pit, and will not straightway pull him out on the sabbath day?

They could not answer him.

¶To those which were bidden, when he marked how they chose out the chief rooms, he put forth a parable, saying,

When thou are bidden of any man to a wedding, sit not down in the highest room; lest a more honorable man than thou be bidden of him; and he that bade thee and him come and say to thee, Give this man place; and thou begin with shame to take the lowest room.

But when thou are bidden, go and sit down in the lowest room; that when he that bade thee cometh, he may say unto thee, Friend, go up higher: then shalt thou have worship in the presence of them that sit at meat with thee.

For whosoever exalteth himself shall be abased; and he that humbleth himself shall be exalted.

¶Then said he to the Pharisee that bade him,

When thou makest a dinner or a supper, call not thy friends, nor thy brethren, neither thy kinsmen, nor thy rich neighbors; lest they also bid thee again, and a recompense be made thee. But when thou makest a feast, call the poor, the maimed, the lame, the blind; and thou shalt be blessed; for they cannot recompense thee: for thou shalt be recompensed at the resurrection of the just.

One of them that sat at meat with Jesus said unto him, Blessed is he that shall eat bread in the kingdom of God. Then said Jesus,

A certain man made a great supper, and bade many: and sent his servant at supper time to say to them that were bidden, Come; for all things are now ready. And they all with one consent began to make excuse.

The first said unto him, I have bought a piece of ground, and I must needs go and see it: I pray thee have me excused. And another said, I have bought five yoke of oxen, and I go to prove them: I pray thee have me excused. And another said, I have married a wife, and therefore I cannot come.

So that servant came and shewed his lord these things. Then the master of the house being angry said to his servant, Go out quickly into the streets and lanes of the city, and bring in hither the poor, and the maimed, and the halt, and the blind.

And the servant said, Lord, it is done as thou hast commanded, and yet there is room.

And the lord said unto the servant, Go out into the highways and hedges, and compel them to come in, that my house may be filled. For I say unto you, That none of those men which were bidden shall taste of my supper.

There went multitudes with Jesus: and he turned, and said unto them,

If any man come to me, and hate not his father, and mother, and wife, and children, and brethren, and sisters, yea, and his own life also, he cannot be my disciple. And whosoever doth not bear his cross, and come after me, cannot be my disciple.

For which of you, intending to build a tower, sitteth not down first, and counteth the cost, whether he have sufficient to finish it? Lest haply, after he hath laid the foundation, and is not able to finish it, all that behold it begin to mock him, saying, This man began to build, and was not able to finish.

Or what king, going to make war against another king, sitteth not down first, and consulteth whether he be able with ten thousand to meet him that cometh against him with twenty thousand? Or else, while the other is yet a great way off, he sendeth an ambassage, and desireth conditions of peace. So likewise, whosoever he be of you that forsaketh not all that he hath, he cannot be my disciple.

¶Salt is good: but if the salt have lost his savor, wherewith shall it be seasoned? It is neither fit for the land, nor yet for the dunghill; but men cast it out. He that hath ears to hear, let him hear.

SERMON IN PARABLES
(CONTINUED)

A.D. 30. Age 33. Perea.

Luke 15, 1-32.

THEN drew near unto Jesus the publicans and sinners for to hear him. The Pharisees and scribes murmured, This man receiveth sinners, and eateth with them.

Jesus spake this parable unto them,

 *What man of you, having a hundred sheep, if he lose one of them, doth not leave the ninety and nine in the wilderness, and go after that which is lost, until he find it? And when he hath found it, he layeth it on his shoulders, rejoicing. And when he cometh home, he calleth together his friends and neighbors, saying unto them, Rejoice with me, for I have found my sheep which was lost.

I say unto you, that likewise joy shall be in heaven over one sinner that repenteth, more than over ninety and nine just persons, which need no repentance.

¶Either what woman having ten pieces of silver, if she lose one piece, doth not light a candle, and sweep the house, and seek diligently till she find it? And when she hath found it, she calleth her friends and her neighbors together, saying, Rejoice with me: for I have found the piece which I had lost.

Likewise, I say unto you, there is joy in the presence of the angels of God over one sinner that repenteth.

A certain man had two sons: and the younger of them said to his father, Father, give me the portion of goods that falleth to me. And he divided unto them his living.

And not many days after, the younger son gathered all together, and took his journey into a far country, and there wasted his substance with riotous living. And when he had spent all, there arose a mighty famine in that land; and he began to be in want.

And he went and joined himself to a citizen of that country; and he sent him into his fields to feed swine. And he would fain have filled his belly with the husks that the swine did eat; and no man gave unto him.

And when he came to himself, he said, How many hired servants of my father's have bread enough and to spare, and I perish with hunger! I will arise and go to my father, and will say unto him, Father, I have sinned against heaven, and before thee, and am no more worthy to be called thy son: make me as one of thy hired servants.

And he arose, and came to his father. But when he was yet a great way off, his father saw him, and had compassion, and ran, and fell on his neck, and kissed him.

And the son said unto him, Father, I have sinned against heaven, and in thy sight, and am no more worthy to be called thy son.

But the father said to his servants, Bring forth the best robe, and put it on him; and put a ring on his hand, and shoes on his feet: and bring hither the fatted calf, and kill it; and let us eat, and be merry: for this my son was dead, and is alive again; he was lost, and is found. And they began to be merry.

Now his elder son was in the field: and as he came and drew nigh to the house, he heard music and dancing. And he called one of the servants, and asked what these things meant. And he said unto him, Thy brother is come; and thy father hath killed the fatted calf, because he hath received him safe and sound. And he was angry, and would not go in: therefore came his father out, and entreated him.

And he answering said to his father, Lo, these many years do I serve thee, neither transgressed I at any time thy commandment; and yet thou never gavest me a kid, that I might make merry with my friends: but as soon as this thy son was come, which hath devoured thy living with harlots, thou hast killed for him the fatted calf.

And he said unto him, Son, thou art ever with me, and all that I have is thine. It was meet that we should make merry, and be glad: for this thy brother was dead, and is alive again; and was lost, and is found.

SERMON IN PARABLES (CONTINUED)

A.D. 30. Age 33. Perea.

Luke 16, 1-31.

JESUS said also to his disciples,

There was a certain rich man, which had a steward; and the same was accused unto him that he had wasted his goods. And he called him, and said unto him, How is it that I hear this of thee? give an account of thy stewardship; for thou mayest be no longer steward.

Then the steward said within himself, What shall I do? for my lord taketh away from me the stewardship: I cannot dig: to beg I am ashamed. I am resolved what to do, that, when I am put out of the stewardship, they may receive me into their houses.

So he called every one of his lord's debtors unto him, and said unto the first, How much owest thou unto my lord? And he said, A hundred measures of oil. And he said unto him, Take thy bill, and sit down quickly, and write fifty.

Then said he to another, And how much owest thou? And he said, A hundred measures of wheat. And he said unto him, Take thy bill, and write four-score.

And the lord commended the unjust steward, because he had done wisely: for the children of this world are in their generation wiser than the children of light.

And I say unto you, Make to yourselves friends of the mammon of unrighteousness; that, when ye fail, they may receive you into everlasting habitations.

He that is faithful in that which is least is faithful also in much: and he that is unjust in the least is unjust also in much.

If herefore ye have not been faithful in the unrighteous mammon, who will commit to your trust the true riches? And if ye have not been faithful in that which is another man's who, shall give you that which is your own?

¶No servant can serve two masters: for either he will hate the one, and love the other, or else he will hold to the one and despise the other. Ye cannot serve God and mammon.

The Pharisees also, who were covetous, heard all these things: and they derided Jesus. He said unto them,

Ye are they which justify yourselves before men; but God knoweth your hearts: for that which is highly esteemed among men is abomination in the sight of God. The law and the prophets were unto John: since that time the kingdom of God is preached, and every man presseth into it. And it is easier for heaven and earth to pass, than one tittle of the law to fail.

Whosoever putteth away his wife, and married another, committeth adultery: and whosoever marrieth her that is put away from her husband committeth adultery. *

¶There was a certain rich man, which was clothed in purple and fine linen, and fared sumptuously every day: and there was a certain beggar named Lazarus, which was laid at his gate, full of sores, and desiring to be fed with the crumbs which fell from the rich man's table: moreover the dogs came and licked his sores.

And it came to pass, that the beggar died, and it was carried by the angels into Abraham's bosom: the rich man also died and was buried; and in hell he lifted up his eyes, being in torments, and seeth Abraham afar off, and Lazarus in his bosom. And he cried and said, Father Abraham, have mercy on me, and send Lazarus, that he may dip the tip of his finger in water, and cool my tongue: for I am tormented in this flame.

But Abraham said, Son, remember that thou in thy lifetime receivedst thy good things, and likewise Lazarus evil things: but now he is comforted, and thou art tormented. And beside all this, between us and you there is a great gulf fixed: so that they which would pass from hence to you cannot; neither can they pass to us, that would come from thence.

Then he said, I pray thee therefore, father, that thou wouldest send him to my father's house: for I have five brethren; that he may testify unto them, lest they also come into this place of torment.

Abraham saith unto him, They have Moses and the prophets; let them hear them.

And he said, Nay, father Abraham: but if one went unto them from the dead, they will repent.

And he said unto him, If they hear not Moses and the prophets, neither will they be persuaded, though one rose from the dead.

SERMON IN PARABLES (CONCLUDED)

A.D. 30. Age 33. Perea. Bethany. Perea.

Luke 17, 1-10: John 11, 1-54.

THEN said Jesus unto the disciples,

It is impossible but that offences will come: but woe unto him, through whom they come! It were better for him that a millstone were hanged about his neck, and he cast into the sea, than that he should offend * one of these little ones.

Take heed to yourselves: If thy brother trespass against thee, rebuke him; and if he repent, forgive him. And if he trespass against thee seven times in a day, and seven times in a day turn again to thee, saying, I repent; thou shalt forgive him.

The apostles said unto the Lord, Increase our faith. And the Lord said,

If ye had faith as a grain of mustard seed, ye might say unto this sycamine tree, Be thou plucked up by the root, and be thou planted in the sea; and it should obey you.

But which of you, having a servant ploughing or feeding cattle, will say unto him by and by, when he is come from the field, Go and sit down to meat? and will not rather say unto him, Make ready wherewith I may sup, and gird thyself, and serve me, till I have eaten and drunken; and afterward thou shalt eat and drink?

Doth he thank that servant because he did the things that were commanded him? I trow not.

So likewise ye, when ye shall have done all those things which are commanded you, say, We are unprofitable servants: we have done that which was our duty to do.

¶Lazarus, of Bethany, the brother of Mary and Martha, was sick. (It was that Mary which anointed the Lord with ointment, and wiped his feet with her hair. †) The sisters sent unto Jesus, saying, Lord, behold, he whom thou lovest is sick. Jesus said,

This sickness is not unto death, but for the glory of God, that the Son of God might be glorified thereby.

Now Jesus loved Martha, and her sister, and Lazarus. He abode two days in the place where he was; then saith he to his disciples,

Let us go into Judea again.

His disciples say, Master, the Jews of late sought to stone thee; and goest thou thither again? Jesus answered,

Are there not twelve hours in the day? If any man walk in the day, he stumbleth not, because he seeth the light of this world. But if a man walk in the night, he stumbleth, because there is no light in him.

Our friend Lazarus sleepeth; but I go, that I may awake him out of his sleep.

Howbeit Jesus spake of Lazarus' death; but they thought that he had spoken of rest in sleep. Then said Jesus plainly,

Lazarus is dead. And I am glad for your sakes that I was not there, to the intent ye may believe; nevertheless let us go unto him.

And when Jesus came, he found that Lazarus had lain in the grave four days.

Martha, as soon as she heard that Jesus was coming, went and met him; but Mary was still in the house. Then said Martha unto Jesus, Lord, if thou hadst been here, my brother had not died. But I know, that even now, whatsoever thou wilt ask of God, God will give it thee. Jesus saith unto her,

Thy brother shall rise again.

Martha answered, I know that he shall rise again in the resurrection at the last day. Jesus said unto her,

I am the resurrection, and the life; he that believeth in me, though he were dead, yet shall he live: and whosoever liveth and believeth in me shall never die. Believest thou this?

Martha saith, Yea, Lord: I believe that thou art the Christ, the Son of God, which should come into the world.

When she had so said, she went her way, and called Mary her sister secretly, saying, The Master is come.

Mary arose quickly, and came unto him in that place where Martha met him. The Jews which were with Mary in the house followed her. She fell at Jesus' feet, saying, Lord, if thou hadst been here, my brother had not died.

Jesus saw her weeping: he groaned in the spirit, and was troubled, and said,

Where have ye laid him?

They say, Lord, come and see.

Jesus wept.

Then said the Jews, Behold how he loved him!

Jesus cometh to the grave. It was a cave, and a stone lay upon it. Jesus said,

Take ye away the stone.

Martha, the sister, saith, Lord, he hath been dead four days. Jesus saith,

Said I not unto thee, that, if thou wouldst believe, thou shouldst see the glory of God?

Then they took away the stone. And Jesus lifted up his eyes, and said,

Father, I thank thee that thou hast heard me. And I knew that thou hearest me always: but because of the people which stand by I said it, that they may believe that thou hast sent me.

When he had thus spoken, he cried,

Lazarus, come forth.

He that was dead came forth, bound with graveclothes. Jesus saith unto them,

Loose him, and let him go.

¶Then gathered the chief priests, and the Pharisees a council, and said, What do we? for this man doeth many miracles. If we let him alone, all men will believe on him: and the Romans shall come and take away both our place and nation.

Then from that day forth they took counsel together for to put Jesus to death.

Jesus therefore walked no more openly among the Jews; but went thence unto a country near to the wilderness, into a city called Ephraim, and there continued with his disciples.

"THE KINGDOM OF GOD IS WITHIN YOU"

A.D. 30. Age 33. Galilee. Samaria. Perea.

Luke 17, 11-37; 18, 1-8.

AS Jesus went to Jerusalem, he passed through Samaria and Galilee. In a certain village ten lepers, which stood far off, lifted up their voices, and said, Jesus, Master, have mercy on us. He said unto them,

Go shew yourselves unto the priests.

As they went, they were cleansed. And one of them turned back, and fell at Jesus' feet, giving him thanks: he was a Samaritan. Jesus said,

Were there not ten cleansed? but where are the nine? There are not found that returned to give glory to God, save this stranger.

And he said unto him,

Arise, go thy way: thy faith hath made thee whole.

¶When Jesus was demanded of the Pharisees, when the kingdom of God should come, he answered,

The kingdom of God cometh not with observation: neither shall they say, Lo here! or, lo there! for, behold, the kingdom of God is within you.

And he said unto his disciples,

The days will come, when ye shall desire to see one of the days of the Son of man, and ye shall not see it. And they shall say to you, See here; or, see there: go not after them, nor follow them. For as the lightning, which lighteneth out of the one part under heaven, shineth unto the other part under heaven; so shall also the Son of man be in his day.

But first must he suffer many things, and be rejected of this generation.

And as it was in the days of Noe, so shall it be also in the days of the Son of man. They did eat, they drank, they married wives, they were given in marriage, until the day that Noe entered into the ark, and the flood came, and destroyed them all.

Likewise also as it was in the days of Lot; they did eat, they drank, they bought, they sold, they planted, they builded; but the same day that Lot went out of Sodom it rained fire and brimstone from heaven, and destroyed them all.

Even thus shall it be in the day when the Son of man is revealed. In that day, he which shall be upon the housetop, and his stuff in the house, let him not come down to take it away: and he that is in the field, let him likewise not return back.

Remember Lot's wife.

Whosoever shall seek to save his life shall lose it; and whosoever shall lose his life shall preserve it.

I tell you, in that night there shall be two men in one bed; the one shall be taken, and the other shall be left. Two women shall be grinding together; the one shall be taken, and the other left. Two men shall be in the field; the one shall be taken, and the other left. *

They said unto Jesus, Where, Lord? He answered,

Wheresoever the body is, thither will the eagles be gathered together.

¶He spake a parable to this end, that men ought always to pray, and not to faint, saying,

There was in a city a judge, which feared not God, neither regarded man: and there was a widow in that city; and she came unto him, saying, Avenge me of mine adversary.

And he would not for a while: but afterward he said within himself, Though I fear not God, nor regard man; yet because this widow troubleth me, I will avenge her, lest by her continual coming she weary me.

And the Lord said,

Hear what the unjust judge saith. And shall not God avenge his own elect, which cry day and night unto him, though he bear long with them? I tell you that he will avenge them speedily. Nevertheless, when the Son of man cometh, shall he find faith on the earth?

"EASIER FOR A CAMEL TO GO THROUGH THE EYE OF A NEEDLE"

A.D. 30. Age 33. Perea.

Luke 18, 9-30: Mark 10, 13-31: Matthew 19, 13-30; and 20, 1-16.

JESUS spake this parable unto certain which trusted in themselves that they were righteous, and despised others:

Two men went up into the temple to pray; the one a Pharisee, and the other a publican.

The Pharisee stood and prayed thus with himself: God, I thank thee, that I am not as other men are, extortioners, unjust, adulterers, or even as this publican. I fast twice in the week, I give tithes of all that I possess.

And the publican, standing afar off, would not lift up so much as his eyes unto heaven, but smote upon his breast, saying, God be merciful to me a sinner.

I tell you, this man went down to his house justified rather than the other: for every man that exalteth himself shall be abased; and he that humbleth himself shall be exalted.

¶Then were brought infants, that Jesus should touch them: but the disciples rebuked them that brought them. Jesus, much displeased, said unto the disciples,

Suffer the little children, and forbid them not, to come unto me: for of such is the kingdom of heaven.

Verily I say unto you, Whosoever shall not receive the kingdom of God as a little child, he shall in no wise enter therein.

He took them up in his arms, put his hands upon them, and blessed them; and he departed thence.

¶When he was gone forth into the way there came one running, a ruler, and kneeled, and asked, Good Master, what good thing shall I do to inherit eternal life? * Jesus answered,

Why callest thou me good? None is good, save one, that is, God: but if thou wilt enter into life, keep the commandments.

He saith, Which? Jesus said,

Thou knowest the commandments, Do not commit adultery, Do not kill, Do not steal, Do not bear false witness, Defraud not, Honor thy father and thy mother: and, Thou shalt love thy neighbor as thyself.

The young man saith, All these things have I kept from my youth up: what lack I yet? Jesus beholding him loved him, and said,

Yet lackest thou one thing; if thou wilt be perfect, go thy way, sell all that thou hast, and distribute unto the poor, and thou shalt have treasure in heaven: and come, take up the cross, and follow me.

The young man went away grieved, for he was rich, and had great possessions.

¶Jesus looked round about, and saith,

How hardly shall they that have riches enter into the kingdom of God? It is easier for a camel to go through the eye of a needle, † than for a rich man to enter into the kingdom of God.

The disciples were amazed at his words. But Jesus saith again,

Children, how hard is it for them that trust in riches to enter into the kingdom of God! Verily I say unto you, That a rich man shall hardly enter into the kingdom of heaven! And again I say unto you, It is easier for a camel to go through a needle's eye, than for a rich man to enter into the kingdom of God.

The disciples were saying among themselves, Who then can be saved? And Jesus answered,

With men this is impossible; but not with God. The things which are impossible with men are possible with God: for with God all things are possible.

¶Then Peter said, Lo, we have left all, and have followed thee. What shall we have therefore? Jesus saith,

Ye which have followed me, in the regeneration when the Son of man shall sit in the throne of his glory, ye also shall sit upon twelve thrones, judging the twelve tribes of Israel.

There is not a man that hath forsaken houses, or father, or mother, or brethren, or sisters, or wife, or children, or lands, for the kingdom of God's sake, for my sake and the gospel's, but he shall receive a hundredfold, and shall inherit everlasting life.

Verily I say unto you, every one that hath left house, or father, or mother, or brethren, or sisters, or wife, or children, or lands, for my name's sake, and the gospel's, shall receive manifold more in this present time: houses, and brethren, and sisters, and mothers, and children, and lands, with persecutions; and shall inherit life everlasting in the world to come.

But many that are first shall be last; and the last shall be first.

¶For the kingdom of heaven is like unto a man that is a householder, which went out early in the morning to hire laborers into his vineyard. And when he had agreed with the laborers for a penny a day, he sent them into his vineyard.

And he went out about the third hour, and saw others standing idle in the marketplace, and said unto them, Go ye also into the vineyard, and whatsoever is right I will give you. And they went their way.

Again he went out about the sixth and ninth hour, and did likewise.

And about the eleventh hour he went out, and found others standing idle, and saith unto them, Why stand ye here all the day idle? They say unto him, Because no man hath hired us. He saith unto them, Go ye also into the vineyard; and whatsoever is right, that shall ye receive.

So when even was come, the lord of the vineyard saith unto his steward, Call the laborers, and give them their hire, beginning from the last unto the first.

And when they came that were hired about the eleventh hour, they received every man a penny.

But when the first came, they supposed that they should have received more; and they likewise received every man a penny. And when they had received it, they murmured against the goodman of the house, saying, These last have wrought but one hour, and thou hast made them equal unto us, which have borne the burden and heat of the day.

But he answered one of them, and said, Friend, I do thee no wrong: didst not thou agree with me for a penny? Take that thine is, and go thy way: I will give unto this last, even as unto thee. Is it not lawful for me to do what I will with mine own? Is thine eye evil, because I am good?

So the last shall be first, and the first last; for many be called, but few chosen.

DIVORCE DENOUNCED

A.D. 30. Age 33. Perea.

Mark 10, 1-12: Matthew 19, 1-12.

INTO the coasts of Judea by the farther side of Jordan, multitudes followed Jesus: and the people resort unto him; and, as he was wont, he taught them.

¶The Pharisees also came, and tempting him asked Jesus, Is it lawful for a man to put away his wife for every cause? * He answered,

What did Moses command you?

They said, Moses suffered to write a bill of divorcement, and to put her away. Jesus answered,

For the hardness of your heart he wrote you his precept. But from the beginning of creation God made them male and female. For this cause shall a man leave his father and mother, and cleave to his wife.

Have ye not read, that he which made them at the beginning made them male and female, and said, For this cause shall man leave father and mother, and shall cleave to his wife: and they twain shall be one flesh? So then they are no more twain, but one flesh. What therefore God hath joined together, let no man put asunder.

They say unto him, Why did Moses then command to give a writing of divorcement and to put her away? He saith,

Moses because of the hardness of your hearts suffered you to put away your wives: but from the beginning it was not so. And I say unto you, Whosoever shall put away his wife, except it be for fornication, and shall marry another, committeth adultery: and whoso marrieth her which is put away doth commit adultery.

In the house his disciples asked Jesus again of the same matter. He saith,

Whosoever shall put away his wife, and marry another, committeth adultery against her. And if a woman shall put away her husband, and be married to another, she committeth adultery.

The disciples say unto him, If the case of the man be so with his wife, it is not good to marry. But Jesus answered,

All men cannot receive this saying, save they to whom it is given. For there are some eunuchs, which were so born from their mother's womb: and there are some eunuchs which were made eunuchs of men: and there be eunuchs, which have made themselves eunuchs for the kingdom of heaven's sake.

He that is able to receive it, let him receive it.

"DRINK INDEED OF MY CUP"

A.D. 30. Age 33. Perea.

Matthew 20, 17-28: Mark 10, 32-45: Luke 18, 31-34.

JESUS going up to Jerusalem took again the disciples apart in the way, and began to tell them what things should happen unto him, saying,

Behold, we go up to Jerusalem; and the Son of man shall be betrayed and delivered unto the chief priests, and unto the scribes; and he shall be spitefully entreated and spitted on; and they shall condemn him to death, and shall deliver him unto the Gentiles.

They shall mock him, and shall scourge him, and shall crucify and kill him: and the third day he shall rise again.

And all the things that are written by the prophets concerning the Son of man shall be accomplished.

They (the twelve) understood none of this saying; neither knew they the things which were spoken.

¶Then came unto Jesus the mother of James and John, the sons of Zebedee, desiring a certain thing of him. * He said unto her,

What wilt thou?

And he said unto them,

What would ye that I should do for you?

She saith, Grant that these my two sons may sit, the one on thy right hand, and the other on the left, in glory in thy kingdom. But Jesus said unto them,

Ye know not what ye ask: are ye able to drink of the cup that I shall drink of, and to be baptized with the baptism that I am baptized with?

And they say, We can. Jesus answered,

Ye shall drink indeed of my cup, the cup that I drink of: and with the baptism that I am baptized withal ye shall be baptized: but to sit on my right hand and on my left hand, is not mine to give, but it shall be given to them for whom it is prepared of my Father.

The ten were moved with indignation against the two brethren. But Jesus called them to him, and said,

Ye know that the princes of the Gentiles exercise dominion over them; ye know that they which are accounted to rule over the Gentiles exercise lordship over them; and their great ones exercise authority upon them.

But so shall it not be among you: but whosoever will be great among you, shall be your minister: and whosoever of you will be the chiefest, shall be servant of all: let him be your servant, even as the Son of man: for even the Son of man came not to be ministered unto, but to minister, and to give his life a ransom for many.

SIGHT RESTORED TO TWO BLIND BEGGARS

A.D. 30. Age 33. Jericho.

Luke 18, 35-43; 19, 1-27: Mark 10, 46-52.

A MULTITUDE followed Jesus. Nigh * unto Jericho, a certain blind man sat by the way side begging: and hearing the multitude, he asked what it meant. They told him, Jesus of Nazareth passeth by.

And he cried, Jesus, thou Son of David, have mercy on me.

Jesus commanded him to be brought; and asked him,

What wilt thou that I shall do unto thee?

And he said, Lord, that I may receive my sight. Jesus said unto him,

Receive thy sight: thy faith hath saved thee.

Immediately he received his sight. And Jesus entered and passed through Jericho.

¶As he went out * of Jericho with his disciples, blind Bartimeus sat by the highway side begging. When he heard that it was Jesus of Nazareth, he began to cry out, Jesus, Son of David, have mercy on me.

Many charged him that he should hold his peace: but he cried the more, Thou Son of David, have mercy on me.

Jesus commanded him to be called. And they call the blind man, saying, Be of good comfort; he calleth thee.

Casting away his garment, he came to Jesus. He said unto the man,

What wilt thou that I shall do unto thee?

The blind man said, Lord, that I might receive my sight. And Jesus said,

Go thy way; thy faith hath made thee whole.

Immediately his eyes received sight, and he followed Jesus in the way.

¶Jesus [had] entered and passed through Jericho. And a man named Zaccheus, which was the chief among the publicans, and rich, sought to see Jesus who he was, and could not for the press, because he was little of stature. He ran before, and climbed into a sycamore tree to see Jesus: for he was to pass that way.

When Jesus came to the place, he looked up, and saw Zaccheus, and said,

Zaccheus, make haste, and come down: for to day I must abide at thy house.

He came down, and received Jesus joyfully. When they saw it, they murmured, He was gone to be guest with a man that is a sinner.

Zaccheus said unto the Lord: Behold, the half of my goods I give to the poor; and if I have taken any thing from any man by false accusation, I restore him fourfold. Jesus said,

This day is salvation come to this house, forasmuch as he also is a son of Abraham.

For the Son of man is come to seek and to save that which was lost.

And he added a parable, because he was nigh to Jerusalem, and they thought that the kingdom of God should immediately appear. He said therefore,

*A certain nobleman went into a far country to receive for himself a kingdom, and to return. And he called his ten servants, and delivered them ten pounds, and said unto them, Occupy till I come.

But his citizens hated him, and sent a message after him, saying, We will not have this man to reign over us.

And it came to pass, that when he was returned, having received the kingdom, then he commanded these servants to be called unto him, to whom he had given the money, that he might know how much every man had gained by trading.

Then came the first saying, Lord, thy pound hath gained ten pounds. And he said unto him, Well, thou good servant: because thou hast been faithful in a very little, have thou authority over ten cities.

And the second came, saying, Lord, thy pound hath gained five pounds. And he said likewise to him, Be thou also over five cities.

And another came, saying, Lord, behold, here is thy pound, which I have kept laid up in a napkin; for I feared thee, because thou art an austere man: thou takest up that thou layest not down, and reapest that thou didst not sow.

And he saith unto him, Out of thine own mouth will I judge thee, thou wicked servant. Thou knewest that I was an austere man, taking up that I laid not down, and reaping that I did not sow: Wherefore then gavest not thou my money into the bank, that at my coming I might have required mine own with usury?

And he said unto them that stood by, Take from him the pound, and give it to him that hath ten pounds. (And they said unto him, Lord, he hath ten pounds.) But those mine enemies, which would not that I should reign over them, bring hither, and slay them before me.

For I say unto you, That unto every one which hath shall be given; and from him that hath not, even that he hath shall be taken away from him.

JESUS GOES TO JERUSALEM

A.D. 30. Age 33. Bethphage. Jerusalem.

John 11, 55-57: Matthew 21, 1-6: Mark 77, 1-11: Luke 19, 28-44.

THE Jews' passover was nigh at hand; and many went out of the country up to Jerusalem, before the passover, to purify themselves. Jesus went before, ascending up to Jerusalem.

Now the chief priests and the Pharisees had given a commandment, that if any man knew where Jesus were, he should shew it, that they might take him. Then they sought for him.

¶When Jesus was come to Bethphage and Bethany, at the mount of Olives, nigh unto Jerusalem, he sendeth forth two disciples, saying,

Go ye your way into the village over against you, in the which, as soon as ye be entered into it, straightway ye shall find an ass tied, and a colt with her, * whereon yet never man sat; loose them, and bring them hither unto me.

And if any man say aught unto you, and ask you, Why do ye this? why do ye loose them? ye shall say, Because the Lord hath need of them; and straightway he will send them hither.

The [two] disciples went, and did as Jesus had commanded. The owners said, Why loose ye them? They answered, The Lord hath need of them. And they let them go.

They brought the ass, and the colt, and put their garments on the colt; and they set Jesus thereon.

As he went, many spread their clothes in the way; and others cut branches off the trees, and strewed them in the way.

At the descent of the mount of Olives, the multitude began to praise God, saying, Blessed be the King that cometh in the name of he Lord. Hosanna in the highest: peace in heaven!

Some of the Pharisees said unto Jesus, Master, rebuke thy disciples. He answered,

I tell you, that if these should hold their peace, the stones would immediately cry out.

¶When Jesus was come near, he beheld the city (Jerusalem), and wept over it, saying,

If thou hadst known, even thou, at least in this thy day, the things which belong unto thy peace! but now they are hid from thine eyes.

For the days shall come upon thee, that thine enemies shall cast a trench about thee, and compass thee round, and keep thee in on every side. And shall lay thee even with the ground, and thy children within thee; and they shall not leave in thee one stone upon another; because thou knewest not the time of thy visitation.

¶When Jesus was come into Jerusalem, he taught daily in the temple. All the city was moved. The blind and the lame came to him, and he healed them.

The wonderful things that he did, and the children crying in the temple, Hosanna to the Son of David, displeased the chief priests and the scribes; and they said unto Jesus, Hearest thou what these say? He answered,

Yea; have ye never read, Out of the mouth of babes and sucklings thou hast perfected praise?

And when he had looked round about upon all things, and now the eventide was come, he went out. With the twelve he went unto Bethany, and lodged there.

THE FIG TREE WITHERED

A.D. 30. Age 33. Near Bethany. Jerusalem.

Mark 11, 12-26: Matthew 21, 12-13; 18-22: Luke 19, 45-48.

NOW on the morrow in the morning, when they were come from Bethany, as Jesus returned into the city, he was hungry: and seeing afar off a fig tree having leaves, he came, if haply he might find any thing thereon. He found nothing but leaves, for the time of the figs was not yet. And he said,

Let no fruit grow on thee henceforward. No man eat fruit of thee hereafter for ever.

Presently the fig tree withered away. The disciples saw it, saying, How soon is the fig tree withered away! Jesus answered,

Verily I say unto you, If ye have faith, and doubt not, ye shall not only do this which is done to the fig tree, but also if ye shall say to this mountain, Be thou removed, and be thou cast into the sea; it shall be done. And all things, whatsoever ye shall ask in prayer, believing, ye shall receive.

¶ *They came to Jerusalem, and Jesus went into the temple, and began to cast out them that sold and bought therein, and overthrew the tables of the money changers, and the seats of them that sold doves; and would not suffer that any man should carry any vessel through the temple. And he taught, saying,

My house is the house of prayer. Is it not written, My house shall be called of all nations the house of prayer? but ye have made it a den of thieves.

The scribes and chief priests heard it, and sought how they might destroy Jesus: for they feared him, because all the people were attentive to hear him.

When even was come, he went out of the city. In the morning, as they came by, they saw the fig tree dried up from the roots. And Peter calling to remembrance saith unto Jesus, Master, behold, the fig tree which thou cursedst is withered away. Jesus answering saith,

Have faith in God. For verily I say unto you, That whosoever shall say unto this mountain, Be thou removed, and be thou cast into the sea; and shall not doubt in his heart, but shall believe that those things which he saith shall come to pass, he shall have whatsoever he saith.

Therefore I say unto you, What things soever ye desire, when ye pray, believe that ye receive them, and ye shall receive them.

And when ye stand praying, forgive, if ye have ought against any; that your Father also which is in heaven may forgive you your trespasses. But if ye do not forgive, neither will your Father which is in heaven forgive your trespasses.

CHRIST'S AUTHORITY CHALLENGED

A.D. 30. Age 33. Jerusalem, in the Temple.

Matthew 21, 23-46: Mark 11, 27-33; 12, 1-12: Luke 20, 1-19.

*ON one of those days, as Jesus was walking in the temple, and preached the gospel, the chief priests, and the scribes came with the elders, saying, By what authority doest thou these things? Jesus answered,

I also will ask of you one question, which if ye will tell me, and answer me, I in like wise will tell you by what authority I do these things: The baptism of John, whence was it? was it from heaven, or of men? Answer me.

They reasoned with themselves, saying, If we shall say, From heaven; he will say, Why then did ye not believe him? But and if we shall say, Of men; the people will stone us: for they be persuaded that John was indeed a prophet.

They feared the people. And they answered, We cannot tell.

Jesus saith unto them,

Neither tell I you by what authority I do these things.

¶Then began he to speak by parables:

But what think ye? A certain man had two sons; and he came to the first, and said, Son, go work to day in my vineyard. He answered and said, I will not: but afterward he repented, and went.

And he came to the second, and said likewise. And he answered and said, I go, sir: and went not.

Whether of them twain did the will of his father?

They say, The first. Jesus saith,

Verily I say unto you, That the publicans and the harlots go into the kingdom of God before you. For John came unto you in the way of righteousness, and ye believed him not: but the publicans and the harlots believed him: and ye, when ye had seen it, repented not afterward, that ye might believe him.

¶Hear another parable: There was a certain householder, which planted a vineyard, and set a hedge round about it, and digged a place in it for the winevat; and digged a winepress in it; and built a tower, and let it out to husbandmen, and went into a far country for a long time.

And at the season when the time of the fruit drew near, he sent a servant to the husbandmen, that he might receive from them of the fruit of the vineyard: but the husbandmen caught him, and beat him, and sent him away empty.

And again he sent unto them another servant; they beat him also, and at him they cast stones, and wounded him in the head, and handled him shamefully, and sent him away empty.

And again he sent a third: and him they wounded also, and killed, and they cast him out: and many others, more than the first: and they did unto them likewise, beating some, and killing some.

Having yet therefore one son, his well beloved, then said the lord of the vineyard, What shall I do? I will send my beloved son: last of all he sent unto them his son, saying, It may be they will reverence him, my son, when they see him.

But when those husbandmen saw the son, they reasoned among themselves, saying, This is the heir; come, let us kill him, and let us seize on his inheritance, and the inheritance shall be ours.

So they caught him, and slew him, and cast him out of the vineyard.

When the lord therefore of the vineyard cometh, what will he do unto those husbandmen? He will come and miserably destroy those wicked men, and will let out his vineyard unto other husbandmen, which shall render him the fruits in their seasons.

When they heard it, they said, God forbid. Jesus beheld them, and said,

Did ye never read in the Scriptures?

What is this then that is written? Have ye not read this Scripture: The stone which the builders rejected, the same is become the head of the corner: this was the Lord's doing, and it is marvellous in our eyes? *

Therefore I say unto you, The kingdom of God shall be taken from you, and given to a nation bringing forth the fruits thereof. And whosoever shall fall on this stone shall be broken: but on whomsoever it shall fall, it will grind him to powder.

The chief priests and Pharisees heard Jesus' parables: they perceived that he had spoken the parables against them. And they sought to lay hold on him, but feared the people, because they took him for a prophet; and they left him, and went their way.

"MANY ARE CALLED"

A.D. 30. Age 33. Jerusalem, in the Temple.

Matthew 22, 1-32: Mark 12, 13-27: Luke 20, 20-38.

JESUS spake unto them again by parables,

The kingdom of heaven is like unto a certain king which made a marriage for his son, and sent forth his servants to call them that were bidden to the wedding: and they would not come.

Again, he sent forth other servants, saying, Tell them which are bidden, Behold, I have prepared my dinner: my oxen and my fatlings are killed, and all things are ready: come unto the marriage. But they made light of it, and went their ways, one to his farm, another to his merchandise: and the remnant took his servants, and entreated them spitefully, and slew them. But when the king heard thereof, he was wroth: and sent forth his armies, and destroyed those murderers, and burned up their city.

Then saith he to his servants, The wedding is ready, but they which were bidden were not worthy. Go ye therefore into the highways, and as many as ye shall find, bid to the marriage. So those servants went out into the highways, and gathered all together as many as they found, both bad and good: and the wedding was furnished with guests.

¶And when the king came in to see the guests, he saw there a man which had not on a wedding garment: and he saith unto him, Friend, how earnest thou in hither not having a wedding garment? And he was speechless.

Then said the king to the servants, Bind him hand and foot, and take him away, and cast him into outer darkness; there shall be weeping and gnashing of teeth.

For many are called, but few are chosen.

¶Then the Pharisees took counsel how they might entangle Jesus in his talk. They sent spies, which should feign themselves just men, to catch him in his words, that so they might deliver him unto the authority of the governor.

When these were come, they say unto Jesus, Master, we know that thou teachest the way of God in truth, neither acceptest the person of men. Tell us, Is it lawful to give tribute to Cesar, or not?

Jesus perceived their craftiness, and said,

Why tempt ye me, ye hypocrites? Shew me the tribute money; bring me a penny, that I may see it. Shew me a penny.

And they brought it. He said unto them,

Whose image and superscription hath it? Whose is this image and superscription?

They answered, Cesar's. Then saith he,

Render therefore unto Cesar the things which be Cesar's; and unto God the things which be God's.

They marvelled at his answers: they held their peace, and left him.

The same day came Sadducees, which say that there is no resurrection: and asked Jesus, saying, Moses wrote, If a man's brother die, and leave his wife behind him, and leave no children, the brother shall marry the wife, and raise up seed unto his brother. *

Now there were seven brethren: the first took a wife, and died without children: the second took her to wife, and he died childless: the third likewise; and in like manner the seven also: they died, and left no children. Last of all, the woman died. Therefore in the resurrection whose wife of them is she?

Jesus answering said,

Do ye not therefore err, because ye know not the Scriptures? Ye do err, not knowing the Scriptures, neither the power of God.

The children of this world marry, and are given in marriage; but they which shall be accounted worthy to obtain that world, and the resurrection from the dead; when they shall rise from the dead, they neither marry, nor are given in marriage: for they are equal unto the angels of God which are in heaven; and are the children of God, being the children of the resurrection.

Now that the dead are raised, even Moses shewed at the bush, when he calleth the Lord the God of Abraham, and the God of Isaac, and the God of Jacob.

And as touching the resurrection of the dead, that they rise, have ye not read in the book of Moses that which was spoken unto you by God: how in the bush God spake unto Moses, saying, I am the God of Abraham, and the God of Isaac, and the God of Jacob?

God is not the God of the dead, but the God of the living; for all live unto him: ye therefore do greatly err.

THE FIRST GREAT COMMANDMENT: AND THE SECOND

A.D. 30. Age 33. Jerusalem, in the Temple.

Matthew 22, 34-46: Mark 12, 28-44: Luke 20, 41-47; 21, 1-4.

THE Pharisees had heard that Jesus had put the Sadducees to silence; and one of them which was a lawyer, perceiving that Jesus had answered the Sadducees well, asked him, tempting him, Master, which is the great commandment in the law? Which is the first commandment of all? Jesus said unto him,

The first of all the commandments is, Hear, O Israel; The Lord our God is one Lord: and thou shalt love the Lord thy God with all thy heart, and with all thy soul, and with all thy mind, and with all thy strength: this is the first and great commandment. And the second is like unto it, namely this, Thou shalt love thy neighbor as thyself. On these two commandments hang all the law and the prophets. There is none other commandment greater than these.

And the scribe (lawyer) said, Well, Master, thou hast said the truth: for there is one God; and there is none other: and to love him with all the heart, and with all the understanding, and with all the soul, and with all the strength; and to love his neighbor as himself, is more than all burnt offerings and sacrifices.

Jesus saw that he answered discreetly; and said unto him,

Thou art not far from the kingdom of God.

¶While the Pharisees were gathered together, Jesus asked them,

What think ye of Christ? whose son is he?

They say unto him, The son of David. He saith unto them,

How then doth David in spirit call him Lord, saying, The Lord said unto my Lord, Sit thou on my right hand, till I make thine enemies thy footstool? If David then call him Lord, how is he his son?

And no man was able to answer him a word: neither durst any man from that day forth ask him questions. The common people heard him gladly.

¶While Jesus taught in the temple, he said,

How say the scribes that Christ is David's son? For in the book of Psalms David himself saith by the Holy Ghost, The Lord said unto my Lord, Sit thou on my right hand, till I make thine enemies thy footstool. David therefore himself calleth him Lord; and how is he then his son?

Then in the audience of all the people he said unto his disciples,

Beware of the scribes, which desire to walk in long robes, and love greetings in the marketplaces, and the highest seats in the synagogues, and the uppermost rooms at feasts; which devour widows' houses, and for a shew make long prayers: these same shall receive greater damnation,

¶Jesus sat over against the treasury. He beheld people cast money and gifts into the treasury. Many that were rich cast in much. He saw also a certain poor widow casting in thither two mites, which make a farthing. He called his disciples, and saith unto them,

Of a truth I say unto you, that this poor widow doth cast in more than they all which have cast into the treasury: for all these have of their abundance cast in unto the offerings of God: but she of her penury did cast in all that she had, even all her living.

"WOE UNTO YOU, SCRIBES AND PHARISEES!"

A.D. 30. Age 33. Jerusalem, in the Temple.

Matthew 23, 1-39.

TO the multitude, and to his disciples spake Jesus, saying,

The scribes and the Pharisees sit in Moses' seat: all therefore whatsoever they bid you observe, that observe and do; but do not ye after their works: for they say, and do not. For they bind heavy burdens and grievous to be borne, and lay them on men's shoulders; but they themselves will not move them with one of their fingers.

But all their works they do for to be seen of men: they make broad their phylacteries, and enlarge the borders of their garments, and love the uppermost rooms at feasts, and the chief seats in the synagogues, and greetings in the markets, and to be called of men, Rabbi, Rabbi. But be not ye called Rabbi: for one is your Master, even Christ; and all ye are brethren.

And call no man your father upon the earth: for one is your Father which is in heaven. Neither be ye called masters: for one is your Master, even Christ.

But he that is greatest among you shall be your servant. And whosoever shall exalt himself shall be abased; and he that shall humble himself shall be exalted.

¶But woe unto you, scribes and pharisees, hypocrites! for ye shut up the kingdom of heaven against men: for ye neither go in yourselves, neither suffer ye them that are entering to go in.

Woe unto you, scribes and Pharisees, hypocrites! for ye pay tithe of mint and anise and cummin, and have omitted the weightier matters of the law, judgment, mercy and faith: these ought ye to have done, and not to leave the other undone. Ye blind guides, which strain at a gnat, and swallow a camel.

Woe unto you, scribes and Pharisees, hypocrites! for ye make clean the outside of the cup and of the platter, but within they are full of extortion and excess. Thou blind Pharisee, cleanse first that which is within the cup and platter, that the outside of them may be clean also.

Woe unto you, scribes and Pharisees, hypocrites! for ye are like unto whited sepulchres, which indeed appear beautiful outward, but are within full of dead men's bones, and of all uncleanness. Even so ye also outwardly appear righteous unto men, but within ye are full of hypocrisy and iniquity.

Woe unto you, scribes and Pharisees, hypocrites! because ye build the tombs of the prophets, and garnish the sepulchres of the righteous, and say, If we had been in the days of our fathers, we would not have been partakers with them in the blood of the prophets.

Wherefore ye be witnesses unto yourselves, that ye are the children of them which killed the prophets. Fill ye up then the measure of your fathers. Ye serpents, ye generation of vipers, how can ye escape the damnation of hell?

¶Wherefore, behold, I send unto you prophets, and wise men, and scribes: and some of them ye shall kill and crucify; and some of them shall ye scourge in your synagogues, and persecute them from city to city: that upon you may come all the righteous blood shed upon the earth, from the blood of righteous Abel unto the blood of Zacharias son of Barachias, whom ye slew between the temple and the altar. Verily I say unto you, All these things shall come upon this generation.

*O Jerusalem, Jerusalem, thou that killest the prophets, and stonest them which are sent unto thee, how often would I have gathered thy children together, even as a hen gathereth her chickens under her wings, and ye would not!

Behold, your house is left unto you desolate. For I say unto you, Ye shall not see me henceforth, till ye shall say, Blessed is he that cometh in the name of the Lord.

"NOW IS MY SOUL TROUBLED"

A.D. 30. Age 33. Jerusalem, in the Temple.

John 12, 20-36; 42-50.

CERTAIN Greeks came up to worship at the feast: the same came to Philip, saying, Sir, we would see Jesus.

Philip and Andrew tell Jesus. Jesus answered them, saying,

The hour is come, that the Son of man should be glorified.

Verily, verily, I say unto you, Except a corn of wheat fall into the ground and die, it abideth alone: but if it die, it bringeth forth much fruit. He that loveth his life shall lose it; and he that hateth his life in his world shall keep it unto life eternal.

If any man serve me, let him follow me; and where I am, there shall also my servant be: if any man serve me, him will my Father honor.

Now is my soul troubled; and what shall I say? Father, save me from this hour? but for this cause came I unto this hour.

Father, glorify thy name.

Then came there a voice from heaven, saying, I have both glorified it, and will glorify it again.

The people that stood by, and heard it, said that it thundered: others said, An angel spake.

Jesus said,

This voice came not because of me, but for your sakes.

Now is the judgment of this world: now shall the prince of this world be cast out. And I, if I be lifted up from the earth, will draw all men unto me.

This he said, signifying what death he should die.

The people answered, We have heard out of the law that Christ abideth for ever; and how sayest thou, The Son of man must be lifted up? Who is this Son of man? Then Jesus said,

Yet a little while is the light with you. Walk while ye have the light, lest darkness come upon you: for he that walketh in darkness knoweth not whither he goeth. While ye have light, believe in the light, that ye may be the children of light.

¶Among the chief rulers many believed on Jesus; but because of the Pharisees they did not confess him, lest they should be put out of the synagogue: for they loved the praise of men more than the praise of God.

¶Jesus cried and said,

He that believeth on me believeth not on me, but on him that sent me. And he that seeth me seeth him that sent me.

I am come a light into the world, that whosoever believeth on me should not abide in darkness. And if any man hear my words, and believe not, I judge him not: for I came not to judge the world, but to save the world.

He that rejecteth me, and receiveth not my words, hath one that judgeth him: the word that I have spoken, the same shall judge him in the last day. For I have not spoken of myself; but the Father which sent me, he gave me a commandment, what I should say, and what I should speak. And I know that his commandment is life everlasting: whatsoever 1 speak therefore, even as the Father said unto me, so I speak.

THE TEMPLE DOOMED

A.D. 30. Age 33. Jerusalem. Mt. of Olives.

Matthew 24, 1-31: Mark 13, 1-27: Luke 21, 5-28.

AS Jesus went out from the temple, his disciples came for to show him the buildings of the temple. One saith, Master, see what buildings are here! Some spake of the temple how it was adorned with goodly stones and gifts. Jesus answering said,

*Seest thou these great buildings? See ye not all these things? Verily I say unto you, As for these things which ye behold, the days will come, in the which there shall not be left here one stone upon another, that shall not be thrown down.

¶As Jesus sat upon the mount of Olives, over against the temple, Peter and James, John and Andrew asked him privately, What sign will there be when these things shall come to pass? What shall be the sign of thy coming, and of the end of the world? Jesus answering them began to say,

Take heed lest any man deceive you. For many shall come in my name, saying, I am Christ; and shall deceive many; and the time draweth near; go ye not therefore after them.

Take heed that ye be not deceived but when ye shall hear commotions, and wars, and rumors of wars, see that ye be not troubled; be not terrified. Such things must needs be: for all these things must first come to pass; but the end shall not be yet (is not by and by).

Nation shall rise against nation, and kingdom against kingdom; and there shall be famines, and troubles, and pestilences, and great earthquakes, in divers places; and fearful sights and great signs shall there be from heaven. All these things are the beginnings of sorrows.

¶But take heed to yourselves: for before all these, they shall lay their hands on you, and persecute you; delivering you up to councils, and into prisons, to be afflicted: and in the synagogues ye shall be beaten: and ye shall be brought before rulers and kings for my name's sake. And it shall turn to you for a testimony against them. Then shall they kill you, and ye shall be hated of all nations for my name's sake.

But the gospel must first be published among all nations.

And when they shall lead you, and deliver you up, take no thought beforehand what ye shall speak, neither do ye premeditate: but whatsoever shall be given you in that hour, that speak ye: for it is not ye that speak, but the Holy Ghost. Settle it therefore in your hearts, not to meditate before what ye shall answer; for I will give you a mouth and wisdom, which all your adversaries shall not be able to gainsay nor resist.

And then shall many be offended, * and shall betray one another. And ye shall be betrayed both by parents, and brethren, and kinsfolks, and friends. Now the brother shall betray the brother to death, and the father the son; and children shall rise up against their parents, and shall cause them to be put to death; and some of you shall they cause to be put to death. And ye shall be hated of all men for my name's sake.

But there shall not a hair of your head perish. In your patience possess ye your souls.

And many false prophets shall rise and shall deceive many. And because iniquity shall abound, the love of many shall wax cold. But he that shall endure unto the end, the same shall be saved. And this gospel of the kingdom shall be preached in all the world for a witness unto all nations; and then shall the end come.

¶When ye therefore shall see the abomination of desolation, spoken of by Daniel the prophet, standing in the holy place, where it ought not (let him that readeth understand): and when ye shall see Jerusalem compassed with armies, then know that the desolation thereof is nigh; then let them which are in Judea flee to the mountains: and let them which are in the midst of it depart out; and let not them that are in the countries enter thereinto. And let him that is on the housetop not come down into the house, neither enter therein, to take anything out of his house; and let him which is in the field not return back for to take his clothes.

For these be the days of vengeance, that all things which are written may be fulfilled.

And woe unto them that are with child, and to them that give suck, in those days! for there shall be great distress in the land, and wrath upon the people. And pray ye that your flight be not in winter, neither on the sabbath day: for in those days shall be great affliction, tribulation such as was not since the beginning of the creation which God created, unto this time; no, nor ever in the world shall be. And except that the Lord had shortened those days, there should no flesh be saved: but for the elect's sake, whom he hath chosen, those days shall be shortened.

And they shall fall by the edge of the sword, and shall be led away captive into all nations: and Jerusalem shall be trodden down of the Gentiles, until the times of the Gentiles be fulfilled.

And then if any man shall say to you, Lo, here is Christ; or, lo, he is there;

believe it not: for there shall arise false Christs and false prophets, and shall show great signs and wonders, to seduce; insomuch that, if it were possible, they shall deceive even the very elect.

But take ye heed: behold, I have foretold you all things.

Wherefore if they shall say unto you, Behold, he is in the desert; go not forth: Behold, he is in the secret chambers; believe it not. For as the lightning cometh out of the east, and shineth even unto the west; so shall also the coming of the Son of man be. For wheresoever the carcass is, there will the eagles be gathered together.

¶But immediately, in those days after that tribulation, there shall be signs in the sun, and in the moon, and in the stars: the sun shall be darkened, and the moon shall not give her light, and the stars of heaven shall fall; and the powers that are in the heavens shall be shaken: and upon the earth [shall be] distress of nations, with perplexity; the sea and waves roaring: men's hearts failing them for fear, and for looking after those things which are coming on the earth: for the powers of heaven shall be shaken.

And then shall appear the sign of the Son of man in heaven: and then shall all the tribes of the earth mourn, and they shall see the Son of man coming in the clouds of heaven with power and great glory.

And then shall he send his angels with a great sound of a trumpet, and they shall gather together his elect from the four winds, from the uttermost part of the earth to the uttermost part of heaven; from one end of heaven to another.

And when these things begin to come to pass, then look up, and lift up your heads; for your redemption draweth nigh.

"MY WORDS SHALL NOT PASS AWAY"

A.D. 30. Age 33. Mount of Olives.

Matthew 24, 32-51; 25, 1-13: Mark 13, 28-37: Luke 21, 29-36.

*NOW learn a parable of the fig tree: Behold the fig tree when her branch is yet tender, and putteth forth leaves; and behold the trees when they now shoot forth: ye see and know of your own selves that summer is nigh at hand.

So in like manner, when ye shall see all these things come to pass, know ye that the kingdom of God is nigh at hand, even at the doors. Verily I say unto you, This generation shall not pass, till all these things be done. Heaven and earth shall pass away, but my words shall not pass away.

¶And take heed to yourselves, lest at any time your hearts be overcharged with surfeiting and drunkenness, and cares of this life; and so that day come upon you unawares. For as a snare shall it come on all them that dwell on the face of the whole earth.

Watch ye therefore, and pray always, that ye may be accounted worthy to escape all these things that shall come to pass, and to stand before the Son of man.

¶But of that day and that hour knoweth no man, no, not the angels which are in heaven, neither the Son, but my Father only.

Take ye heed, watch and pray: for ye know not when the time is. *But as the days of Noe were, so shall also the coming of the Son of man be. For as in the days that were before the flood they were eating and drinking, marrying and giving in marriage, until the day that Noe entered into the ark, and knew not till the flood came, and took them all away: so shall also the coming of the Son of man be. Then shall two be in the field; the one shall be taken, and the other left. Two women shall be grinding at the mill; the one shall be taken, and the other left.

¶Watch therefore: for ye know not what hour your Lord doth come.

For the Son of man is as a man taking a far journey, who left his house, and gave authority to his servants, and to every man his work, and commanded the porter to watch.

Watch ye therefore: for ye know not when the master of the house cometh, at even, or at midnight, or at the cockcrowing, or in the morning: lest coming suddenly he find you sleeping.

And what I say unto you I say unto all, Watch.

†But know this, that if the goodman of the house had known in what watch the thief would come, he would have watched, and would not have suffered his house to be broken up. Therefore be ye also ready: for in such an hour as ye think not the Son of man cometh. And what I say unto you I say unto all, Watch.

Who then is a faithful and wise servant, whom his lord hath made ruler over his household, to give them meat in due season?

Blessed is that servant, whom his lord when he cometh shall find so doing. Verily I say unto you, That he shall make him ruler over all his goods.

But and if that evil servant shall say in his heart, My lord delayeth his coming; and shall begin to smit his fellow servants, and to eat and drink with the drunken; the lord of that servant shall come in a day when he looketh not for him, and in an hour that he is not aware of, and shall cut him asunder, and appoint him his portion with the hypocrites: there shall be weeping and gnashing of teeth.

¶Then shall the kingdom of heaven be likened unto ten virgins, which took their lamps, and went forth to meet the bridegroom. And five of them were wise, and five were foolish. They that were foolish took their lamps, and took no oil with them. But the wise took oil in their vessels with their lamps.

While the bridegroom tarried, they all slumbered and slept. And at midnight there was a cry made, Behold, the bridegroom cometh; go ye out to meet him.

Then all those virgins arose, and trimmed their lamps. And the foolish said unto the wise, Give us of your oil; for our lamps are gone out.

But the wise answered, saying, Not so; lest there be not enough for us and you, but go ye rather to them that sell, and buy for yourselves.

And while they went to buy, the bridegroom came: and they that were ready went in with him to the marriage: and the door was shut.

Afterward came also the other virgins, saying, Lord, Lord, open to us. But he answered and said, Verily I say unto you, I know you not.

Watch, therefore, for ye know neither the day nor the hour wherein the Son of man cometh.

PARABLE OF THE TALENTS

A.D. 30. Age 33. Mount of Olives.

Matthew 25, 14-46.

*FOR the kingdom of heaven is as a man travelling into a far country, who called his own servants, and delivered unto them his goods. And unto one he gave five talents, to another, two, and to another, one; to every man according to his several ability; and straightway took his journey.

Then he that had received the five talents went and traded with the same, and made them other five talents. And likewise he that had received two, he also gained other two. But he that had received one went and digged in the earth, and hid his lord's money.

After a long time the lord of those servants cometh, and reckoned with them.

And so he that had received five talents came and brought other five talents, saying, Lord, thou deliveredst unto me five talents: behold, I have gained beside them five talents more. His lord said unto him, Well done, thou good and faithful servant: thou hast been faithful over a few things, I will make thee ruler over many things: enter thou into the joy of thy lord.

He also that had received two talents came and said, Lord, thou deliveredst unto me two talents: behold, I have gained two other talents beside them. His lord said unto him, Well done, good and faithful servant: thou hast been faithful over a few things, I will make thee ruler over many things: enter thou into the joy of thy lord.

Then he which had received the one talent came and said, Lord, I knew thee that thou art a hard man, reaping where thou hast not sown, and gathering where thou hast not strewed; and I was afraid, and went and hid thy talent in the earth: lo, there thou hast that is thine.

His lord answered and said unto him, Thou wicked and slothful servant, thou knewest that I reap where I sowed not, and gather where I have not strewed: Thou oughtest therefore to have put my money to the exchangers, and then at my coming I should have received mine own with usury.

Take therefore the talent from him, and give it unto him which hath ten talents.

For unto every one that hath shall be given, and he shall have abundance: but from him that hath not shall be taken away even that which he hath. And cast ye the unprofitable servant into outer darkness: there shall be weeping and gnashing of teeth.

¶When the Son of man shall come in his glory, and all the holy angels with him, then shall he sit upon the throne of his glory: and before him shall be gathered all nations: and he shall separate them one from another, as a shepherd divideth his sheep from the goats: and he shall set the sheep on his right hand, but the goats on the left.

Then shall the King say unto them on his right hand, Come, ye blessed of my Father, inherit the kingdom prepared for you from the foundation of the world: for I was a hungered, and ye gave me meat: I was thirsty, and ye gave me drink: I was a stranger, and ye took me in: naked, and ye clothed me: I was sick, and ye visited me: I was in prison, and ye came unto me.

Then shall the righteous answer him, saying, Lord, when saw we thee a hungered, and fed thee? or thirsty, and gave thee drink? When saw we thee a stranger, and took thee in? or naked, and clothed thee? Or when saw we thee sick, or in prison, and came unto thee?

And the King shall answer and say unto them, Verily I say unto you, Inasmuch as ye have done it unto one of the least of these my brethren, ye have done it unto me.

Then shall he say also unto them on the left hand, Depart from me, ye cursed, into everlasting fire, prepared for the devil and his angels: for I was a hungered, and ye gave me no meat: I was thirsty, and ye gave me no drink: I was a stranger, and ye took me not in: naked, and ye clothed me not; sick, and in prison, and ye visited me not.

Then shall they also answer him, saying, Lord, when saw we thee a hungered, or athirst, or a stranger, or naked, or sick, or in prison, and did not minister unto thee?

Then he shall answer them, saying, Verily I say unto you, Inasmuch as ye did it not to one of the least of these, ye did it not to me.

And these shall go away into everlasting punishment: but the righteous into life eternal.

"ME YE HAVE NOT ALWAYS"

A.D. 30. Age 33. Bethany.

John 12, 1-11: Matthew 26, 6-13: Mark 14, 3-9.

JESUS came, six days before the passover, to Bethany, where Lazarus was, whom he had raised from the dead. In the house of Simon the leper there, they made Jesus a supper; and Martha served. Lazarus was one of them at the table with Jesus.

Mary, having an alabaster box of ointment of spikenard very precious, brake the box, and poured it on Jesus' head as he sat at meat, and anointed his feet, and wiped his feet with her hair. *

Some disciples had indignation, saying, To what purpose is this waste? Judas Iscariot [which should betray Jesus] saith, Why was not this ointment sold for three hundred pence, and given to the poor? And they murmured against Mary.

When Jesus understood it, he said.

Let her alone: why trouble ye the woman? Against the day of my burying hath she done this.

For ye have the poor with you always, and whensoever ye will ye may do them good: but me ye have not always. She hath wrought a good work upon me; for she hath done what she could: for in that she hath poured this ointment on my body, she is come aforehand to anoint my body to the burying (she did it for my burial). Why trouble ye her?

Verily I say unto you, Wheresoever this gospel shall be preached throughout the whole world, there shall also this that this woman hath done, be told for a memorial of her.

The Jews knew that Jesus was there: and they came, not for Jesus' sake only, but that they might see Lazarus, whom he had raised from the dead.

But the chief priests consulted that they might put Lazarus also to death; because that by reason of him many of the Jews believed on Jesus.

THE THIRTY PIECES OF SILVER

A.D. 30. Age 33. Bethany. Jerusalem: Upper Room.

Luke 21, 37-38; 22, 1-18: Matthew 26, 1-5; 14-20: Mark 14, 1-2; 10-17: John 13, 2-17.

NOW the feast of unleavened bread drew nigh, which is called the passover. In the daytime Jesus was teaching in the temple. At night he abode in the mount of Olives; in the morning the people came early to the temple for to hear him.

Two days before the feast, the chief priests, the scribes, and the elders of the people, assembled unto the palace of the high priest Caiaphas, and consulted that they might take Jesus by craft. But they said, Not on the feast day, lest there be an uproar of the people.

¶Then Judas surnamed Iscariot, one of the twelve, went and said unto the chief priests, What will ye give me, and I will deliver Jesus unto you? They were glad, and covenanted to give Judas thirty pieces of silver. Judas promised: and sought opportunity how he might conveniently betray Jesus unto them in the absence of the multitude.

¶Now before the feast of the passover, when Jesus knew that his hour was come that he should depart out of this world unto the Father, he said unto his disciples,

Ye know that after two days is the feast of passover, and the Son of man is betrayed to be crucified.

Then came the first day of the feast of unleavened bread, when the passover must be killed; and Jesus sent Peter and John, saying,

Go and prepare the passover, that we may eat.

And they said, Where wilt thou that we prepare? He said,

When ye are entered into the city, behold, there shall meet you a man bearing a pitcher of water: go ye into the city to such a man, and follow him into the house where he entereth in. And wheresoever he shall go in, say ye to the goodman of the house, The Master saith unto thee, My time is at hand; I will keep the passover at thy house with my disciples. Where is the guestchamber, where I shall eat the passover with my disciples?

And he will shew you a large upper room furnished and prepared: there make ready for us.

They went, and found as he had said: and they made ready the passover. In the evening Jesus cometh with the twelve apostles, and when the hour was come, he sat down, the twelve with him.

And he said unto them,

With desire I have desired to eat this passover with you before I suffer: for I say unto you, I will not any more eat thereof, until it be fulfilled in the kingdom of God.

And he took the cup and gave thanks, and said,

Take this, and divide it among yourselves: for I say unto you, I will not drink of the fruit of the vine, until the kingdom of God shall come.

Supper being ended, Jesus riseth; and he laid aside his garments, and took a towel, and girded himself. After that he poureth water into a basin, and began to wash the disciples' feet, and to wipe them with the towel.

Then Simon Peter saith, Lord, dost thou wash my feet? Jesus answered,

What I do thou knowest not now; but thou shalt know hereafter.

Peter saith unto him, Thou shalt never wash my feet. Jesus answered,

If I wash thee not, thou hast no part with me.

Peter saith, Lord, not my feet only, but also my hands and my head. Jesus saith unto him,

He that is washed needeth not save to wash his feet, but is clean every whit: and ye are clean, but not all.

For he knew who should betray him; therefore said he,

Ye are not all clean.

So after he had washed their feet, and had taken his garments, and was set down again, he said unto them,

Know ye what I have done to you?

Ye call me Master and Lord: and ye say well; for so I am. If I then, your Lord and Master, have washed your feet: ye also ought to wash one another's feet. For I have given you an example, that ye should do as I have done to you.

Verily, verily, I say unto you, The servant is not greater than his lord: neither he that is sent greater than he that sent him. If ye know these things, happy are ye if ye do them.

THE LAST SUPPER

A.D. 30 Age 33. Jerusalem: Upper Room.

Paul I. Corinthians 11, 24-25: Matthew 26, 21-29: Mark 14, 18-25: Luke 22, 19-38: John 13, 18-38; 14, 1-4.

THE same night in which he was betrayed, the Lord Jesus took bread, and gave thanks, and blessed it, and brake it, and gave it to his disciples, and said,

Take, eat; this is my body, which is given * for you: this do in remembrance of me.

As they sat and did eat, Jesus said,

Verily I say unto you, that one of you shall betray me.

¶But, behold, the hand of him that betrayeth me is with me on the table. And truly the Son of man goeth, as it was determined: but woe unto that man by whom he is betrayed!

I speak not of you all: I know whom I have chosen: but that the Scripture may be fulfilled, He that eateth bread with me hath lifted up his heel against me.

Now I tell you before it come, that, when it is come to pass, ye may believe that I am he.

Verily, verily, I say unto you, He that receiveth whomsoever I send receiveth me; and he that receiveth me receiveth him that sent me.

When Jesus had thus said, he was troubled in spirit; and testified,

Verily, verily, I say unto you, that one of you which eateth with me shall betray me.

The disciples looked one on another, doubting of whom he spake. They were exceeding sorrowful, and began every one of them to say unto Jesus, one by one, Lord, is it I? and another, Is it I? He answered,

It is one of the twelve: he that dippeth his hand with me in the dish, the same shall betray me.

The Son of man indeed goeth, as it is written of him; but woe to that man by whom the Son of man is betrayed! good were it for that man if he had never been born.

Now there was leaning on Jesus' bosom one whom Jesus loved. † Simon Peter beckoned to him, that he should ask who it should be of whom Jesus spake. He then lying on Jesus' breast saith, Lord, who is it? Jesus answered,

He it is, to whom I shall give a sop, when I have dipped it.

He dipped the sop: he gave it to Judas Iscariot: then said unto him,

That thou doest, do quickly.

Judas said, Master, is it I? Jesus said unto him,

Thou hast said.

Judas went immediately out: and it was night. When he was gone, Jesus said,

Now is the Son of man glorified, and God is glorified in him. If God be glorified in him, God shall also glorify him in himself, and shall straightway glorify him.

Little children, yet a little while I am with you. Ye shall seek me: and as I said unto the Jews, * so now I say to you, Whither I go, ye cannot come.

A new commandment I give unto you, That ye love one another; as I have loved you, that ye also love one another. By this shall all men know that ye are my disciples, if ye have love one to another.

¶Simon Peter said unto him, Lord, whither goest thou? Jesus answered,

Whither I go, thou canst not follow me now: but thou shalt follow me afterwards.

Peter said, Lord, why cannot I follow thee now? I will lay down my life for thy sake. Jesus answered,

Wilt thou lay down thy life for my sake? Verily, verily, I say unto thee, The cock shall not crow, till thou hast denied me thrice.

¶There was a strife among the disciples, which of them should be accounted the greatest. And Jesus said unto them,

The kings of the Gentile exercise lordship over them; and they that exercise authority upon them are called benefactors. But ye shall not be so; but he that is greatest among you, let him be as the younger; and he that is chief, as he that doth serve.

For whether is greater, he that sitteth at meat, or he that serveth? is not he that sitteth at meat? but I am among you as he that serveth.

Ye are they which have continued with me in my temptations. And I appoint unto you a kingdom, as my father hath appointed unto me; that ye may eat and drink at my table in my kingdom, and sit on thrones judging the twelve tribes of Israel.

¶And the Lord said,

Simon, Simon, behold, Satan hath desired to have you, that he may sift you as wheat: but I have prayed for thee, that thy faith fail not: and when thou art converted, strengthen thy brethren.

And Simon said, Lord, I am ready to go with thee, both into prison, and to death. And Jesus said,

I tell thee, Peter, the cock shall not crow this day, before that thou shalt thrice deny that thou knowest me.

And he said unto them,

When I sent you without purse, and scrip, and shoes, lacked ye anything?

They said, Nothing. Then said Jesus,

But now, he that hath a purse, let him take it, and likewise his scrip: and he that hath no sword, let him sell his garment, and buy one.

For I say unto you, that this that is written must yet be accomplished in me, And he was reckoned among the transgressors.

For the things concerning me have an end.

And they said, Lord, behold, here are two swords. And he answered,

It is enough.

When he had supped, Jesus after the same manner took the cup, and when he had given thanks, gave it to them, saying,

Drink ye all of it.

And they all drank of it. And he said unto them,

This cup is the new testament in my blood, which is shed for you; for this is my blood of the new testament which is shed for many for the remission of sins: this do ye, as oft as ye drink it, in remembrance of me.

Verily I say unto you, I will drink henceforth no more of this fruit of the vine, until that day when I drink it new with you in the kingdom of God, my Father's kingdom.

Let not your heart be troubled: ye believe in God, believe also in me.

In my Father's house are many mansions: if it were not so, I would have told you. I go to prepare a place for you. And if I go and prepare a place for you, I will come again, and receive you unto myself; that where I am, there ye may be also. And whither I go ye know, and the way ye know.

THE LAST SUPPER (CONTINUED)

A.D. 30. Age 33. Jerusalem: Upper Room.

John 14, 5-31.

THOMAS saith unto Jesus, Lord, we know not whither thou goest; and how can we know the way. Jesus saith unto him,

I am the way, the truth, and the life: no man cometh unto the Father, but by me. If ye had known me, ye should have known my Father also: and from henceforth ye know him, and have seen him.

Philip saith, Lord, shew us the Father, and it sufficeth us. Jesus answered,

Have I been so long time with you, and yet hast thou not known me, Philip? he that hath seen me hath seen the Father; and how sayest thou then, Shew us the Father?

Believest thou not that I am in the Father, and the Father in me? The words I speak unto you, I speak not of myself: but the Father that dwelleth in me, he doeth the works. Believe me that I am in the Father, and the Father in me: or else believe me for the very works' sake.

Verily, verily, I say unto you, He that believeth on me, the works that I do shall he do also; and greater works than these shall he do; because I go unto my Father.

And whatsoever ye shall ask in my name, that will I do, that the Father may be glorified in the Son. If ye shall ask anything in my name, I will do it.

¶If ye love me keep my commandments. And I will pray the Father, and he shall give you another Comforter, that he may abide with you for ever; even the Spirit of truth; whom the world cannot receive, because it seeth him not, neither knoweth him: but ye know him; for he dwelleth with you, and shall be in you. I will not leave you comfortless; I will come to you.

Yet a little while, and the world seeth me no more; but ye see me: because I live, ye shall live also. At that day ye shall know that I am in my Father, and ye in me, and I in you.

He that hath my commandments, and keepeth them, he it is that loveth me: and he that loveth me shall be loved of my Father, and I will love him, and will manifest myself to him.

Judas, not Iscariot, saith unto him, Lord, how is it that thou wilt manifest thyself unto us, and not unto the world? Jesus answered,

If a man love me, he will keep my words: and my Father will love him, and we will come unto him, and make our abode with him. He that loveth me not keepth not my sayings: and the word which ye hear is not mine, but the Father's which sent me.

These things have I spoken unto you, being yet present with you.

But the Comforter, which is the Holy Ghost, whom the Father will send in my name, he shall teach you all things, and bring all things to your remembrance, whatsoever I have said unto you. Peace I leave with you, my peace I give unto you: not as the world giveth, give I unto you.

Let not your heart be troubled, neither let it be afraid. Ye have heard how I said unto you, I go away, and come again unto you. If ye loved me, ye would rejoice, because I said, I go unto the Father: for my Father is greater than I.

And now I have told you before it come to pass, that, when it is come to pass, ye might believe.

Hereafter I will not talk much with you: for the prince of this world cometh, and hath nothing in me. But that the world may know that I love the Father; and as the Father gave me commandment, even so I do.

THE LAST SUPPER (CONTINUED)

A.D. 30. Age 33. Jerusalem: Upper Room.

John 15, 1-27; 16, 1.

I AM the true vine, and my Father is the husbandman. Every branch in me that beareth not fruit he taketh away: and every branch that beareth fruit, he purgeth it, that it may bring forth more fruit. Now ye are clean through the word which I have spoken unto you.

Abide in me, and I in you. As the branch cannot bear fruit of itself, except it abide in the vine; no more can ye, except ye abide in me. I am the vine, ye are the branches; he that abideth in me, and I in him, the same bringeth forth much fruit; for without me ye can do nothing.

If a man abide not in me, he is cast forth as a branch, and is withered; and men gather them, and cast them into the fire, and they are burned. If ye abide in me, and my words abide in you, ye shall ask what ye will, and it shall be done unto you.

Herein is my Father glorified, that ye bear much fruit; so shall ye be my disciples.

As the Father hath loved me, so have I loved you: continue ye in my love. If ye keep my commandments, ye shall abide in my love; even as I have kept my Father's commandments and abide in his love.

These things have I spoken unto you, that my joy might remain in you, and that your joy might be full. This is my commandment, that ye love one another, as I have loved you.

Greater love hath no man than this, that a man lay down his life for his friends. Ye are my friends, if ye do whatsoever I command you. Henceforth I call you not servants; for the servant knoweth not what his lord doeth; but I have called you friends; for all things that I have heard of my Father I have made known unto you.

Ye have not chosen me, but I have chosen you, and ordained you, that ye should go and bring forth fruit, and that your fruit should remain: that whatsoever ye shall ask of the Father in my name, he may give it you. These things I command you, that ye love one another.

If the world hate you, ye know that it hated me before it hated you. If ye were of the world, the world would love his own: but because ye are not of the world but I have chosen you out of the world, therefore the world hateth you.

Remember the word that I said unto you, The servant is not greater than his lord.

If they have persecuted me, they will also persecute you; if they have kept my saying, they will keep yours also. But all these things will they do unto you for my name's sake, because they know not him that sent me.

If I had not come and spoken unto them, they had not had sin: but now they have no cloak for their sin. He that hateth me hateth my Father also.

If I had not done among them the works which none other man did, they had not had sin: but now have they both seen and hated both me and my Father.

But this cometh to pass, that the word might be fulfilled that is written in their law, They hated me without a cause.

But when the Comforter is come, whom I will send unto you from the Father, even the Spirit of truth, which proceedeth from the Father, he shall testify of me: and ye also shall bear witness, because ye have been with me from the beginning.

These things have I spoken unto you, that ye should not be offended. *

THE LAST SUPPER (CONTINUED)

A.D. 30. Age 33. Jerusalem: Upper Room.

John 16, 2-33.

THEY shall put you out of the synagogues: yea, the time cometh, that whosoever killeth you, you will think that he doeth God service. And these things will they do unto you, because they have not known the Father, nor me.

But these things have I told you, that when the time shall come, ye may remember that I told you of them. And these things I said not unto you at the beginning, because I was with you.

But now I go my way to him that sent me; and none of you asketh me, Whither goest thou? But because I have said these things unto you, sorrow hath filled your heart. Nevertheless I tell you the truth; It is expedient for you that I go away: for if I go not away, the Comforter will not come unto you; but if I depart, I will send him unto you. And when he is come, he will reprove the world of sin, and of righteousness, and of judgment: of sin, because they believed not on me; of righteousness, because I go to my Father, and ye see me no more; of judgment, because the prince of this world is judged.

I have yet many things to say unto you, but ye cannot bear them now. Howbeit when he, the Spirit of truth, is come, he will guide you into all truth: for he shall not speak of himself; but whatsoever he shall hear, that shall he speak: and he will shew you things to come. He shall glorify me: for he shall receive of mine, and shall shew it unto you.

All things that the Father hath are mine: therefore said I, that he shall take of mine, and shall shew it unto you.

A little while, and ye shall not see me: and again, a little while, and ye shall see me, because I go to the Father.

Then said some of his disciples among themselves, What is this that he saith, A little while, and ye shall not see me: and again, A little while, and ye shall see me: and, Because I go to the Father?

Now Jesus knew that they were desirous to ask him, and he said,

Do ye inquire among yourselves of that I said, A little while, and ye shall not see me: and again, a little while, and ye shall see me?

Verily, verily, I say unto you, That ye shall weep and lament, but the world shall rejoice; and ye shall be sorrowful, but your sorrow shall be turned into joy.

A woman when she is in travail hath sorrow, because her hour is come: but as soon as she is delivered of the child, she remembereth no more the anguish, for joy that a man is born into the world. And ye now therefore have sorrow: but I will see you again, and your heart shall rejoice, and your joy no man taketh from you.

And in that day ye shall ask me nothing. Verily, verily, I say unto you, Whatsoever ye shall ask the Father in my name, he will give it you. Hitherto have ye asked nothing in my name: ask, and ye shall receive, that your joy may be full.

These things have I spoken unto you in proverbs: but the time cometh, when I shall no more speak unto you in proverbs, but I shall shew you plainly of the Father. At that day ye shall ask in my name: and 1 say not unto you, that I will pray the Father for you: for the Father himself loveth you, because ye have loved me, and have believed that I came out from God.

I came forth from the Father, and am come into the world: again, I leave the world, and go to the Father.

His disciples said unto him, Lo, now speakest thou plainly, and speakest no proverb. Now are we sure that thou knowest all things: by this we believe that thou camest forth from God. Jesus answered,

Do ye now believe? Behold, the hour cometh, yea, is now come, that ye shall be scattered, every man to his own, and shall leave me alone: and yet I am not alone, because the Father is with me.

These things I have spoken unto you, that in me ye might have peace. In the world ye shall have tribulation: but be of good cheer; I have overcome the world.

THE LAST SUPPER
(CONTINUED)

A.D. 30. Age 33. Jerusalem: Upper Room.

John 17, 1-26.

THESE words spake Jesus, and lifted up his eyes to heaven,

Father, the hour is come; glorify thy Son, that thy Son also may glorify thee: as thou hast given him power over all flesh, that he should give eternal life to as many as thou hast given him. And this is life eternal, that they might know thee the only true God, and Jesus Christ whom thou hast sent. I have glorified thee on the earth: I have finished the work which thou gavest me to do. And now, O Father, glorify thou me with thine own self with the glory which I had with thee before the world was.

I have manifested thy name unto the men which thou gavest me out of the world: thine they were, and thou gavest them me; and they have kept thy word. Now they have known that all things whatsoever thou hast given me are of thee. For I have given unto them the words which thou gavest me; and they have received them, and have known surely that I came out from thee, and they have believed that thou didst send me.

I pray for them: I pray not for the world, but for them which thou hast given me; for they are thine. And all mine are thine, and thine are mine; and I am glorified in them. And now I am no more in the world, but these are in the world, and I come to thee. Holy Father, keep through thine own name those whom thou hast given me, that they may be one, as we are. While I was with them in the world, I kept them in thy name: those that thou gavest me I have kept, and none of them is lost, but the son of perdition: that the Scripture might be fulfilled.

And now come I to thee; and these things I speak in the world, that they might have my joy fulfilled in themselves. I have given them thy word; and the world hath hated them, because they are not of the world, even as I am not of the world. I pray not that thou shouldest take them out of the world, but that thou shouldest keep them from the evil. They are not of the world, even as I am not of the world. Sanctify them through thy truth: thy word is truth. As thou hast sent me into the world, even so have I also sent them into the world. And for their sakes I sanctify myself, that they also might be sanctified through the truth.

Neither pray I for these alone, but for them also which shall believe on me through their word; that they all may be one; as thou, Father, art in me, and I in thee, that they also may be one in us: that the world may believe that thou hast sent me. And the glory which thou gavest me I have given them: that they may be one, even as we are one; I in them, and thou in me, that they may be made perfect in one; and that the world may know that thou hast sent me, and hast loved them, as thou hast loved me.

Father, I will that they also, whom thou hast given me, be with me where I am; that they may behold my glory, which thou hast given me: for thou lovedst me before the foundation of the world.

O righteous Father, the world hath not known thee: but I have known thee, and these have known that thou hast sent me. And I have declared unto them thy name, and will declare it: that the love wherewith thou hast loved me may be in them, and I in them.

Arise, let us go hence.

IN GETHSEMANE

A.D. 30. Age 33. Mount of Olives. Gethsemane.

Matthew 26, 30-47: Mark 14, 26-43: Luke 22, 39-47: John 18, 1-9.

*WHEN they had sung a hymn, Jesus came out; and he went as he was wont, to the mount of Olives; and his disciples followed him. Then saith Jesus unto them,

All ye shall be offended † because of me this night: for it is written, I will smite the Shepherd, and the sheep of the flock shall be scattered abroad.

But after that I am risen again, I will go before you into Galilee.

Peter answered, Although all shall be offended because of thee, yet will not I. I will never be offended. Jesus saith unto him,

Verily I say unto thee, That this day, even in this night, before the cock crow twice, thou shalt deny me thrice.

But Peter spake the more vehemently, Though I should die with thee, yet will I not deny thee in any wise. Likewise said they all.

¶They came to a place named Gethsemane, over the brook Cedron, where was a garden, into the which Jesus entered and his disciples. And he said unto them,

Sit ye here, while I go and pray yonder. Pray that ye enter not into temptation.

He was withdrawn from them about a stone's cast; with him Peter, James, and John. Then saith he unto them,

My soul is exceeding sorrowful, even unto death: tarry ye here, and watch with me.

He went forward a little, and kneeled, and prayed,

Abba, Father, all things are possible unto thee: Father, if it be possible, if thou be willing, remove this cup from me: nevertheless not my will, but thine, be done. ‡

Being in an agony he prayed more earnestly: and his sweat was as it were great drops of blood.

And he cometh unto the disciples, and findeth them sleeping. He saith unto Peter,

Simon, sleepest thou? What, couldest not thou watch with me one hour? Watch ye and pray, lest ye enter into temptation. The spirit truly is willing, but the flesh is weak.

Jesus went away the second time, and prayed,

O my Father, if it be possible, let this cup pass from me: if this cup may not pass away from me, except I drink it, thy will be done.

When he rose up, and was come to the disciples, he found them sleeping for sorrow, and he said unto them,

Why sleep ye? rise and pray, lest ye enter into temptation.

He went away again, and prayed the third time, saying the same words,

Father, take away this cup from me: nevertheless not what I will, but what thou wilt.

And he cometh the third time, and again he found the disciples asleep; and he saith,

Sleep on now, and take your rest: it is enough: behold, the hour is come; behold, the hour is at hand, and the Son of man is betrayed into the hands of sinners. Rise up, let us be going: lo, he is at hand that doth betray me.

¶Judas knew the place: for Jesus ofttimes resorted thither with his disciples.

Immediately, while Jesus yet spake, cometh Judas, and with him a multitude: a band of men from the chief priests and Pharisees; and the scribes and elders of the people, with lanterns and torches, and weapons: swords and staves.

Jesus knowing all things that should come upon him, went forth, and said unto them,

Whom seek ye?

They answered, Jesus of Nazareth. Jesus saith,

I am he.

They went backward, and fell to the ground. Then asked he them again,

Whom seek ye?

They said, Jesus of Nazareth. Jesus answered,

I have told you that I am he: if therefore ye seek me, let these go their way.

That the saying might be fulfilled, which he spake,

Of them which thou gavest me have I lost none.

THE BETRAYAL: JUDAS' KISS

A.D. 30. Age 33. Gethsemane. Jerusalem.

Matthew 26, 48-58: Mark 14, 44-50; 53-54: Luke 22, 47-55: John 18, 10-16; 19-23.

NOW Judas had given them a token (sign), saying, Whomsoever I shall kiss, that same is he: hold him fast.

*Judas went before, and drew near unto Jesus, to kiss him: and saith, Hail, Master; and kissed him.

Jesus said unto Judas,

Friend, wherefore art thou come? † Judas, betrayest thou the Son of man with a kiss?

Then they laid hands on Jesus.

They which were about him said, Lord, shall we smite them with the sword?

And Simon Peter having a sword smote the high priest's servant, Malchas, and cut off his right ear. Jesus said,

Suffer thus far.

And he touched his ear and healed him. Then said Jesus unto Peter,

Put up again thy sword into his place in the sheath: for all they that take the sword shall perish with the sword: the cup which my Father hath given me, shall I not drink it? Thinkest thou that I cannot now pray to my Father, and he shall presently give me more than twelve legions of angels? But how then shall the Scriptures be fulfilled, that thus it must be?

In that same hour said Jesus unto the multitude,

Be ye come out, as against a thief, with swords and staves for to take me?

When I sat daily with you, teaching in the temple, ye stretched forth no hands against me: ye laid no hold on me: ye took me not: but this is your hour, and the power of darkness. But all this was done that the Scriptures of the prophets might be fulfilled. The Scriptures must be fulfilled.

Then all the disciples forsook him, and fled.

¶The officers of the Jews bound Jesus and led him away. They brought him into the palace of the high priest, Caiaphas that year.

Simon Peter followed, to see the end. And so did another disciple: that disciple was known to Caiaphas, and went with Jesus into the palace. But Peter stood at the door without. Then went out that disciple and spake unto her that kept the door, and brought in Peter.

When they had kindled a fire in the midst of the hall, Peter sat amongst the servants, and warmed himself at the fire.

¶With Caiaphas the high priest were assembled the chief priests and the elders and the scribes.

Caiaphas asked Jesus of his disciples, and of his doctrine, Jesus answered,

I spake openly to the world: I ever taught in the synagogues, and in the temple, whither the Jews always resort: and in secret have I said nothing. Ask them which heard me, what I have said unto them: behold, they know what I said. Why askest thou me?

When Jesus had thus spoken, one of the officers struck him with the palm of his hand, saying, Answerest thou the high priest so? Jesus answered,

If I have spoken evil, bear witness to the evil: but if well, why smitest thou me?

CHRIST'S TRIAL

A.D. 30. Age 33. Jerusalem.

Matthew 26, 59-75; 27, 1-7: Mark 14, 55-72: Luke 22, 56-71: John 18, 17-27.

THE chief priests and all the council sought witness against Jesus, to put him to death. Many bare false witness against him, but their witness agreed not together. At the last came two, saying, We heard this fellow say, I am able to destroy the temple of God, that is made with hands, and within three days I will build another made without hands.

The high priest arose, and asked Jesus, Answerest thou nothing? But Jesus held his peace, and answered nothing.

The high priest said, Tell us whether thou be the Christ, the Son of God. And Jesus said,

Thou hast said. I am. Nevertheless I say unto you, Hereafter shall ye see the Son of man sitting on the right hand of power, and coming in the clouds of heaven.

Then saith the high priest, Now ye have heard his blasphemy: what need ye any further witnesses? What think ye?

They answered, He is guilty of death.

When they had blindfolded Jesus, they struck him on the face, and say unto him, Prophesy, who is it that smote thee?

¶Now Peter was beneath in the palace: and the damsel that kept the door came and looked upon him as he sat by the fire, and said, Thou also wart with Jesus of Galilee.

But he denied before them all, saying, I know him not: I know not, neither understand I what thou sayest.

And he went into the porch; and the cock crew.

After a little while another saw Peter, and said, Thou art also of them, for thou art a Galilean: thy speech agreeth thereto: thy speech betrayeth thee.

And Peter denied again, Man, I am not.

About the space of an hour after, another confidently affirmed, Of a truth this fellow was with Jesus.

But Peter began to swear, saying, I know not this man of whom ye speak.

And the second time the cock crew. Then Peter called to mind the word that Jesus said unto him,

Before the cock crow twice, thou shalt deny me thrice.

And when Peter thought thereon, he wept. *

¶As soon as it was day, the elders of the people, and the chief priests and the scribes led Jesus into their council, saying, Art thou the Christ? And he said,

If I tell you, ye will not believe: and if I also ask you, ye will not answer me, nor let me go. Hereafter shall the Son of man sit on the right hand of the power of God.

Then said they, Art thou then the Son of God? And Jesus said,

Ye say that I am.

They said, We ourselves have heard of his own mouth.

And the whole council held a consultation, to put Jesus to death.

¶Judas, when he saw that Jesus was condemned, repented, and brought the thirty pieces of silver to the chief priests, saying, I have sinned in that I have betrayed the innocent blood.

They said, What is that to us? see thou to that.

Then Judas cast down the pieces of silver in the temple, and went and hanged himself.

The chief priests said, It is the price of blood: it is not lawful to put them into the treasury. They took counsel, and bought with them the potter's field, to bury strangers in.

CHRIST BEFORE PILATE"CRUCIFY HIM"

A.D. 30. Age 33. Jerusalem.

John 18, 28-40; 19, 1-16: Luke 23, 1-11; 13-25: Mark 15, 1-15: Matthew 27, 11-26.

THE whole council arose and led Jesus away from the high priest, Caiaphas, and delivered him to Pontius Pilate the governor, in the hall of judgment.

Pilate went out unto them, and said, Take ye him, and judge him according to your law.

The Jews answered, It is not lawful for us to put any man to death.

Then Pilate entered into the judgment hall again, and called Jesus, and said unto him, Art thou the King of Jews? Jesus answered,

Sayest thou this thing of thyself, or did others tell it thee of me?

Pilate answered, Am I a Jew? Thine own nation have delivered thee unto me: what hast thou done? Jesus answered,

My kingdom is not of this world: if my kingdom were of this world, then would my servants fight, that I should not be delivered to the Jews: but now is my kingdom not from hence.

Pilate therefore said, Art thou a king then? Jesus answered,

Thou sayest that I am a king. To this end was I born, and for this cause came I into the world, that I should bear witness unto the truth. very one that is of the truth heareth my voice.

Pilate answered, What is truth? And when he had said this, he went out again unto the Jews, and saith unto them, I find in him no fault at all. But ye have a custom that I should release unto you one at the passover: will ye that I release the King of the Jews?

Then cried they all, Not this man, but Barabbas.

Now Barabbas was a robber.

The chief priests and the officers cried out, Crucify him, crucify him.

Pilate saith, Take ye him, and crucify him: for I find no fault in him.

The Jews answered, By our law he ought to die, because he made himself the Son of God.

¶When Pilate heard that saying, he saith unto Jesus, Whence art thou? But Jesus gave no answer.

Then saith Pilate, Speakest thou not unto me? knowest thou not that I have power to crucify thee, and have power to release thee? Jesus answered,

Thou couldest have no power at all against me, except it were given thee from above: therefore he that delivered me unto thee hath the greater sin.

Thenceforth Pilate sought to release Jesus: but the Jews cried out, We found this fellow forbidding to give tribute to Cesar, saying that he himself is Christ a king. If thou let this man go, thou art not Cesar's friend: whosoever maketh himself a king speaketh against Cesar.

Pilate asked him, Art thou the King of the Jews? And Jesus saith,

Thou sayest it.

The chief priests accused him of many things: but he answered nothing.

And Pilate asked him again, Answerest thou nothing? hearest thou not how many things they witness against thee?

Jesus answered him to never a word; so that Pilate marvelled: and he said to the people, I find no fault in this man.

They were the more fierce, saying, He stirreth up the people throughout Jewry, from Galilee to this place.

When Pilate heard of Galilee, he asked whether the man were a Galilean. And as soon as he knew that Jesus belonged unto Herod's jurisdiction, he sent him to Herod, who was at Jerusalem at that time.

¶Herod was exceeding glad: for he had heard many things of Jesus; and had hoped to see some miracle done by him. He questioned with Jesus in many words; but Jesus answered him nothing. And Herod sent him back to Pilate.

¶Pilate called together the chief priests and the rulers of the people; and he said unto them, Ye have brought this man unto me, as one that perverteth the people; and, behold, I, having examined him before you, have found no fault in him touching those things whereof ye accuse him: no, nor yet Herod.

¶Now at that feast the governor must of necessity release unto the people a prisoner, whom they would.

Pilate therefore said, Will ye that I release unto you Barabbas? or Jesus which is called the Christ?

They cried out all at once, Release Barabbas.

Pilate saith, What shall I do then with Jesus?

They cried out again, Let him be crucified.

Pilate saith, Shall I crucify your King?

The chief priests answered, We have no king but Cesar.

¶When Pilate saw that he could prevail nothing, he took water, and washed his hands before the multitude, saying, I am innocent of the blood of this just person: see ye to it.

Then answered the people, His blood be on us, and on our children.

And so Pilate, willing to content the people, gave sentence that it should be as they required. He released him that for sedition and murder was cast into prison: but he delivered Jesus, when he had scourged him, to their will, to be crucified.

THE CRUCIFIXION—"FATHER, FORGIVE THEM"

A.D. 30. Age 33. Jerusalem. Golgotha: Calvary.

Matthew 27, 27-38: Mark 15, 16-27: Luke 23, 26-34: John 19, 17-20.

THE soldiers of the governor led Jesus into the common hall, called Pretorium. They stripped him, and clothed him with purple (put on him a scarlet robe): they platted a crown of thorns, and put it about his head.

¶Then came Jesus forth wearing the crown of thorns, and the purple robe. They mocked him, saying, Hail, King of the Jews!

After they had mocked him, they took off the purple from him, put his own raiment on him, smote him with their hands, and led him away to crucify him.

There followed a great company of people, and of women, which bewailed him. But Jesus turning said,

Daughters of Jerusalem, weep not for me, but weep for yourselves, and for your children. For, behold, the days are coming, in the which they shall say, Blessed are the barren, and the wombs that never bare, and the paps which never gave suck.

Then shall they begin to say to the mountains, Fall on us: and to the hills, Cover us.

For if they do these things in a green tree, what shall be done in the dry?

And Jesus bearing his cross went forth.

As they came out, one Simon, a man of Cyrene, passed by, coming out of the country: him they compelled, and on him they laid the cross, that he might bear it after Jesus.

¶When they were come to a place called the place of a skull, which is in the Hebrew, Golgotha: to the place called Calvary, they gave to Jesus wine mingled with myrrh (vinegar mingled with gall): when he had tasted thereof, he would not drink. It was the third hour.

And there they crucified Jesus: him and the two malefactors: one on the right hand, and the other on the left, and Jesus in the midst. Then said Jesus,

Father, forgive them; for they know not what they do.

Pilate wrote a title, and put it on the cross. It was written in Hebrew, and Greek, and Latin: JESUS OF NAZARETH THE KING OF THE JEWS.

"IT IS FINISHED"

A.D. 30. Age 33. Jerusalem. Golgotha: Calvary.

Matthew 27, 39-56: Mark 15, 29-41: Luke 23, 35-49: John 19, 23-30.

THE soldiers, when they had crucified Jesus, took his garments, and made four parts, to every soldier a part: casting lots upon them.

The people that passed by derided him, wagging their heads, and saying, Ah, thou that destroyest the temple, and buildest it in three days, save thyself!

The soldiers also mocked him, saying, If thou be the King of the Jews, save thyself!

Likewise the chief priests mocking said among themselves with the scribes, He saved others; himself he cannot save!

One of the two thieves which were crucified with him cast the same in his teeth; but the other rebuked him, saying, Dost thou not fear God? We receive the due reward of our deeds: but this man hath done nothing amiss.

And he said unto Jesus, Lord, remember me when thou comest into thy kingdom.

Jesus said unto him,

Verily I say unto thee, To day shalt thou be with me in paradise.

¶Now there stood by the cross Jesus' mother, and his mother's sister; Mary the wife of Cleophas, and Mary Magdalene. Jesus saw his mother, and the disciple standing by, whom he loved: * and he saith unto his mother,

Woman, behold thy son!

Then saith he to the disciple,

Behold thy mother!

And from that hour that disciple took her unto his own home.

¶Now from the sixth hour there was darkness over all the land until the ninth hour. At the ninth hour Jesus cried with a loud voice, saying,

My God, my God, why hast thou forsaken me?

After this, Jesus knowing that all things were now accomplished, saith,

I thirst.

Straightway one of them ran, and filled a sponge with vinegar, put it upon hysop (on a reed), and put it to Jesus' mouth. When he had received the vinegar, he said,

It is finished.

And when he had cried again with a loud voice, he said,

Father, into thy hands I commend my spirit!

Having said thus, Jesus bowed his head, and yielded up the ghost.

¶All his acquaintance stood afar off, beholding these things. There were also women looking on: among which was Mary Magdalene; and Mary the mother of James the less and of Joses; and Salome the mother of Zebedee's children; and many other women which came up with Jesus into Jerusalem.

LAID IN THE TOMB

A.D. 30. Age 33. Jerusalem: The Sepulchre.

Mark 15, 42-47: Luke 23, 50-56: John 19, 38-42: Matthew 27, 57-66.

AND now when the even was come, because it was the preparation, that is, the day before the sabbath, Joseph of Arimathea went in unto Pilate, and craved the body of Jesus.

A rich man of Arimathea, a city of the Jews, Joseph was an honorable counsellor, a good man, and a just (he had not consented to the counsel and deed of them). He also waited for the kingdom of God, being a disciple of Jesus, but secretly for fear of the Jews.

This man went boldly in unto Pilate, and begged that he might take away the body of Jesus. Pilate gave him leave.

Joseph came therefore, and took the body of Jesus. And there came also Nicodemus (which at the first came by night *), and brought a mixture of myrrh and aloes.

Then took they the body, and wound it in a clean cloth of fine linen, with the spices, as the manner of the Jews is to bury.

Now in the place where Jesus was crucified there was a garden; and in the garden a new sepulchre, wherein was never man yet laid.

When Joseph had laid the body in his own new tomb which he had hewn out in the rock, he rolled a great stone, nigh at hand, to the door of the sepulchre, and departed.

The women which came with Jesus from Galilee beheld the sepulchre, and how the body was laid. And there was Mary Magdalene, and the other Mary, the mother of Joses, sitting over against the sepulchre. That day was the preparation. They returned (home) and prepared spices and ointments: and rested the sabbath day,

¶Now the next day, that followed the day of preparation, the chief priests and Pharisees came unto Pilate, saying, Sir, that deceiver said, while he was yet alive,

After three days I will rise again.

Command therefore that the sepulchre be made sure until the third day, lest his disciples come by night, and steal him away, and say unto the people, He is risen from the dead: so the last error shall be worse than the first.

Pilate said, Ye have a watch: make it as sure as you can. So they went, and made the sepulchre sure, sealing the stone, and setting a watch.

THE RESURRECTION

A.D. 30. Age 33. Jerusalem: The Sepulchre.

Matthew 28, 1, and 8-10: Mark 16, 1-11: Luke 24, 1-9: John 20, 11-18.

IN the end of the sabbath, as it began to dawn toward the first day of the week, came Mary Magdalene and the other Mary, to see the sepulchre at the rising of the sun. They came bringing the sweet spices which they, and Salome, had prepared, that they might anoint him.

They said among themselves, Who shall roll away the stone from the door? and they found the stone rolled away.

They entered in, and found not the body of the Lord Jesus. And it came to pass, as they were perplexed, behold, two men stood by them in shining garments: they said, Why seek ye the living among the dead? he is not here: he is risen: remember how he spake when yet in Galilee, saying,

The Son of man must be delivered into the hands of sinful men, and be crucified, and the third day rise again.

They remembered: they trembled, and went out quickly, with great joy; and did run to bring his disciples word. And, behold, Jesus met them, saying,

All hail!

And they worshipped him. Then said Jesus unto them,

Be not afraid: go tell my brethren that they go into Galilee, and there shall they see me.

Mary (Magdalene) stood without at the sepulchre weeping: and she looked into the sepulchre, and seeth two angels in white, sitting. They say, Why weepest thou?

She saith, They have taken away my Lord.

When she had thus said, she turned, and saw Jesus standing, and knew not that it was Jesus. He saith,

Woman, why weepest thou? whom seekest thou?

She, supposing him to be the gardener, saith, Sir, if thou have borne him hence, tell me where thou hast laid him, and I will take him away. Jesus saith,

Mary.

She turned, and saith unto him, Master. Jesus saith unto her,

Touch me not; for I am not yet ascended to my Father: but go to my brethren, and say unto them, I ascend unto my Father, and your Father; and to my God, and your God.

Mary Magdalene came and told the disciples that she had seen the Lord, that he was alive, and that he had spoken these things unto her.

And they believed her not.

AFTER THE RESURRECTION

A.D. 30. Age 33. Emmaus. Jerusalem.

Mark 16, 12-13: Luke 24, 13-31; 33-43: John 20, 19-29.

AFTER that, Jesus appeared in another form unto two of them, that same day, as they walked to Emmaus, a village which was from Jerusalem about three-score furlongs.

While they talked together of all these things which had happened, Jesus himself drew near. But their eyes were holden that they should not know him. And he said unto them,

What manner of communications are these that ye have one to another, as ye walk, and are sad?

One of them (Cleopas) answering said, Art thou a stranger in Jerusalem, and hast not known the things which are come to pass there in these days? Jesus said,

What things?

They answered, Concerning Jesus of Nazareth: and how our rulers have crucified him. But we trusted that it had been he which should have redeemed Israel.

Jesus said unto them,

O fools *, and slow of heart to believe all that the prophets have spoken: ought not Christ to have suffered these things, and to enter into his glory?

And beginning at Moses, he expounded the things in all the Scriptures concerning himself.

¶They drew nigh unto the village whither they went: and Jesus made as though he would have gone further. But they constrained him, saying, Abide with us: for it is toward evening. And he went in to tarry with them.

As he sat at meat with them, he took bread, and blessed it, and brake, and gave to them. And their eyes were opened, and they knew him; and he vanished out of their sight.

The same hour, they returned to Jerusalem, and found the eleven gathered together, saying, The Lord is risen indeed, and hath appeared to Simon. They (the two) told what things were done in the way, and how Jesus was known of them in breaking of bread.

¶As they spake, the same day at evening, being the first day of the week, when the doors were shut where the disciples were assembled for fear of the Jews, Jesus himself stood in the midst of them, and saith,

Peace be unto you.

But they supposed they had seen a spirit, and were affrighted. And he said,

Why are ye troubled? and why do thoughts arise in your hearts? Behold my hands and my feet, that it is myself: handle me, and see; for a spirit hath not flesh and bones, as ye see me have.

While they wondered, he said,

Have ye here any meat?

They gave him of a fish, and of a honeycomb; and he did eat before them. Then said he to them again,

Peace be unto you; as my Father hath sent me, even so I send you.

Receive ye the Holy Ghost. Whosesoever sins ye remit, they are remitted unto them: and whosesoever sins ye retain, they are retained.

¶But Thomas was not with them. When the other disciples said unto him, We have seen the Lord, he said, Except I shall see in his hands the print of the nails, and put my finger into the print of the nails, and thrust my hand into his side, I will not believe.

After eight days, again the disciples were within, and Thomas with them: then came Jesus, as they sat at meat, the doors being shut, and stood in the midst, and said,

Peace be unto you.

Then saith he to Thomas,

Reach hither thy finger, and behold my hands; and reach hither thy hand, and thrust it into my side: and be not faithless, but believing.

Thomas answered, My Lord and my God. Jesus said unto him,

Thomas, because thou hast seen me, thou hast believed: blessed are they that have not seen, and yet have believed.

AT THE SEA OF TIBERIAS

A.D. 30. Age 33. Sea of Galilee.

John 21, 1-25.

JESUS shewed himself again to the disciples at the sea of Tiberias; * and on this wise: there were together Simon Peter and Thomas called Didymus, and Nathanael of Cana in Galilee, and the sons of Zebedee, and two others of his disciples.

Simon Peter saith unto them, I go a fishing. They say, We go with thee. They entered into a ship immediately; and that night they caught nothing.

But when the morning was come, Jesus stood on the shore: but the disciples knew not that it was Jesus. Then saith he unto them,

Children, have ye any meat?

They answered, No. And he said,

Cast the net on the right side of the ship, and ye shall find.

They cast; and as soon as they were come to land, they saw a fire of coals there, and fish laid thereon, and bread. Jesus saith,

Bring of the fish which ye have now caught.

Peter drew the net to land full of great fishes, and for all there were so many; yet was not the net broken.

Jesus saith unto them,

Come and dine.

Jesus then taketh bread, and giveth them, and fish likewise.

¶So when they had dined, Jesus saith,

Simon, son of Jonas, lovest thou me more than these?

He saith, Yea, Lord; thou knowest that I love thee. Jesus saith,

Feed my lambs.

He saith the second time,

Simon, son of Jonas, lovest thou me?

He saith, Yea, Lord; thou knowest that I love thee. Jesus saith,

Feed my sheep.

He saith the third time,

Simon, son of Jonas, lovest thou me?

Peter was grieved because he said the third time, Lovest thou me? And he said, Lord, thou knowest all things; thou knowest that I love thee. Jesus saith unto him,

Feed my sheep.

Verily, verily, I say unto thee, When thou wast young, thou girdedst thyself, and walkedst whither thou wouldest: but when thou shall be old, thou shalt stretch forth thy hands, and another shall gird thee, and carry thee whither thou wouldest not.

This spake he, signifying by what death he should glorify God. And he saith unto Peter,

Follow me.

Peter, turning about, seeth the disciple following, whom Jesus loved. * Seeing him, Peter saith, Lord, and what shall this man do? Jesus answered,

If I will that he tarry till I come, what is that to thee? follow thou me.

This is the disciple * which testifieth of these things: and wrote these things. And there are also many other things which Jesus did, the which, if they should be written every one, I suppose that even the world itself could not contain the books that should be written.

THE ASCENSION

A.D. 30. Age 33. Galilee. Mt. Olivet. Bethany.

Matthew 28, 16-20: Mark 16, 12-18: Luke 24, 44-53; and Luke's Acts of The Apostles 1, 12.

THE eleven disciples went into a mountain in Galilee, where Jesus had appointed them. And he came, saying,

Go ye into all the world, and preach the gospel to every creature.

He that believeth and is baptized shall be saved; but he that believeth not shall be damned.

And these signs shall follow them that believe: In my name shall they cast out devils; they shall speak with new tongues; they shall take up serpents; and if they drink any deadly thing, it shall not hurt them; they shall lay hands on the sick, and they shall recover.

All power is given unto me in heaven and in earth.

Go ye therefore, and teach all nations, baptizing them in the name of the Father, and of the Son, and of the Holy Ghost: teaching them to observe all things whatsoever I have commanded you: and, lo, I am with you alway, even unto the end of the world.

And Jesus said unto them (the eleven),

These are the words which I spake unto you, while I was with you, That all things must be fulfilled, which were written in the law of Moses, and in the prophets, and in the psalms, concerning me.

Then opened he their understanding, that they might understand the Scriptures; and said unto them,

Thus it is written, and thus it behooved Christ to suffer, and to rise from the dead the third day: and that repentance and remission of sins should be preached in his name among all nations, beginning at Jerusalem.

And ye are witnesses of these things.

And, behold, I send the promise of my Father upon you: but tarry ye in the city of Jerusalem, until ye be endued with power from on high.

¶And he led them out as far as to Bethany; and he lifted up his hands, and blessed them.

And it came to pass, while he blessed them, he was parted from them, and carried up into heaven; and a cloud received him out of their sight.

¶Then returned they with great joy unto Jerusalem, from the mount called Olivet, which is from Jerusalem a sabbath day's journey.

They were continually in the temple praising and blessing God.

APOSTLES' QUESTION
ANSWERED_SAUL'S
CONVERSION

A.D. 35. Mount of Olives.

Luke: Acts 1, 2-9.

UNTO the apostles whom he had chosen Jesus shewed himself alive after his passion: and, being assembled with them, * commanded them that they should not depart from Jerusalem: saith he,

Wait (tarry in Jerusalem) for the promise of the Father, which ye have heard of me. For John truly baptized with water; but ye shall be baptized with the Holy Ghost not many days hence.

They asked him, Lord, wilt thou at this time restore again the kingdom to Israel? He said,

It is not for you to know the times or the seasons, which the Father hath put in his own power. But ye shall receive power, after that the Holy Ghost is come upon you: and ye shall be witnesses unto me both in Jerusalem, and in all Judea, and in Samaria, and unto the uttermost parts of the earth.

When he had spoken, while they beheld, he was taken up.

Luke: Acts 8, 3; 9, 1-20. Damascus. A.D. 34-35.

SAUL † made havoc of the church, entering into every house, and haling men and women to prison.

Breathing out threatenings against the disciples of the Lord, he went unto the high priest, and desired of him letters to the synagogues, that if he found any of this way, whether men or women, he might bring them bound to Jerusalem.

As he journeyed, he came near Damascus: and suddenly there shined about him a light from heaven: and he fell to the earth, and heard a voice saying,

Saul, Saul, why persecutest thou me?

Saul said, Who art thou? And the Lord said,

I am Jesus whom thou persecutest: it is hard for thee to kick against the pricks.

Saul astonished said, Lord, what wilt thou have me to do? The Lord answered,

Arise, and go into the city, and it shall be told thee what thou must do.

The men which journeyed with Saul stood speechless, hearing a voice, but seeing no man. Saul arose from the earth; and when his eyes were opened, he saw no man.

They led him by the hand into Damascus. And he was three days without sight, and neither did eat nor drink.

¶There was a certain disciple at Damascus, named Ananias; and to him said the Lord in a vision,

Ananias! Arise, and go into the street which is called Straight, and inquire in the house of Judas for one called Saul of Tarsus: for, behold, he prayeth, and hath seen in a vision a man named Ananias coming in, and putting his hand on him, that he might receive his sight.

Ananias answered, Lord, much evil he hath done to thy saints at Jerusalem.

But the Lord said,

Go thy way: for he is a chosen vessel unto me, to bear my name before the Gentiles, and kings, and the children of Israel: for I will show him how great things he must suffer for my name's sake.

Ananias entered into the house; and putting his hands on him said, Brother Saul, the Lord, even Jesus, hath sent me, that thou mightest receive thy sight, and be filled with the Holy Ghost.

Immediately there fell from Saul's eyes as it had been scales; and he received sight forthwith, and arose, and was baptized.

Straightway Saul preached Christ in the synagogues, that he is the Son of God.

A.D. 41 Cesarea.

Luke: Acts 10, 44-45; and 11, 16.

WHILE Peter spake, the Holy Ghost fell on all them which heard, They of the circumcision which believed were astonished, because that on the Gentiles also was poured out the gift of the Holy Ghost.

Then remembered Peter how that the Lord said,

John indeed baptized with water; but ye shall be baptized with the Holy Ghost.

And he commanded them to be baptized.

THE LORD TO PAUL IN A VISION

A.D. 54. Corinth.

Luke: Acts 18, 7-11.

PAUL entered into a certain man's house, named Justus one that worshipped God, whose house joined hard to the synagogue.

Then spake the Lord to Paul in the night by a vision,

Be not afraid, but speak, and hold not thy peace; for I am with thee, and no man shall set on thee to hurt thee; for I have much people in this city.

And Paul continued there for a year and six months, teaching the word of God.

PAUL'S FAREWELL TO THE EPHESIANS

A.D. 66. Miletus.

Luke: Acts 20, 17-19, 22, 25, 32-38.

FROM Miletus he (Paul) sent to Ephesus, and called the elders of the church.

When they were come, he said unto them, Ye know, from the first day that I came into Asia, after what manner I have been with you at all times, serving the Lord with humility, with temptations which befell me by the lying in wait of the Jews.

Now I go bound in the spirit unto Jerusalem. not knowing the things that shall befall me there. I know that ye all, among whom I have gone, preaching the kingdom of God, shall see my face no more.

Brethren, I commend you to God.

I have coveted no man's silver, or gold, or apparel. Yea, ye know, that these hands * have ministered unto my necessities. I have shewed you how that so laboring ye ought to support the weak, and to remember the words of the Lord Jesus, how he said,

It is more blessed to give than to receive.

When Paul had thus spoken, he prayed with them all. They all wept, sorrowing for the words which he spake, that they should see his face no more. And they accompanied him unto the ship.

APPENDIX
PAUL'S WITNESS
PAUL AT CESAREA AND JERUSALEM

A.D. 60.

Luke: Acts (parts of) Chapters 21, 22, 23, 24, 25, 26, 27.

WE * that were of Paul's company came unto Cesarea, into the house of Philip the evangelist. As we tarried there many days, there came down to us from Judea a certain prophet, named Agabus.

And Agabus took Paul's girdle, and bound his own hands and feet, and said, Thus saith the Holy Ghost, So shall the Jews at Jerusalem bind the man that owneth this girdle, and shall deliver him into the hands of the Gentiles.

We besought Paul not to go up to Jerusalem. He would not be persuaded; and we went up to Jerusalem. The brethren received him gladly.

¶Paul entered into the temple. When the Jews which were of Asia saw him in the temple, they stirred up the people, and laid hands on him, and drew him out of the temple. But when they went about to kill him, the chief captain and the soldiers took him, demanded who he was, and what he had done.

Some cried one thing, some another, crying out, Men of Israel, help: This is the man that teacheth all men every where against the people, and the law: and further brought Greeks also into the temple, and hath polluted this holy place.

Paul said, I am verily a man which am a Jew, born in Tarsus, a city in Cilicia, yet brought up in this city, and taught according to the perfect manner of the law of the fathers, and was zealous toward God. I persecuted this way unto the death, binding and delivering into prisons both men and women.

The high priest doth bear me witness: from whom I received letters unto the brethren, and went to Damascus, to bring them which were there bound unto Jerusalem, for to be punished.

As I made my journey, and was come nigh unto Damascus about noon, suddenly there shone from heaven a great light round about me. I fell unto the ground, and heard a voice saying,

Saul, Saul, why persecutest thou me?

I answered, Who art thou, Lord? And he said unto me,

I am Jesus of Nazareth, whom thou persecutest.

I said, What shall I do, Lord? And the Lord said unto me,

Arise, and go into Damascus; and there it shall be told thee of all things which are appointed for thee to do.

I could not see for the glory of that light. Led by the hand of them that were with me, I came into Damascus.

¶One Ananias, a devout man according to the law, came and said, Brother Saul, receive thy sight.

And I looked up upon him. And he said, The God of our fathers hath chosen thee, that thou shouldest know his will, and see that Just One, and hear the voice of his mouth. For thou shalt be his witness unto all men of what thou hast seen and heard.

When I was come again to Jerusalem, even while I prayed in the temple, I was in a trance; and saw him saying unto me,

Make haste, and get thee quickly out of Jerusalem: for they will not receive thy testimony concerning me.

I said, Lord, they know that I imprisoned and beat in every synagogue them that believed on thee: and when the blood of thy martyr Stephen was shed, I also was standing by, and consented unto his death.

He said unto me,

Depart: for I will send thee far hence unto the Gentiles.

¶The Jews gave Paul audience unto this word, and then lifted up their voices, and said, Away with such a fellow from the earth: for it is not fit that he should live.

The chief captain, fearing lest Paul should have been pulled in pieces of them, commanded the soldiers to take him by force from among them, and to bring him into the castle.

The night following the Lord stood by Paul, and said,

Be of good cheer, Paul: for as thou hast testified of me in Jerusalem, so must thou bear witness also at Rome.

When it was day, certain of the Jews banded together, under a curse, neither to eat nor drink till they had killed Paul.

Paul's sister's son heard of their lying in wait. One of the centurions brought the young man to the chief captain. He told him.

So the chief captain called two centurions, saying, Make ready two hundred soldiers to go to Cesarea, and horsemen three score and ten, and spearmen two hundred, at the third hour of the night. Provide them beasts, that they may set Paul on, and bring him safe unto Felix the governor.

And he wrote a letter unto the governor after this manner: This man was taken of the Jews, and should have been killed of them: then came I with an army, and rescued him, having understood that he was a Roman.

The horsemen, when they came to Cesarea and delivered the epistle to the governor, presented Paul also before him. He commanded Paul to be kept in Herod's judgment-hall.

After certain days Felix (the governor) sent for Paul, and heard him. And as Paul reasoned of righteousness, temperance, and judgment to come, Felix trembled, and answered, Go thy way for this time; when I have a convenient season, I will call for thee.

But after two years Porcius Festus came into Felix' room: and Felix, willing to shew the Jews a pleasure, left Paul bound.

¶Festus, willing to do the Jews a pleasure, said to Paul, Wilt thou go up to Jerusalem, and there be judged of these things before me?

Then said Paul, I stand at Cesar's judgment seat, where I ought to be judged: to the Jews have I done no wrong, as thou very well knowest. For if I be an offender, or have committed any thing worthy of death, I refuse not to die: but if there be none of these things whereof these accuse me, no man may deliver me unto them. I appeal unto Cesar.

¶After certain days king Agrippa came unto Cesarea to salute Festus.

Festus declared Paul's cause unto the king, saying, There is a certain man left in bonds by Felix: about whom, when I was at Jerusalem, the chief priests and the elders of the Jews informed me, desiring to have judgment against him. To whom I answered, It is not the manner of the Romans to deliver any man to die, before that he which is accused have the accusers face to face, to answer for himself.

But Paul appealed to be reserved unto the hearing of Augustus.

Then Agrippa said unto Festus, I would also hear the man myself.

And on the morrow, when Agrippa was come with great pomp into the place of hearing, with the chief captains, and principal men of the city, Paul was brought forth.

Festus said, King Agrippa, the Jews have dealt with me, crying that he ought not to live. But when I found that he had committed nothing worthy of death, and that he himself hath appealed to Augustus, I have determined to send him. Of whom I have no certain thing to write unto my lord. Wherefore I have brought him forth before you, O king Agrippa, that, after examination had, I might have somewhat to write.

PAUL'S DEFENCE BEFORE AGRIPPA

A.D. 62. Cesarea.

Luke: Acts 26, 1-32.

AGRIPPA said unto Paul, Thou art permitted to speak. Then Paul answered:

I think myself happy, king Agrippa, because I shall answer for myself this day before thee: especially, because I know thee to be expert in all customs and questions which are among the Jews: wherefore I beseech thee to hear me patiently.

My manner of life from my youth, which was at the first among mine own nation at Jerusalem, know all the Jews; which knew me from the beginning (if they would testify), that after the most straitest sect of our religion, I lived a Pharisee.

And now I stand, and am judged for the hope of the promise made of God unto our fathers: unto which promise our twelve tribes, instantly serving God day and night, hope to come. For which hope's sake, king Agrippa, I am accused of the Jews.

Why should it be thought a thing incredible with you, that God should raise the dead?

I verily thought with myself, that I ought to do many things contrary to the name of Jesus of Nazareth: and many of the saints did I shut up in prison; and when they were put to death, I gave my voice against them. And I punished them oft in every synagogue, and compelled them to blaspheme; and being exceedingly mad against them, I persecuted them even unto strange cities.

Whereupon, as I went to Damascus, with authority and commission from the chief priests, at midday, O king, I saw in the way a light from heaven, above the brightness of the sun, shining round about me. And when we were all fallen to the earth, I heard a voice saying in the Hebrew tongue,

Saul, Saul, why persecutest thou me? it is hard for thee to kick against the pricks.

I said, Who art thou, Lord? And he said,

I am Jesus whom thou persecutest.

But rise, and stand upon thy feet: for I have appeared unto thee for this purpose, to make thee a minister and a witness both of these things which thou hast seen, and of those things in the which I will appear unto thee; delivering thee from the people, and from the Gentiles, unto whom now I send thee, to open their eyes, and to turn them from darkness to light, and from the power of Satan unto God, that they may receive forgiveness of sins, and inheritance among them which are sanctioned by faith that is in me.

Whereupon, O king Agrippa, I was not disobedient unto the heavenly vision: but shewed first unto them of Damascus, and at Jerusalem, and throughout all the coast of Judea, and then to the Gentiles, that they should repent and turn to God, and do works meet for repentance.

For these causes the Jews caught me in the temple, and went about to kill me.

Having therefore obtained help of God, I continue unto this day, witnessing both to small and great, saying none other things than those which the prophets and Moses did say should come: That Christ should suffer, and that he should be the first that should rise from the dead, and should shew light unto the people, and to the Gentiles.

¶As Paul thus spake for himself, Festus said with a loud voice, Paul, thou art beside thyself; much learning doth make thee mad.

Paul said, I am not mad, most noble Festus, but speak forth the words of truth and soberness. For the king knoweth of these things, before whom also I speak freely: for I am persuaded that none of these things are hidden from him; for this thing was not done in a corner.

King Agrippa, believest thou the prophets? I know that thou believest. Then Agrippa said unto Paul, Almost thou persuadest me to be a Christian.

Paul said, I would to God, that not only thou, but also all that hear me this day, were both almost, and altogether such as I am, except these bonds.

Then said Agrippa unto Festus, This man might have been set at liberty, if he had not appealed unto Cesar.

A.D. 62. En route to Rome.

Luke: Acts 27, 1-6.

WHEN it was determined that we * should sail into Italy, they delivered Paul and certain other prisoners unto one named Julius, a centurion of Augustus' band.

Entering into a ship of Adramyttium, we launched, meaning to sail by the coasts of Asia. The next day we touched at Sidon.

When we had launched from thence, we sailed under Cyprus, because the winds were contrary. We came to Myra, a city of Lycia. There the centurion found a ship of Alexandria sailing into Italy; and he put us therein.

Paul: II. Corinthians 12, 7-9.

THERE was given to me a thorn in the flesh, the messenger of Satan to buffet me, lest I should be exalted above measure.

For this thing I besought the Lord thrice, that it might depart from me. And he said unto me,

My grace is sufficient for thee: for my strength is made perfect in weakness.

THE REVELATION

A.D. 96.

Revelation 1, 1-3; 9-20.

THE Revelation of Jesus Christ, which God gave unto him: sent unto his servant John: who bare record of the word of God, and of the testimony of Jesus Christ, and of all things that he saw. Blessed is he that readeth, and they that hear the words of this prophecy, and keep those things which are written therein: for the time is at hand.

¶I, John, was in the Spirit on the Lord's day, and heard behind me a great voice as of a trumpet, saying, †

I am Alpha and Omega, the first and the last, the beginning and the ending:

What thou seest, write in a book, and send it unto the seven churches which are in Asia; unto Ephesus, and unto Smyrna, and unto Pergamos, and unto Thyatira, and unto Sardis, and unto Philadelphia, and unto Laodicea.

And I turned to see the voice that spake:

I saw seven golden candlesticks; and in the midst of the seven candlesticks one like unto the Son of man, clothed with a garment down to the foot, and girt about the paps with a golden girdle. His head and his hairs were white like wool, as white as snow; and his eyes were as a flame of fire; and his feet like unto fine brass, as if they burned in a furnace; and his voice as the sound of many waters. And he had in his right hand seven stars: and out of his mouth went a sharp twoedged sword: and his countenance was as the sun shineth in his strength. And when I saw him, I fell at his feet as dead.

He laid his right hand upon me, saying unto me,

Fear not; I am the first and the last: I am he that liveth, and was dead; and, behold, I am alive forever more, Amen; and have the keys of hell and of death.

Write the things which thou hast seen, and the things which are, and the things which shall be hereafter; the mystery of the seven stars which thou sawest in my right hand, and the seven golden candlesticks. The seven stars are the angels of the seven churches: and the seven candlesticks which thou sawest are the seven churches.

TO THE CHURCH OF EPHESUS

A.D. 96.

Revelation 2, 1-7.

UNTO the angel of the church of Ephesus write;

These things saith he that holdeth the seven stars in his right hand, who walketh in the midst of the seven golden candlesticks;

I know thy works, and thy labor, and thy patience, and how thou canst not bear them which are evil: and thou hast tried them which say they are apostles, and are not, and hast found them liars: and hast borne, and hast patience, and for my name's sake hast labored, and hast not fainted.

Nevertheless I have somewhat against thee, because thou hast left thy first love.

Remember therefore from whence thou art fallen, and repent, and do the first works; or else I will come unto thee quickly, and will remove thy candlestick out of his place, except thou repent.

But this thou hast, that thou hatest the deeds of the Nicolaitans, which I also hate.

He that hath an ear, let him hear what the Spirit saith unto the churches;

To him that overcometh will I give to eat of the tree of life, which is in the midst of the paradise of God.

TO THE CHURCH IN SMYRNA—"BE THOU FAITHFUL UNTO DEATH"

A.D. 96

Revelation 2, 8-11.

AND unto the angel of the church in Smyrna write;

These things saith the first and the last, which was dead, and is alive;

I know thy works, and tribulation, and poverty (but thou art rich); and I know the blasphemy of them which say they are Jews, and are not, but are the synagogue of Satan.

Fear none of those things which thou shalt suffer: behold, the devil shall cast some of you into prison, that ye may be tried; and ye shall have tribulation ten days: be thou faithful unto death, and I will give thee a crown of life.

He that hath an ear, let him hear what the Spirit saith unto the churches;

He that overcometh shall not be hurt of the second death.

TO THE CHURCH IN PERGAMOS—"REPENT, OR ELSE I WILL COME QUICKLY"

A.D. 96

Revelation 2, 12-17.

AND to the angel of the church in Pergamos write;

These things saith he which hath the sharp sword with two edges;

I know thy works, and where thou dwellest, even where Satan's seat is; and thou holdest fast my name, and hast not denied my faith, even in those days wherein Antipas was my faithful martyr, who was slain among you, where Satan dwelleth.

But I have a few things against thee, because thou hast there them that hold the doctrine of Balaam, who taught Balak to cast a stumbling-block before the children of Israel, to eat things sacrificed unto idols, and to commit fornication.

¶So hast thou also them that hold the doctrine of the Nicolaitans, which thing I hate.

Repent; or else I will come unto thee quickly, and will fight against them with the sword of my mouth.

He that hath an ear, let him hear what the Spirit saith unto the churches;

To him that overcometh will I give to eat of the hidden manna, and will give him a white stone, and in the stone a new name written, which no man knoweth saving he that receiveth it.

TO THE CHURCH IN THYATIRA—"I WILL GIVE UNTO EVERY ONE OF YOU ACCORDING TO HIS WORKS"

A.D. 96.

Revelation 2, 18-29.

AND unto the angel of the church in Thyatira write;

These things saith the Son of God, who hath his eyes like unto a flame of fire, and his feet are like fine brass;

I know thy works, and charity, and service, and faith, and thy patience, and thy works; and the last to be more than the first.

Notwithstanding I have a few things against thee, because thou sufferest that woman Jezebel, which calleth herself a prophetess, to teach and to seduce my servants to commit fornication, and to eat things sacrificed unto idols. And I gave her space to repent of her fornication; and she repented not. Behold, I will cast her into a bed, and them that commit adultery with her into great tribulation, except they repent of their deeds. And I will kill her children with death; and all the churches shall know that I am he which searcheth the reins and hearts: and I will give unto every one of you according to your works.

But unto you I say, and unto the rest in Thyatira, as many as have not this doctrine, and which have not known the depths of Satan, as they speak; I will put upon you none other burden. But that which ye have already, hold fast till I come.

And he that overcometh, and keepeth my works unto the end, to him will I give power over the nations: and he shall rule them with a rod of iron; as the vessels of a potter shall they be broken to shivers: even as I received of my Father. And I will give him the morning star.

He that hath an ear, let him hear what the Spirit saith unto the churches.

TO THE CHURCH IN SARDIS—"BE WATCHFUL: I WILL COME AS A THIEF"

A.D. 96.

Revelation 3, 1-6.

AND unto the angel of the church in Sardis write;

These things saith he that hath the seven Spirits of God, and the seven stars;

I know thy works, that thou hast a name that thou livest, and art dead. Be watchful, and strengthen the things which remain, that are ready to die: for I have not found thy works perfect before God.

Remember therefore how thou hast received and heard, and hold fast, and repent. If therefore thou shalt not watch, I will come on thee as a thief, and thou shalt not know what hour I will come upon thee.

Thou hast a few names even in Sardis which have not defiled their garments; and they shall walk with me in white; for they are worthy. He that overcometh, the same shall be clothed in white raiment; and I will not blot out his name out of the book of life, but I will confess his name before my Father, and before his angels.

He that hath an ear, let him hear what the Spirit saith unto the churches.

TO THE CHURCH IN PHILADELPHIA—"I HAVE SET BEFORE THEE AN OPEN DOOR"

A.D. 96.

Revelation 3, 7-13.

AND to the angel of the church in Philadelphia write;

These things saith he that is holy, he that is true, he that hath the key of David, he that openeth, and no man shutteth; and shutteth, and no man openeth;

I know thy works: behold, I have set before thee an open door, and no man can shut it: for thou hast a little strength, and hast kept my word, and hast not denied my name.

Behold, I will make them of the synagogue of Satan, which say they are Jews, and are not, but do lie; behold, I will make them to come and worship before thy feet, and to know that I have loved thee.

Because thou hast kept the word of my patience, I also will keep thee from the hour of temptation, which shall come upon all the world, to try them that dwell upon the earth.

Behold, I come quickly; hold that fast which thou hast, that no man take thy crown.

Him that overcometh will I make a pillar in the temple of my God, and he shall go no more out: and I will write upon him the name of my God, and the name of the city of my God, which is new Jerusalem, which cometh down out of heaven from my God; and I will write upon him my new name.

Him that hath an ear, let him hear what the Spirit saith unto the churches.

TO THE CHURCH OF THE LAODICEANS—I STAND AT THE DOOR, AND KNOCK

A.D. 96.

Revelation 3, 14-22.

AND unto the angel of the church of the Laodiceans write;

These things saith the Amen, the faithful and true witness, the beginning of the creation of God;

I know thy works, that thou art neither cold nor hot: I would thou wert cold or hot. So then because thou art lukewarm, and neither cold nor hot, I will spew thee out of my mouth. Because thou sayest, I am rich, and increased with goods, and have need of nothing; and knowest not that thou art wretched, and miserable, and poor, and blind, and naked: I counsel thee to buy of me gold tried in the fire, that thou mayest be rich; and white raiment, that thou mayest be clothed, and that the shame of thy nakedness do not appear; and anoint thine eyes with eyesalve, that thou mayest see.

As many as I love, I rebuke and chasten; be zealous, therefore, and repent.

Behold, I stand at the door, and knock: if any man hear my voice, and open the door, I will come in to him, and will sup with him, and he with me.

To him that overcometh will I grant to sit with me in my throne, even as I also overcame, and am set down with my Father in his throne.

He that hath an ear, let him hear what the Spirit saith unto the churches.

"I AM ALPHA AND OMEGA."

A.D. 96.

Revelation 4, 1-2; 14, 13; 16, 15; 19, 9-10; 21, 5-8; 22, 6-21.

AFTER this I looked, and, behold, a door was opened in heaven: and the first voice which I heard was as it were of a trumpet talking with me; which said, Come up hither, and I will shew thee things which must be hereafter. And immediately I was in the Spirit: and, behold, a throne was set in heaven, and one sat on the throne.

And I heard a voice from heaven saying unto me,

Write, Blessed are the dead which die in the Lord from henceforth: Yea,

Saith the Spirit,

That they may rest from their labors: and their works do follow them.

And I heard a great voice saying,

Behold, I come as a thief.

Blessed is he that watcheth, and keepeth his garments, lest he walk naked, and they see his shame.

And he saith unto me,

Write, Blessed are they which are called unto the marriage supper of the Lamb.

And he saith unto me,

These are the true sayings of God.

And I, John, fell at his feet to worship him. And he said unto me,

See thou do it not: I am thy fellow servant, and of thy brethren that have the testimony of Jesus: worship God: for the testimony of Jesus is the spirit of prophecy.

And he that sat upon the throne said,

Behold, I make all things new.

And he said unto me,

Write: for these words are true and faithful.

And he said unto me,

It is done. I am Alpha and Omega, the beginning and the end. I will give unto him that is athirst of the fountain of the water of life freely.

He that overcometh shall inherit all things; and I will be his God, and he shall be my son. But the fearful, and unbelieving, and the abominable, and murderers, and whoremongers, and sorcerers, and idolaters, and all liars, shall have their part in the lake which burneth with fire and brimstone: which is the second death.

And he said unto me,

These sayings are faithful and true: and the Lord God of the holy prophets sent his angel to shew unto his servants the things which must shortly be done.

Behold, I come quickly: blessed is he that keepeth the sayings of the prophecy of this book.

And I, John, saw these things, and heard them. And when I had heard and seen, I fell down to worship before the feet of the angel which shewed me these things.

Then saith he unto me,

See thou do it not: for I am thy fellow servant, and of thy brethren the prophets, and of them which keep the sayings of this book: worship God.

And he saith unto me,

Seal not the sayings of the prophecy of this book: for the time is at hand.

He that is unjust, let him be unjust still: and he which is filthy, let him be filthy still: and he that is righteous, let him be righteous still: and he that is holy, let him be holy still.

And, behold, I come quickly; and my reward is with me, to give every man according as his work shall be.

I am Alpha and Omega, the beginning and the end, the first and the last.

Blessed are they that do his commandments, that they may have right to the tree of life, and may enter in through the gates into the city. For without are dogs, and sorcerers, and whoremongers, and murderers, and idolaters, and whosoever loveth and maketh a lie.

I Jesus have sent mine angel to testify unto you these things in the churches. I am the root and the offspring of David, and the bright and morning star.

And the Spirit and the bride say, Come. And let him that heareth say, Come. And let him that is athirst come. And whosoever will, let him take the water of life freely.

For I testify unto every man that heareth the words of the prophecy of this book, If any man shall add unto these things, God shall add unto him the plagues that are written in this book. And if any man shall take away from the words of the book of this prophecy, God shall take away his part out of the book of life, and out of the holy city, and from the things which are written in this book.

He which testifieth these things saith,

Surely I come quickly. Amen.

Even so, come, Lord Jesus.
The grace of our Lord Jesus Christ be with you all. Amen.

Printed in Great Britain
by Amazon

48050597R00178